CARTEL
WIVES

CARTEL WIVES

A True Story of
Deadly Decisions,
Steadfast Love,
and Bringing Down
El Chapo

Mia Flores and Olivia Flores

GRAND CENTRAL
PUBLISHING

NEW YORK   BOSTON

A NOTE TO THE READER

In writing this book, we have recreated events, locales, and conversations based on our memories of them. In order to protect our own safety and that of various friends and loved ones, it was necessary to condense, omit, or alter certain events and timelines and to change the names and identifying details of certain individuals. In all events, however, we have striven to convey the true and unvarnished essence of our experience. Lastly, this is our memoir and not that of our husbands, and we have neither discussed, consulted, nor otherwise confirmed our recollections with them.

Grand Central Publishing
Hachette Book Group
1290 Avenue of the Americas, New York, NY 10104
grandcentralpublishing.com
twitter.com/grandcentralpub

First edition: April 2017

Grand Central Publishing is a division of Hachette Book Group, Inc. The Grand Central Publishing name and logo is a trademark of Hachette Book Group, Inc.

The publisher is not responsible for websites (or their content) that are not owned by the publisher.

Library of Congress Cataloging-in-Publication Data has been applied for.

ISBNs: 978-1-4555-3940-6 (hardcover), 978-1-4555-3938-3 (ebook)

Printed in the United States of America

LSC-C

10 9 8 7 6 5 4 3 2 1

*To my husband. Without you, I wouldn't be who I am today.
You have been my everything since the day I said, "I love you."
A lifetime with you wouldn't be enough. I can't wait to
spend forever with you.*

—Mia

*To my husband, my best friend. You were right again. When you
told me I'd get a record deal and a book deal, I couldn't see it.
You believed in me, built me up, and supported me. When I wanted to
quit, you encouraged me to finish. You said the tough times would
help me grow and see how blessed I am. It took writing this book
to realize that. You've inspired me, motivated me, and have been
my biggest fan. With you by my side, I can accomplish anything
I put my heart into. You've always put me first, seen the good in me,
and brought out the best in me. You made every dream of mine
come true, and I will love you and cherish you for
the rest of my life.*

—Olivia

In loving memory of Margarito Flores, Sr.

You will never be forgotten. May you rest in peace. We love you.

Contents

Cast of Major Characters

(in alphabetical order)

Tomas Arevalo-Renteria: Nicknamed **"Tommy."** He was from Sinaloa and became Junior Flores's best friend. In Chicago, he was the twins' first supplier from Mexico and soon began to work for them. The Flores twins later helped secure his indictment.

Alfredo Beltrán Leyva: Nicknamed **"Mochomo."** He is the younger brother of Arturo, and along with his four other brothers, founder of the Beltrán Leyva Organization (BLO), one of Mexico's top cartels. When his brother, Arturo, was killed, he became the BLO's boss. The Flores brothers' cooperation was a major factor in him not going to trial, and on February 23, 2016, Mochomo pled guilty to conspiracy charges and is now awaiting sentencing.

Arturo Beltrán Leyva: Nicknamed **"La Barba"** and the self-proclaimed *Jefe de Jefes* or "Boss of Bosses." Along with his four brothers, he was one of the founders of the Beltrán Leyva Organization (BLO), one of Mexico's most powerful cartels. The BLO was allied with the Sinaloa Cartel until they started warring in 2008. He was the cartel's head boss until he was killed by Navy SEALs during a raid on December 16, 2009.

Joe Bonelli: The longtime lawyer of Peter and Junior Flores, who defended their brother Adrian against drug charges and took their case when they decided to become federal informants. During the brothers' incarceration, Joe felt he was such a target of retaliation by the cartels that he asked his name never be used, and in all public documents, it's been redacted.

Ruben Castillo: The chief judge for the United States Court of the Northern District of Illinois, who presided over the federal cases of Peter and Junior Flores.

David: Junior Flores's lawyer, who was hired while Junior was negotiating his plea agreement.

Eric Durante: A special agent for the Chicago bureau of the DEA. He became one of the leading agents who oversaw the Flores brothers' case when they became informants.

Manuel Fernández Valencia, aka "La Puerca" or "El Animal": A Sinaloa and BLO associate who controlled a series of tunnels from Mexicali to Calexico and became a trusted business partner of the Flores brothers. He was captured and arrested in late 2010.

Adrian Flores: The older brother of Pedro and Margarito Flores, Jr. He was arrested for drug conspiracy in August 1998. Despite the constant pressure he put on his younger brothers to make an honest living, his arrest left a financial vacuum in his family, causing the twins to build their own drug enterprise.

Amilia Flores: The widow of Margarito Flores, Sr. She has seven children with her late husband.

Daniela Flores: The wife of Adrian Flores, she fled Mexico in 2008 along with the rest of the Flores family.

Margarito Flores, Jr.: Nicknamed **"Junior."** He and his identical twin, Pedro, were born on June 12, 1981, in Chicago, the youngest of seven children. He and his brother became two of the most important cooperators in US history and are scheduled to be released from prison no later than 2021.

Margarito Flores, Sr.: Born in 1937 in central Mexico. This father of twelve dropped out of school in third grade, married his wife in 1959, and immigrated to Chicago in 1969. In 1981, he was sentenced to ten years in prison for possession of a controlled substance, and after his release, he taught his young sons the drug trade. He returned to Mexico in 2009 and was never seen again.

Mia Flores: Born in Chicago in 1980 and raised by an officer in the Chicago Police Department's Gang Unit. She married Peter Flores in 2005 and now lives in hiding with her two young children.

Olivia Flores: Born in Chicago in 1975 to a Chicago police officer. She married Margarito Flores, Jr. in 2005 and now lives in hiding with her two young children.

Pedro Flores: Nicknamed **"Peter"** or **"P."** He and his identical twin, Margarito Jr., were born on June 12, 1981, in Chicago, the youngest of seven children. He and his brother became two of the most important cooperators in US history and are scheduled to be released from prison no later than 2021.

Kevin Garcia: Known to most people as **"K."** This high-ranking member of the Latin Kings was Olivia Flores's second husband. He was gunned down by rival gang members in Chicago in June 2003.

Joaquín Guzmán Loera: Nicknamed **"El Chapo."** He was born in poverty to a cattle farmer from the Mexican state of Sinaloa on April 4, 1957. He rose to become the head of the Sinaloa Cartel and the most powerful and sought-after drug lord in the world.

Mark Jones: The high school and college boyfriend of Mia Flores. He became a CPD beat cop. In 2012, in a massive police corruption scandal, he pleaded guilty to stealing cash from suspected drug dealers and other

Chicago citizens. Because of his work undercover, he was sentenced to just two months in prison.

Leo: The first husband of Olivia Flores. He gave prosecutors information about Saul Rodriguez's plot to kidnap Olivia Flores's parents, hoping for a lenient sentence.

Matthew McCarthy: A special agent for the Milwaukee bureau of the DEA. He originally raided the Flores brothers' homes in 2004, an event that led to them becoming fugitives. He worked closely with Eric Durante on the Flores brothers' case when they became informants.

Músico: Arturo Beltrán Leyva's right-hand man and top lieutenant in the BLO.

German Olivares: El Chapo's accountant and trusted lieutenant. He controlled the Juárez Plaza.

Rubén Oseguera Cervantes: Nicknamed **"El Mencho."** This feared leader of the New Generation Cartel once barricaded Guadalajara and set fire to banks, buses, and gas stations, then posted it on YouTube. He's been known to murder Mexican Army soldiers and shoot down military helicopters with shoulder-held rocket launchers. After the capture of El Chapo, he is now the most wanted drug lord in Mexico.

Pablo: Known as **"Uncle Pablo"** to Peter and Junior Flores. He was an old family friend and associate of the Sinaloa Cartel who for many years served as their supplier. He was behind the April 2005 kidnapping of Peter Flores and the December 2005 kidnapping of Margarito Flores, Sr. After betraying El Chapo and not settling his debts with him, he was kidnapped and executed by the drug lord's *sicarios*.

Payo: One of Junior Flores's closest friends. Músico was his boss in the BLO, and he was Chapillo Lomas's *compadre*. He was in charge of collecting $300,000 monthly to pay Mexican officials to open up drug routes.

Rambo: El Chapo's top *sicario*, or hitman, and head of a cell of hitmen in Jalisco, Mexico.

Saul Rodriguez: A paid informant of the Chicago Police Department beginning in the late 1990s. Rodriguez was behind the 2003 kidnapping of Peter Flores in Chicago. With the assistance of corrupt police officers, it's estimated he kidnapped and robbed at least twenty-nine other drug dealers over the years. In 2015, Rodriguez was sentenced to forty years in prison. At his sentencing, he sobbed for ten minutes and said, "I don't want to be bad no more."

Tom Shakeshaft: An assistant US Attorney for the Northern District of Illinois from 2004 to 2015. Shakeshaft led the investigation and prosecution of the Flores brothers and the dozens of superseding indictments that spun out of their case. He left government service for private practice in February 2015.

Alfredo Vásquez-Hernández: A *compadre* and longtime friend of El Chapo's whom the Flores brothers partnered with to open a furniture transport company that would help them secretly transport drugs in rail cars. In November 2014 he pleaded guilty to drug conspiracy and was sentenced to twenty-two years in prison.

Ismael Zambada García: Nicknamed **"El Mayo."** He was born on New Year's Day 1948. He is one of the founders and leaders of the Sinaloa Cartel, along with El Chapo Guzmán. He is currently under indictment by the United States and Mexico, with over $5 million in reward money for his capture, and with the imprisonment of El Chapo, he is the current head of the Sinaloa Cartel.

Ismael Zambada Imperial, aka "Mayito Gordo": The younger brother of Vicente and Mayito Flaco, this narco junior son of El Mayo was arrested near Culiacán in November 2014 and is due to be extradited to San Diego to stand trial for drug trafficking.

Ismael Zambada Sicairos, aka "Mayito Flaco": The younger brother of Vicente and older brother of Mayito Gordo. His indictment for drug trafficking was unsealed in San Diego in January 2015. He is now a fugitive.

Vicente Zambada Niebla: Nicknamed **"El Vicentillo"** or **"El Niño."** He is one of the sons of El Mayo. Vicente rose to become number 3 in the Sinaloa Cartel. He was arrested in 2009 and extradited to the United States in 2010, where he became a US informant. He is currently awaiting sentencing for narcotics trafficking.

Introduction

To our kids' friends, we're just average soccer moms.

In truth, we're the wives of identical twin brothers who are almost single-handedly responsible for the meteoric rise of narcotics in the United States over the last two decades. From 1998 to 2008, our husbands, Pedro and Margarito Flores, Jr., grew to become high-level traffickers who blazed a drug-riddled trail across the Mexican border, dramatically increasing the volume of cocaine, heroin, methamphetamines, and marijuana passing into the United States, traveling through their hub in Chicago, and then fanning out to almost a dozen major cities across the United States and Canada.

In 2008, at the height of their criminal enterprise, Peter and Junior, as we know them and will call them in this book, made the difficult and life-changing decision to cooperate with the federal government, become informants, and ultimately turn themselves in. This was a family decision, made by the four of us while sitting at the kitchen table one night, and we did it to spare our children from the horrors of the recent Mexican drug wars, with their torture, murder, and complete destruction of far too many families and communities. More than that, we needed to stop the cycle of crime that our husbands were born into; we didn't want our children to see this as their future. We were never drug users, and our husbands weren't—and never had been—proud of their day-to-day work. They did it only because it was the only life they'd ever known. In their family, drugs weren't just normal and accepted, they were the trade their father taught them. Even in America—the supposed land of opportunity—when you're poor, uneducated, and Mexican, drug dealing is often thought to be the only way up.

After Peter and Junior became informants and told the US

Attorney's office every detail of their criminal career, they spent almost all of 2008 secretly recording conversations with the highest-level cartel members in Mexico, including notorious narcocriminal Joaquín "El Chapo" Guzmán. Their unprecedented cooperation helped secure the indictments of sixty-nine major drug figures, from the architects of border-crossing tunnels to the bosses of several cartels, who practically ran Mexico. Additionally, they assisted in eleven superseding indictments that netted over one hundred people. Today, not all of these people are in jail, but with our husbands' testimony, they soon will be. And some of the worst of the worst are dead, killed by the mouths they once helped feed.

In 2015, Peter and Junior were sentenced for their crimes and sent to off-the-radar federal Witness Security Unit prisons, and we went into hiding. We now live in undisclosed locations with our young children, visit our husbands on weekends and holidays, and lie to our friends and neighbors about who we are. While we sit in the carpool line waiting to pick up our kids, we wonder if it's time to change our cell phone numbers for the second time that month, fret over whether our husbands' upcoming testimony against a cartel head will cause a hitman to track us down, and try as hard as possible to imagine a distant future when our families will be reunited, under the watchful eye of the Witness Protection Program.

Even if you've never touched drugs, they've changed your life. While you may not realize it, narcotics are all around you, and they're altering the very fabric of the world we live in. The innocent-looking cashier at your neighborhood convenience store may be hiding a kilo of cocaine behind the counter, or the sweet, quiet lady you sit next to on a plane may have a balloon full of heroin in her stomach. The smiling class parent who greets you at your son's junior high school dance might secretly be battling an addiction to prescription painkillers. Our husbands stashed millions of dollars' worth of cocaine and heroin in a luxury townhouse down the street from Harpo Studios, and did the same at a home in tony Calabasas, a few miles from where the Kardashians live. Yet none of the neighbors suspected a thing. Or, look at us. We tell people we're just stay-at-home moms who are separated from our husbands, but in truth, we were once on a first-name basis with men who put bullets into the backs of people's heads. While most mothers like us are hosting the Boy Scout troop on Sunday nights, we're coming back from a day visiting our husbands in federal prison.

You can blame a lot of things for the pervasiveness of drugs in this country, but the truth is that Peter and Junior Flores, two baby-faced Mexican American identical twin brothers from the West Side of Chicago, are behind much of it. While we knew—and know—them as the gentle, loving, mild-mannered men who treated us with nothing but love and respect, the law knows them as the most significant drug informants in US history.

As kids, Peter and Junior learned the business from their father. When they were in their teens, they started off dealing drugs on the streets of Little Village, the heavily Mexican area of Chicago around where we all grew up. Over the next few years, they established a contact in Mexico's Sinaloa Cartel, and they graduated to become distributors rather than dealers. They set up their business, ran it like a well-oiled machine, and soon became Chicago's most prominent traffickers.

In Chicago, their business was strictly US-based. But when they fled to Mexico in 2003, they hit the international stage. Within a few years, they befriended the major cartel heads and became responsible for hundreds of tons of narcotics crossing the border and being distributed throughout the United States and Canada. Then they funneled $2 billion in cash back into the hands of the Mexican cartels. In their five years living in Mexico, they weren't in any cartel, but they were the only American drug kingpins allowed to work directly with the bosses of the Sinaloa Cartel—headed by El Chapo and Ismael Zambada Garcia (aka "El Mayo")—and the Beltrán Leyva Organization (BLO), run by El Chapo's relatives and sworn enemies, Arturo and Alfredo ("Mochomo") Beltrán. They were wholesalers who bought vast volumes of narcotics from the cartels on credit and then arranged for its transport from Mexico to LA to Chicago. They took a business of tons and siphoned it into a business of kilos, then shipped the money back to their suppliers. Their operations didn't stop once the drugs reached the United States, though; they kept men on the ground in Chicago to process the money and make sure the narcotics reached their destinations across the United States and Canada.

No one in Mexico did what they did—or as well as they did—so El Chapo Guzmán, El Mayo Zambada, and the Beltrán Leyva brothers peacefully vied for their attention. What better way to move billions of dollars in drugs into the United States than with the genius of twins who'd already built an empire there, who had intimate knowledge of US drug trafficking, and who, best of all, were American citizens living in Mexico?

In early 2008, though, everything changed. The Sinaloa Cartel went to war with the BLO, and the average number of drug-related murders per month in Mexico shot up from two hundred to five hundred. Junior and Peter were working in a culture where it became normal for heads to roll into neighborhood bars, right up to people's feet, or to hear of entire families shot to death on the streets of Guadalajara. Our husbands saw men lying in the hot sun, strapped to trees, and skinned alive. Suddenly, the drug trade in Mexico had become a grudge match on a macro scale. Sinaloa and the BLO wanted to destroy each other, and that meant killing everyone who was on the opposing side. Unfortunately for our husbands, they were the biggest assets of both cartels and, as such, caught between the two of them.

At this point—the height of their career—our husbands had warehouses, stash houses run by their many employees, and legitimate businesses—such as shipping companies—as fronts. Their financial ledgers were so sophisticated and extensive that when they turned them over to US authorities, the feds had to hire a team of forensic accountants to sort through them. An official said that they ran their business like a Fortune 500 company, and that if they hadn't been drug traffickers, they could have been CEOs of legitimate corporations. In the years 2006 to 2008, their peak, they transported between two thousand and three thousand pounds of cocaine each month. If you consider that a kilo is 2.2 pounds, that's almost $50 million worth of cocaine a month. That's *$600 million* a year.

But they were stuck between two warring factions, and they hated the example they were setting for their families. So they gave it all up.

When they did, they spent most of 2008 acting as informants, recording every business conversation they had and handing over massive shipments of drugs that had crossed the border on their watch. After several months, they voluntarily turned themselves in to Drug Enforcement Administration officials at the Guadalajara International Airport and were immediately flown back to Chicago. Over the next six years, they were held in protective custody. Because of their testimony, the city of Chicago named El Chapo as public enemy number 1, a title previously only given to Al Capone. On January 27, 2015, they were sentenced to fourteen years in a maximum security prison, with credit given for the six years they'd already served.

If we're lucky—and alive—we'll see them released in 2021, when our kids are practically grown up.

While they're behind bars, they can't tell the world about the horrors we all witnessed and the redemption we've sought. But we can.

We've remained silent in the eight long years since we kissed the beaches of Mexico goodbye, fleeing back to Chicago and toward our new, uncharted futures. Now, we can only trust each other, and we certainly can't tell anything to our neighbors or families. We've considered granting interviews to the press, but we wanted to hold off until we could tell our full stories, without interruption. We want you to hear what our families have gone through in our own words.

We're not writing this book to become rich. We've been wealthy beyond our wildest dreams, and the truth is, we don't miss it. If we'd wanted our lives to stay the same, we would have begged our husbands to stay in Mexico, where we drove luxury cars, lived in penthouses, vacationed on the beach in Puerto Vallarta whenever we felt like it, and had more cash than our parents had ever dreamed of. But it was dirty money, with a trail of bodies behind it. Through it all, we would have done anything to have husbands with nine-to-five jobs like our fathers had. For different reasons, we fell in love with criminals, and we're not here to justify it, but we'd like to tell you how and why it happened.

Our lives are tarnished and secretive, and our pasts are shameful, but we have a story to tell. We've had greater access to the cartels than almost any other American citizen, so we can provide an unprecedented window into how they work, the damage they've caused, and why putting them out of business has proven so difficult.

As for the personal side of this story, we want to provide an unfiltered look into why people enter a life of crime. Unfortunately, for many, especially poor Mexican workers, it's the only choice they feel they have.

You're probably surprised we're still with our husbands, and trust us, we understand why. The idea of one of our kids marrying someone involved in any kind of illegal activity—let alone drug trafficking—is unthinkable. We're not asking that you like Peter and Junior, and, in fact, you may wish they could spend the rest of their lives in prison for all the harm they've caused. Neither of us is here to try to save our reputations. We just want to open up a window into our culture, show how it shaped us, and help you visualize a life we wouldn't wish on our worst enemies. Sometimes, stories don't have heroes. We just hope to illuminate how and why people are pulled into the drug trade, how it ruins them, and what it's like to live the rest of your life as a consequence of the mistakes you've made in the past.

PART ONE

THE AMERICAN DREAM

CHAPTER 1

Olivia

I was born in 1975 in Pilsen, a predominantly Mexican-American neighborhood in Chicago's Lower West Side, about three miles southwest of the Loop.

Pilsen was about as inner city as you can get, and growing up I thought it was normal to see crowds of gangbangers on the corner near my house. I just assumed everywhere was like that. But now that I'm an adult, I get it. My husband and I had a conversation recently, and he was like, "Pilsen is a low-income neighborhood."

I said, "No, it's middle class."

"Babe, you were *not* middle class."

"Yeah, I guess you're right." I hadn't even realized it till he said something.

In my mind, we lived in a great neighborhood because my parents did everything they could to make my older sister and I feel comfortable. My grandfather came from Mexico when my dad was seven or eight, then saved enough money to bring his family over, too. The immigration process wasn't easy, and it took a few years because he chose to do it legally. But he was an honest, hardworking man, and he wouldn't have had it any other way.

Dad came to Pilsen not speaking any English, and as he grew up his mentality was the same as his dad's: work hard, buy property, and save, save, save. Dad was determined to be someone who would make his family proud, so he got his first job at fourteen, put in overtime, went back to school, and became a US citizen. Then he became a Chicago police officer and patrolled the streets all day, bravely wearing his blue uniform.

He and Mom wanted us to have the very best, so they sent my sister and me to Catholic school. We got braces in middle school when no one else had them. They saved all year, and when there was enough in the bank, they took us on family vacations to Disney World. By all accounts, we were living the American dream.

Like my dad, Mom always wanted more. She sold furs at Marshall Field's, so she got a discount on designer furniture, and she filled our house with it. Our home was small, but Mom was a great decorator, so I felt like we had money. Mom was also super smart. She was very driven, very determined, and so strong and powerful that she usually got whatever she wanted. Coming from my neighborhood, she was unique. Mom was Puerto Rican, had a gorgeous body, and held her head high; when she walked into a room, everybody knew she was there. She was always glamorous and well dressed—makeup and heels and great jewelry, even if it didn't cost much. Most importantly, though, she had a great heart to match. She always wanted something different from our neighborhood, and she dreamed of her family having a better life.

At home I was so shy, and I wasn't really able to be myself. My sister was my best friend and my biggest teacher; she had started going over multiplication tables with me when I was in kindergarten and she was in second grade. She took care of me, and I followed her around like her little shadow. I was such a daddy's girl; I clung to my dad and just showed my mom what she wanted to see or told her what she wanted to hear. She was such a firecracker and so controlling that if I crossed her, I wouldn't have heard the end of it. But outside the house, I was completely the opposite. I mimicked my mom—loud, impressive, and in charge. I was the cool girl in school, and I had my shit together.

I met my first boyfriend in middle school, and even though he was sixteen, he didn't mind that I was only fourteen. I had a great body and was so confident, trying to be all mature and sophisticated like my mom. I was a virgin, but I was so infatuated with him that I wasn't all that scared when we became sexually active early on. What did I know at fourteen? I thought I was going to spend the rest of my life with this guy.

After a few months of being with him, I began throwing up and missed my period. I didn't make much of it, though; I wasn't keeping track of stuff like that. But when I found out I was pregnant, I was shocked. I remember thinking, *How could this possibly happen to me?* I came from a good family, I studied like crazy, and I'd always gotten straight As.

Even though Mom pushed for open communication with her girls, I was too scared and embarrassed to open up to her. My sister always told her everything, but I was so shy I covered my ears every time Mom tried to talk about sex. That's why it took me forever to work up the courage to tell her I was pregnant. When I finally did, she was so hurt and disappointed.

"What do you mean?" she said. "You're only fifteen! I put you through private school! I gave you everything!"

When my dad found out, he hugged me tight, tears streaming down his face.

"Olivia, your mom told me you're pregnant. I love you, and I'd do anything for you. I don't want you to be scared. Whatever you decide to do, your mom and I are here."

My sister, who was away at college, even got on a Greyhound bus to come home to be with me. Mom and Dad had always made it clear that family was everything, so all of them were going to support me, no matter what.

In the back of my mind, though, having this baby was going to make me a *woman*. I was finally going to be my own person. My mom wasn't going to be able to run my life, and I wasn't going to have any rules. I was going to have my baby, finish school, and spend the rest of my life with my boyfriend. I was in love, I was mature, and my mom couldn't tell me a damn thing.

That didn't happen. After I had Xavier, I hated how strict my parents were, making me follow the same rules and giving me the same curfew. My boyfriend would come over and see our son, and my mom would scream at me, "You can't sit on his lap in my house! You can't be in the same room together alone!" Not one fucking thing had changed.

But thank God they hadn't—thank God I still had the stability of home—because my boyfriend started to cheat on me. When I told him I wanted to break up, he punched me in the face. This was the first time anyone had ever put their hands on me. I lied to my parents and told them I'd gotten hit in the eye with a snowball, then I stayed with him for two more years because I thought I was doing the best thing for my son. Here I was, this supposedly strong, mature, teenage woman, and I was letting this man control me.

The person who finally saved me was Xavier, who was all of two years old. I couldn't let him see me falling apart, so I broke up with his dad and never looked back. I felt nothing but animosity toward my ex, but for the sake of my son, Mom always told me never to speak badly or negatively about him.

"If you put Xavier's father down, he'll feel like a failure. As a mother, it's your responsibility to always protect him."

My mom was really wise, and I respected her wishes. I didn't want to influence Xavier's feelings in any way, so I quickly learned to contain my feelings about his father. I wanted him to be the dad Xavier needed him to be, without my influence. It was the right thing to do.

My parents were pretty much saints those first few years with Xavier. I was working at Dunkin' Donuts or some other minimum wage job and spending my whole paycheck on diapers, trying so hard to be responsible, and Mom told me she'd put my son through private school once the time came. My dad became a real father figure to him, signing him up for T-ball and hanging out with him every chance he got. "He's my little man," he'd say, and then run off and put my son in his car seat so they could go to the park together. I'd always been my dad's baby girl, and he was just as sweet with my son.

Whether you're fifteen or forty, every mom wants what's best for her kids, but we're not perfect. We all have our breaking points. Toward the middle of high school, I had mine.

Just before I had Xavier, I'd begged my mom to enroll me in public school.

"It's a great high school," I said. "It's really changing. They have all these new programs, and I'll be closer to home for the baby."

For the first time in her life, my mom just gave in and let me have my way. Maybe she actually believed me, or maybe she was just tired of fighting. Either way, I think it was the worst decision she ever made.

That school was so ghetto. It was gang infested. It was drug infested. The Chicago PD patrolled it, and so many people brought knives to school that they installed metal detectors. Nobody *ever* went to class. Instead, they all went to daytime parties.

During my freshman and sophomore years, I'd been so responsible and avoided all of that. I'd been the first girl in my high school to start freshman year with a full-on belly, and since then I'd been working my butt off to be a good mom. I'd gone straight from school to work to home so I could put my baby to bed, but after a while, I just couldn't take it anymore. I'd always put my son first, but being young and selfish, I just wanted to make myself happy.

I started hanging out with the gangbangers and drug dealers, and all of a sudden, I was around nice cars, money, and jewelry. I loved every single bit of it. But when I'd get home, all mom and I would do was fight, fight, fight.

"I raised you better than this," she'd say. "Xavier needs you!"

I'd turn it around on her and scream about how strict she'd always been with me. "What do you expect from me? I'm young, and I need to have a life, too. Besides, I'm still making straight As!" I might have had twenty absences from cutting school and hanging out at parties all day, but I was making good grades at that shithole school.

I thought I was the bomb, and no one could tell me otherwise. I was voted "Smartest," "Best Dressed," and "Most Popular" in my class, and I graduated in three years, at the young age of seventeen. I got a full ride to the University of Illinois at Chicago, and my parents couldn't have been happier. But after my second semester, I threw it all away. There was no way I was going to wait four long years until I started making money, so I told my parents that I was enrolling in cosmetology school.

"It's my dream to open up a salon," I said, trying to sell them on the idea of me dropping out.

They were heartbroken. My sister was getting ready to graduate college and was figuring out where to go to get her master's degree, and here I was, going to beauty school.

Before it was all said and done, my nine-month cosmetology program turned into two years. It just wasn't my priority; what I was seeing on the streets was too exciting for me to stay away. It wasn't the drugs; it was the money. Gangbangers have nice cars with rims, and diamond studs and expensive watches. They were bringing home mad cash, and it wasn't from Dunkin' Donuts. It was from the great state of California.

When I was seventeen, I started taking trips to California to smuggle weed. I'd hop on a bus and ride for two days out there, then a handful of guys and I would meet up with the connect. I'd watch them scoop up a few pounds of marijuana, put it into a potato sack, and then compress it with a machine. The weed would become a hard, square block, and they'd pass it over to me and let me put it into my suitcase. I'd get on a bus back home, and when I arrived, I'd collect around $10,000. *I'm the hottest, richest girl in Chicago,* I thought.

I made a few trips like that and never had a problem. But on one trip back, I had to change buses in Denver. When I hopped off and tried to claim my suitcase, it wasn't there.

"It's on a different bus," the station agent said. "You'll have it in two days."

I just wanted to die. I ran out of the bus station as fast as I could, took a cab to the airport, and bought a one-way ticket back to Chicago. When I got home, I drove myself crazy trying to figure out how in the hell I was going to claim the stash I'd left behind. Then, I decided to just go for it. Two days later I showed up to the Greyhound station with my ID in hand and picked up my load, no questions asked.

I was fearless, and people started to respect me for it. Traffickers looked at me and said, "That girl knows her shit," so they decided to trust me and give me a little promotion. When one of them asked me to travel to Mexico and drive some weed back in the gas tank of my car, I didn't hesitate to say yes.

Before I'd leave town, I'd lie and tell my parents I was staying at a girlfriend's house. For all they knew I was just hanging out with my friends, drinking and partying the day away while they were taking care of Xavier. Mom was always furious.

"When the hell are you coming back?" she'd yell.

"In a few days."

There was no "I'll miss you," or "Thank you for taking care of my son while I'm away." Soon, she stopped talking to me altogether, and my only communication with Xavier was through my dad. It broke his heart, and deep down, it broke mine, too.

I told myself I was making money to take care of my son, but really, it was for me. All I cared about was having my freedom and earning a better, faster, shinier life, which came from getting rich. On the streets I'd been hanging out on, money came from one place: drugs.

I went to Mexico a handful of times for the next year or so. Most of the time things went well, but I did run into a few problems along the way. On one trip, my friend Maria and I were interrogated for hours while border patrol put my car on a lift and tried to remove the gas tank. Maria tried to blame it on me, saying, "It's not my car, it's hers." I don't know if it was sheer determination or if I could just talk myself out of anything, but they let us go. I was so furious at Maria I made her get out on the side of the highway next to the road kill so she could hitchhike home. After about fifteen minutes, I started to feel bad, but more than that, I was worried about her snitching. Even though I turned around and picked her up, I sent her a clear message: *Don't mess with me.*

I was making real money, so I bought a black SUV with gold rims and a gold Rolex to match. I started walking around in those Versace gold coin silk shirts. All those nice things and all that power got to my head, and I began demanding more control. I wanted in. I recruited my own drivers and got my own crew. On weekdays I'd put together my trips, call up my drivers, and fly down to Mexico. I'd pay them $10,000 and keep all the profit. If I wasn't below the border, my weekends were all about going to clubs, popping bottles, and networking. It was validation that I was big time.

Before one trip, my driver stood me up. *I could do this in my sleep,* I said to myself, and I decided to do the job on my own.

Sure enough, I got caught. I was pulled over at a roadblock—I don't know if it was random, if I looked suspicious, or if someone had tipped them off—but it was clear I wasn't getting off this time.

"I don't have anything," I said.

"Step to the side." There weren't just police officers there, there were federal agents, too, and they looked serious.

I watched one of the *federales* drive my car to the side of the road, just like they had that time with Maria. He put my car on the lift and spent the next hour or so trying to pull the tank down.

"I told you, I don't have anything." I was starting to get nervous, but I tried to play it cool.

I heard some rattling and clanking around, and the *federale* pulled down the tank.

Shit, this is it, I thought. *Game over.*

He pulled a brick of weed out of my gas tank, held it above his head, then tossed it toward another agent. Then he peeled off his gloves, came toward me, pulled my arms behind me, and cuffed me.

I don't think I knew what scared was till that moment. All that pride, all that defiance against my mom, all the hours and hours I'd spent at clubs rather than home with Xavier, all the diamonds and bottles of champagne I'd bought over the last year. It had all come to this. What the fuck had I been thinking?

The agent shoved me into the car and walked away. Looking through the window, I watched him enter a little glassed-in booth nearby, where there were a few other *federales*. But instead of working, these dudes had their faces planted on the table, doing lines of coke. After a few minutes, two of them left the booth. One got behind the wheel of the car I was in and another slid into the backseat next to me. As we were driving, he reached over and touched my chest.

"Please don't hurt me," I said in English because my Spanish was terrible. All I could think was, *Oh my God, they're going to rape me.*

He placed his palm on my heart, leaned over, and looked me in the eyes.

"Your heart isn't even racing. You must not be scared. But you should be; I'm not going to hurt you, but someone else will. You're going to prison for a very long time."

I was too ashamed to call my parents, so I reached out to my sister. She hopped on a plane immediately and made it just in time for sentencing, which happened within seventy-two hours of my arrest. When the judge sentenced me, she was right by my side.

I got ten years in a maximum security prison.

Mexican prison is about as bad as you'd imagine it to be, especially if you're a scared little girl like I was. The living conditions were unimaginably filthy and disgusting, and being American in a third world prison was torture every single day. I slept on a cement bed surrounded by cement walls. There was no glass on the windows, only bars, so roaches, mice, spiders, and sometimes even cats crept in at night. I ate black beans with my hands because they wouldn't give us spoons, and the water they made us drink from the faucets was contaminated, dirty, and brown. I vomited or had diarrhea pretty much every single day. On Thanksgiving, we got a real feast, which was five animal crackers and tea, and I thought it was the best thing in the whole fucking world.

Three months passed slowly, and I missed Xavier so much it burned. I was given one phone call a month, and I mustered up the courage to call my parents.

"I'm sorry. I'm so ashamed. I'm just so sorry."

"It's okay, baby, we love you. You have to stay strong."

They told me my sister had been sleeping on her cold tile floor so she could understand my pain. But all of their love and support made me feel unworthy. I regretted everything I'd put my family through, and I hated myself for covering my ears instead of listening to my mom.

Every night, I got on my knees and prayed to the Virgin Mary. "Please, get me out of here," I'd cry and plead. I made all kinds of promises to her. "I'll change my life. I'll be a good mother." On the concrete floor, my knees turned raw and bled, but I just kept praying, every single night.

Before I'd gone to prison I'd met a guy named Leo who owned a body shop. I had a nice car, with rims on it, really nice and shiny. When

I took it to get painted, I met Leo, and he was into me right away. I was very independent. I had my own money. I had this nice car and was living the life. For a girl in our neighborhood, that was rare. Leo didn't talk down to me; he was respectful and totally impressive. Pretty soon, we were dating.

I knew he was a drug dealer because I'd gone to his condo and had seen a triple-beam scale and money counter, but I didn't care. I liked his nice car and his nice house, and he had a business that my parents actually believed was real. He was polite and well mannered, and he dressed well, not super flashy like the gangbangers I used to hang out with when I was younger.

A few months into my prison sentence, Leo came to visit, unannounced.

"Oh my God, Leo, what are you doing here?" I said when I saw him. I'd thought a little bit about him, but I hadn't used my one call a month on him, much less asked him to come down. We'd *just* started dating. But here was this real, live person from home, not a coked up *federale* or a perverted prison guard. He was like a vision of the Holy Mother herself.

Leo stayed for a month and visited me every weekend. He had the warden on payroll, so he even managed to pull off conjugal visits once a week. I was in the federal side of the prison, which was better than the state side, where all the killers and thieves were. In my section there were a bunch of older boss ladies who were in for drugs, and Leo really took to them. He'd bring us lobster and steak and matching sneakers, and we'd hang out together like a big family. It almost felt like a scene from *Goodfellas*. I knew he was paying off the prison guards to make every visit as long as possible, but if that's the way things worked, that's the way it would be. In the position I was in, Leo was in charge.

One weekend, he made an announcement. "I paid your judge $250,000, and he's letting you go."

Just like that, I was gonna get the hell out of there.

No one had ever done anything like that for me, so I was shocked. I'd spent six months in that shithole, and I practically sprinted out of there the day they let me go. Leo had saved me, giving me that second chance to become a better person.

I married him after he whisked me away from Mexican prison, not because I loved him, but because I loved what he'd done for me. I felt obligated. What had I done to deserve this? What hadn't I done, really? Maybe I'd spent my life reacting to a mom who I thought was too strict, or maybe there was too much of her brashness in me. But all I know is that it all came down to wanting a bigger, better life, one that was far away from a single family home off the Blue Line in Pilsen. I wanted to open a hair salon one day, but that didn't guarantee me a life outside the ghetto. Like way too many people I knew, I'd turned to drugs. They were just how people got money in our neighborhood. You had to stick bricks of weed in your gas tank, deal it on the street, or hook up with a guy like Leo to be able to afford more than what a paycheck from Dunkin' Donuts got you.

We had a big, beautiful wedding and went to Hawaii for our honeymoon. I'd wanted to protect my parents from the truth about why I'd gotten out of prison early, so I'd told them that Leo had hired an attorney in Mexico, who'd successfully appealed my case. In reality, it was Leo's money that actually got me out. My parents thought he was the best thing to ever happen to me. They thought Leo was legitimate. But his body shop? It was just a front.

Our problems started almost immediately. Leo became so controlling, refusing to let me go out with my cousins or girlfriends. He put a recording device under the driver's seat of my brand new Lexus and installed a tracking device in it. One night he followed me to a salsa club with my girlfriends and threw a drink at me when I refused to leave with him. My face, my hair, my white dress and jewelry were all soaked, and I told myself I wouldn't go home with him, but I did. After all, I had everything I thought I'd always wanted. Leo was going to help me get ahead in the world. With him, I could go back to school and open my salon. With him, I was wearing Versace and Chanel, and going to Bulls championship games, with courtside seats. I'd seen Michael Jordan get his fifth and sixth rings! For a girl from Pilsen who had a kid at fifteen, that's a dream come true.

Yet my husband was turning into a monster right before my eyes.

Then there was Xavier. He'd just enrolled at a great school, and I was finally acting like the mom I should have been all along. Yet he had to see me with some asshole.

My parents had just celebrated their silver wedding anniversary. Twenty-five years, and they still had an incredible relationship that they worked at every day. I believed marriage was supposed to last forever, and I wanted to make it work. But the more I tried, the more controlling Leo became. We kept up appearances, hired an architect, and started to build this big, beautiful house in the suburbs. It was my dream. I thought, *If I can have that, I can deal with his bullshit, right?* Sure. We moved into my parents' lower level while it was under construction, and one morning, while Leo was walking out the door to take Xavier to school, the feds appeared. They were there for him. Right in front of my poor son, they cuffed Leo and dragged him to the squad car. Xavier started to scream, which made my mom run downstairs.

"Oh my God, they're taking Leo!" I heard her say. She was frantic. "What are you doing in my house? Why are you taking my son-in-law?" Of course, she had no idea he was a dealer.

I was still downstairs when they came, and I was like, *Oh, shit.* I spent the next ten minutes running around the basement like a chicken with its head cut off, ripping up every scrap of paper and receipt I could find. I didn't want the feds to find out anything more than they knew already.

Of course, it wasn't enough because they had everything they needed. Leo was charged with conspiracy to distribute drugs and money laundering, and the feds seized our house, a million dollars in jewelry, our Navigator and Lexus, and a bunch of our assets. The case against Leo was rock solid. He was going to go away for a long time.

I tried to be supportive, to be a good wife, and I visited him in prison every chance I got. He could call as much as he wanted, too—there was no three-hundred-minute limit at that time. He rang me nonstop and was just as controlling as he'd been when he wasn't locked away.

I wasn't just embarrassed; I was crushed. I'd never wanted to hurt my parents, yet I'd broken their hearts again. My dad had trusted me, and I'd disrespected and betrayed him by letting a drug dealer come into his home, his sanctuary. For the first time in her life, my mom was at a loss for words, but her silence said enough.

Leo sat in prison with no house and a wife he couldn't really control from behind bars, and he felt like he had nothing else to lose. He realized that if he didn't work with the authorities he might spend even more time in jail, so he decided to cooperate with them.

I screamed at him when I found out. "You what? How dare you!" In my world, being a snitch was the worst possible thing you could be. It was the ultimate betrayal of everything you stood for and made you less than a person.

"I had to," he said. "Things are only going to get worse for me if I don't."

"You fucking rat," I said. "I just cannot be with you. I don't respect you. You knew exactly what you were involved in. You're not a man. I have more balls than you."

I left him that day and never went back. I wanted nothing more to do with him, and I decided to file for divorce. Stalking me had been bad, and tossing a drink on me had been worse. But being a snitch was just too much. Was it an excuse for me to leave him? Probably. But it was just the last fucking straw for me.

And apparently, it was soon going to be the last straw for him, too.

Luckily, at that point, I'd already moved on.

CHAPTER 2

Mia

My mom was born in Brazil, while my dad's family came from Mexico. My parents got married when my mom was just a teenager, and I was born not long after that, in 1980.

When I was a baby, my biological father was a drummer in a popular band. He wasn't the best provider, so my mom had to take on a lot of responsibility when he went on tour, which was a lot. She'd have two or three jobs at once, and she'd leave me with her mother or sister when she was at work. Things weren't great with my grandmother and aunt, though, and I just cried for my mom all day. Then my mom and my grandmother started fighting all the time. Pretty soon Mom couldn't take it anymore, and she became estranged from her parents.

I can't imagine how lonely she felt, all of twenty years old with a baby, a husband who was never there, and only herself to depend on. Then she split up with my biological father when I was one, and she was *really* alone. Thank God she met my dad when she did. I don't remember it—I was just a toddler—but my dad helped give us stability, even though times were hard and our life wasn't great.

We were living in the slums on 26th Street in Little Village. Little Village is just a few blocks southwest of Pilsen, where Olivia is from, and it's known as the "Mexico of the Midwest" because it's almost entirely Mexican American. When you drive down 26th Street, which is the neighborhood's main drag, you see *taquerías*, auto body shops, *supermercados*, and a big sign that says "Welcome to Little Village" in Spanish. Every September thousands of people flock there for the Mexican

Independence Day parade, which is even bigger than Chicago's St. Patrick's Day parade. In fact, next to LA, Chicago has the largest Mexican American population in the United States, so there are always tons of people there.

But even with all that business and all that pride, 26th Street was a real dump when I was a kid. The life we had wasn't great.

My dad is four years younger than my mom, so he was away at college and earning his degree while she was at home and working. With only one paycheck, we couldn't even afford the rent. Our landlord would knock on the door, demanding a check, and my poor mom would hide from him with me. Of course, the landlord would come back the next day, but she'd just hide again.

My dad was great at baseball, and he was going to try to become a professional. His coach said, "Just do it! You're going to make it. Get into the minors, stay on, and I promise you you'll make it all the way to the majors."

But he gave that all up for me. He said to his coach, "I have a family to raise," and that was that. He married my mom, got his associate's degree, and adopted me when I was in the third grade.

I'd see my biological dad every now and then, but he was just this guy that I would hang out with once in a while. There was no heaviness to it, like, "Oh my God, now I have to see my *father*." I didn't feel like I was missing anything because his mom and dad had become second parents to me, and I had my mom and dad at home. I never had to worry if I was loved.

When my parents got married, we moved into my dad's parents' three-bedroom bungalow. It was close by, still in Little Village but a little south, in the 40s. When you moved up in numbers things got nicer, so the 40s were a step up from the 20s, but not by much. The house was maybe one thousand square feet, and it was *so* cramped. We had ten people living there once, and there was only one bathroom. One bathroom for ten people! God bless my grandmother, though. She tried to make things as neat as possible, and that house was spotless. It always smelled like Pine Sol and her perfume, and in the corner of each room she had a little cabinet that held her beloved knickknacks and every photo anyone had ever given her.

Outside on the streets, things weren't half that orderly. There were gang emblems, graffiti, and murals on every garage door and corner building. People refused to become immune to the mess, like they had on 26th Street, so they'd buy white paint to cover them all up. But no matter how much our neighbors tried keeping up the neighborhood, it never stopped the gangbangers from writing on the walls the next day. I knew an old Mexican man who was so worried that one of them would see a rival's graffiti on his house, then do a random drive-by, that he used his hard-earned paycheck to buy paint every single week.

Believe it or not, though, when I was that young, it didn't affect me. I was more concerned with how uncomfortable things were in our house than outside of it. I think people stereotype low-income, minority communities like Little Village as being "bad neighborhoods," where terrible things happen right out in the open and you're in danger all the time. I didn't feel that way. When I was little, I didn't witness anyone shooting up or sniffing lines of coke on the street corners. There weren't any crackheads stumbling down the street. You just didn't see those things out in the open. I wasn't naïve enough to believe that people didn't do drugs, but it just seemed like there was order. My father told me early on that there were rules and laws called "street codes." He said, "If a gang member's caught doing hardcore drugs, he'll get beaten up by other gang members. It's called 'a violation.'" Sure, you could see the gang members and dealers from a mile away because of their flashy cars and their gold jewelry, but they still had rules, so to speak.

Just before I turned ten, my dad started going to the Chicago police academy. If there was anyone who was meant to be a cop, it was him. You know when a police officer walks into a room, you can just *see* their whole aura? That was my dad. My mom had been working for years in the transportation business, and living with my grandparents had allowed them to save some money. My mom was pregnant with my sister, and the thought of having one more person cramped into that house was terrible. It was high time to move.

I'd been going to a private school on 69th Street, on the South Side, and my parents had been looking around there for a house for years. Finally, they found something they could afford, and we packed up our things and moved. The neighborhood, West Lawn, was only five miles away from my grandparents' place in Little Village, but it seemed like a different world. *This is wonderful,* I thought. *This is where people with real jobs live.* West Lawn was populated by city workers and their families, so it was solidly working class, but everybody wanted to create a better life for their families. And they did; it was basically little kid heaven. You could ride your bike and be outside all day long, like you were in a small town rather than the city. Our neighbors became our good friends, and we looked forward to block parties every summer. Everyone would sit on their front porches and talk to each other while the kids played games on the sidewalk. All my little neighbor friends went to the same Catholic school, and our parents were all living the same life, trying to make the same dreams come true—through honest means.

Sure, the "bad neighborhoods" were just a few miles away, where my own grandparents still lived and where we visited every weekend, but we felt like we were far from that. Unlike Olivia, I never had to learn to navigate the divisions within that type of neighborhood. Olivia knew the dynamics of gangs and drugs, and how to avoid crossfire by never driving down certain streets. I didn't have to do that; by the time I moved, I was above the fray. Where Olivia knew boundaries, I just saw streets.

Because my dad was a cop, though, I'd hear stories. Chicago was sort of a war zone in the early 1990s, and you'd constantly hear about innocent people losing their lives because of violence. When Dad left the house every day, sometimes in the morning and sometimes at night, depending on what hours he'd been assigned, I'd feel a pit in my stomach. Every now and then I'd see on the news about a cop getting shot, and I'd think, *Oh, God. That could have been my sweet dad.* If he was on the night shift, Mom would sleep maybe three hours all night. This was before cell phones were popular, so when he was on the streets he couldn't call us. We'd just have to wait for him to get back to his desk or show up at the front door when he got off duty.

Then he joined the gang unit and traded in his blue uniform for street clothes, and the danger he faced every day really started to hit home.

One Sunday night when I was in middle school my family went out to dinner at one of the nicer Mexican restaurants in Little Village. They had a mariachi band playing, and we were all sitting around the table, my little sister on a booster seat and my baby brother in his high chair. Dad loved mariachi bands—we all did—and we were just happily sitting there listening to them and trying to pick out what to order.

Suddenly, I saw my dad's face change from completely sunny and happy to white, like he'd just seen a ghost.

"What is it, Dad?" I asked.

"Nothing. Just order."

He was trying to play it cool, but his face said it all. He was scared out of his fucking mind. I was facing him, and I turned around and saw a crowd of gang members getting situated at a large table. They were glaring at my dad.

"Turn around. Don't look their way. I need to go make a call." He pushed his chair back and got up.

We just sat there looking at each other. Probably five minutes went by, and then, finally, my mom broke the ice. Under her breath she whispered, "He put a few of those guys away, and I think they just got out."

I wanted to get up and run, but I forced myself to stay seated. The gangbangers kept looking at our table, then one of them would stand up and go outside. He'd return, then another one would get up. Every time they did their chairs would scrape against the floor, making this loud *errrrr* sound, and I swear to God the mariachi guys would start to sing louder, like they were nervous, too.

Finally, my dad returned, but he had a uniformed cop in tow.

"Let's go," he said.

I stood up and lifted my baby brother out of his high chair, and my dad led us out as fast as he could. As we marched by, all the gang members stood up, in unison.

That was the last time we ever went to that restaurant.

We never saw those kinds of people in West Lawn, at least not for many years. At some point when I was in high school, though, the gangs started to migrate to the neighborhood, just a few people here and there at first, then crowds of them. You'd see them driving around in their jacked-up Chevys with rims, blaring music so loud it trembled through the streets. They wore their colors and their hats tilted to one side to represent whichever gang they belonged to. Even though someone could have shot them with just one look at their colors, they weren't afraid. *Maybe they're proud of who they are,* I wondered, and then I realized that it was more than that. They just weren't afraid. Most of them had teardrops tattooed on their faces, showing everybody how many people they'd killed.

Every single time I saw them, I hated them. These guys were completely disgusting. They would yell out obscene words to my girlfriends and me while we walked to and from school. At first we just ignored them, then eventually we started yelling back.

"Leave us the fuck alone!"

They'd answer, "You stuck-up bitches."

Other than yelling, what was I really going to do? Nothing, that's what. My dad was a police officer putting guys like that away, and our home was safe and normal. Mom and Dad made sure of it. I went to a nice private school right down the road and had had the same best friend since kindergarten. I made good grades and became a cheerleader. I did my homework on the kitchen table. I went to Catholic church on Sunday with my grandma, and like every kid, pretended I was sick one Sunday a month so I could skip it. Other than that, I was as good a daughter as you could ever wish for, and I did it because it was expected of me. Succeeding and making a good life was what people in my neighborhood did. And if I slacked off, I wouldn't be letting just my parents down, but my little brother and sister as well.

My mom had always taken her career seriously, and by the time I was in high school her intelligence and drive had helped her to reach the top: she'd become a supervisor at her job. She'd done it without a college education, too. She was happy with what she did—really happy—and after living with my grandparents cramped in a tiny house for so long, she deserved it. "Find something you love, and work at it!" she'd always say to me, and I admired her for it. She put in long hours and traveled all across the Midwest, and with my dad working nights a lot, there was really no one to take care of the house and my little brother and sister. Except me.

My little brother was just a baby then, and I spent every day after school and all summer babysitting him. If I ever wanted to go out on a weekend, I would do all my chores Monday through Friday. They weren't even chores; it was deep cleaning. Then I'd start cooking, so by the time my mom got home at seven thirty or eight, we would have dinner together, as a family. That's what mom wanted, so it's what she got.

My responsibilities were never-ending, but today, I'm grateful I had them. I learned the importance of taking care of your family, and while they might have sucked at the time, they served me well in the long run. Now I know how to be a great mother, and my brother and sister are still like my own kids.

Was I perfect then? Maybe I tried to be, but in the end, who really is? My biggest mistake came when I started dating in high school. During my sophomore year, I met a guy named Mark Jones. He was three years older than me, and his dream in life was to be a cop. Of course, I grew up with police officers, and I worshipped my dad. I knew how hard they all worked, sometimes two or three side jobs to be able to afford Chicago's sky-high taxes. I liked what those guys stood for, so I was drawn to Mark right away. Soon, I was falling for him in that high school way, when you think you've got everything figured out, even though you're only fifteen. *This is exactly the kind of person I should be with,* I thought. *You grow up with this life, you stick with it.*

I dated him for three years, through his time in the academy and during his first year as a cadet. We broke up when I was eighteen, and I'm so glad I did. He was arrogant, and he was a cheater. He thought he was God's gift to the world, and after a few years I really started to see him for who he was. I knew he wasn't the kind of person I wanted to be with, and thank God I figured that out because he ended up being a criminal as well as an asshole.

In 2012, Mark was sentenced to two months in jail after one of the biggest corruption scandals in the Chicago police force's history. Over the course of his career, he assisted his colleagues in stealing hundreds of thousands of dollars from suspected drug dealers during traffic stops and unlawful searches of their homes. From all the good things cops do, like protecting the city and your family, you'd think they'd all be loyal and honest. Nine times out of ten, I think they are. Look at my dad. But there are bad apples in the bunch, like my ex.

It would take getting to know my future husband and seeing what he went through with the police to show me how true that is.

CHAPTER 3

Junior

Olivia

After Leo went to prison in 1998, I was done with him, so I filed for divorce. That's when I hooked up with K.

Everybody called Kevin Garcia by his nickname, K. He was a high-ranking leader of the Latin Kings and ran in Little Village. He didn't look like your average gangbanger—you didn't see him on a street corner dressed in black and gold—but he didn't have to. He was somebody important. I'd seen him around for a while, starting back when I was going to house parties in high school, and I'd always felt an attraction to him. He was so powerful, and I was drawn to that. He had nice cars and iced-out jewelry. He was flashy and flamboyant, which was right up my alley because that's what I liked: loud. He moved a lot of drugs through Little Village and all over Chicago, but he owned a restaurant, which made him legit on paper.

Before Leo got arrested, and we had to forfeit everything, I was always in designer clothes. I'd gotten a boob job—back when no one else was getting one—and people called me the "Million-Dollar Bitch." It was hard not to notice me, and K had—from the first time he saw me out one night. He didn't start to go after me until my husband went to prison, though. The case was all over the news. He started pursuing me because he wanted to be with me, not because I had money. After all, he had plenty of his own.

He'd come by my mom's house constantly, trying to seek me out. I never gave in, until finally, one day, I did.

"Okay, I'll go out with you." A big smile spread across his face.

My dad walked the streets as a cop every day, and he knew trouble when he saw it. He was protective of his little girl, and he hated K on sight.

"How can you be with someone like that?" he asked. "He's a punk."

Even though I knew he was right, I was so in love that I didn't give a shit. "He's not like that anymore," I said. "Everybody changes." Then I flipped it on him. "You're so judgmental."

K had a rap sheet a mile long, but at first, he treated me like gold. He was a ghetto superstar. He knew everybody, and everybody knew him: the Spanish gangs, the black gangs, drug dealers, and people whose names I never learned. Every night, he and I would go to a basketball court downtown named Hoops, and he and all the moneymakers would rent it out starting at midnight. After games, they'd talk business.

One day in 1999, these two sweet-looking eighteen-year-old identical twins drove up in separate luxury cars. They were baby-faced, handsome, and well dressed, and even though they wore iced-out custom jewelry, designer man bags, and nice, fresh cuts, they seemed humble. I just knew they were somebody from the way everyone gravitated to them.

"Olivia, these are my little brothers, Peter and Junior," said K as he pulled them into a big hug.

One of them put his hand out to shake mine. *Get the fuck outta here!* I thought. Nobody did that anymore; people usually just stared at my boobs, but these guys looked me straight in the eye and greeted me like I was a real, proper lady.

I started talking with Junior, and I didn't realize he was so much younger than me because he was so mature. He couldn't have been sweeter, either. K was so flamboyant, with his Gucci and Armani clothes and his big personality. But sometimes, I could see right through him. Junior was just as impressive, but he was genuine and sincere. He seemed so different. I was surprised he was in this life.

"You're so sweet. I have to hook you up with one of my girlfriends," I said after we stopped talking.

"Sure," he said. "Just tell K to call me."

K told me that night that he'd started working closely with the twins. They were making big moves on the streets, and they were supplying him with quality work from Mexico. K wasn't a street-level dealer anymore, but he oversaw them, and he was such an opportunist that Peter and Junior had become a big asset to him. In return, he gave them protection and prevented anyone from robbing them.

Even though they were only eighteen, Peter and Junior were a big deal. They'd developed a sophisticated network of suppliers, stash houses, and workers, and they were selling narcotics to gangs like the Latin Kings. They'd made their first drug deal the year before—thirty kilos of cocaine, with a street value of almost a million dollars—and their business had boomed from that day on.

K and the twins had all grown up in Little Village, but their motivations had been different. The twins didn't know a life outside of the drug trade; it was something they'd been born into. Their mom had her first baby when she was only twelve, then had six more children. The twins were the youngest. Their dad had grown up in poverty on a farm in Mexico, dropped out of school in the third grade, then moved to Chicago in the 60s and started working as a forklift operator at Brach's Candy. He made $14,000 a year, which is hard to support seven kids on, so he became what they call a coyote, smuggling illegal immigrants over the border. Then he moved up to cocaine. Pretty soon, he was bringing about thirty-five kilos over the border every month. He bought a two-story house and a new Chevrolet station wagon, living out his version of the American Dream.

But just before Junior and Peter were born in 1981, the feds arrested their dad for possession, taking him away while his pregnant wife and kids stood there and watched. He spent the next seven years in prison while his wife suffered, working two jobs to make ends meet, cooking, cleaning, paying bills, raising newborn twins plus five other children, and visiting her husband every chance she could. When Junior and

Peter's dad got out, they were so happy to have him in their lives and were eager to learn from him.

Unfortunately, he wasn't the best role model. When they were seven, he asked them to put their little hands into gas tanks to fish out bricks of marijuana, then taught them to use a triple-beam scale. At eight, they translated drug deals for him. By nine, they were riding in flatbed trucks across the border with him, sitting on top of tarps that covered shipments of drugs. Their dad went on the run when they were twelve, fleeing another drug charge, and their older brother, Adrian, stepped in to help raise them. Unfortunately, he went to prison for drug conspiracy, too, then after five years was deported to Mexico on the day he was released. Peter and Junior had to do something to support their family, so they used the only skill they'd ever known: drug trafficking, using their dad's connections back in Mexico.

Unlike K, they weren't in a gang, and they were peaceful. K had gone to prison for aggravated battery and attempted murder, and the Latin Kings praised him while his enemies feared him. Peter and Junior didn't even carry weapons. They *needed* the money; K just wanted it.

I kept seeing Peter and Junior out more and more, and every time I'd see Junior, my face would light up. He made me feel alive. It just felt good to talk to somebody who was always so positive. He was like a breath of fresh air, always laughing and joking, and I loved the person he was. I wanted K to hang out more with him, to be more like him. Even though we had chemistry, it was just an innocent friendship, but K would sometimes notice us together, and he'd watch us out of the corner of his eye. He genuinely loved Junior, but seeing me happy with someone else caused his insecurities to get the best of him.

Still, I was all K's at this point because my divorce from Leo had gone through easily. He started treating me like gold, even helping me start up the salon I'd always dreamed of. I hired over ten stylists, and the place was booked out for months. I was working from the start of the day to midnight every day. Because business was booming, K and I opened up a massive car wash that we named Hot Boyz. It was the coolest spot ever, with neon lights shaped like flames surrounding the outside, which lit up the whole street. Finally, at only twenty-three, I had my own thing, my own *two* things: real, legitimate jobs. For the first time ever, I loved what I was doing.

On top of being super busy, making sure both businesses were running smoothly, I purchased my first house and completely gutted it. Interior design was my thing, so I went all-out decorating it and put in an awesome gaming room for Xavier. My house was modern, warm, and well put together all at once. Just like me.

Unfortunately, things with K had become up and down. We'd started breaking up all the time, usually because he'd cheated on me. Once, I kicked him out because he got an ex-girlfriend pregnant, and I swore there was no coming back from this one. It was over for good, and I decided to go to a club to hang out with my girlfriends. We were sitting in the VIP section, talking and laughing, and as I raised my champagne glass to make a toast to being single, I glanced out into the crowd. There was Junior. We made eye contact, and he walked through his entourage to greet me.

"Liv, what are you doing here? You're the last person I thought I'd see. Do you want to join me for a drink?"

"Can we go outside instead?" I asked. There was no harm in getting one little drink, but I was worried word would get back to K, and he'd come and find me and drag me out of the club. Even though it was over, just saying hello to Junior felt like a betrayal.

"Of course," he said. "Let's go to my car."

We sat in his car and talked for three or four hours, until the sun came up. Few things had ever seemed so natural, so right, but on the drive home I started thinking, *What am I doing?* I'd felt an attraction to Junior, and it was something deeper than I had with K. I hadn't done anything, and besides, K and I weren't even together, but my stomach was in knots, like I'd just cheated.

Every time I tried to make positive steps in my life, I faced heartache. So even though I'd broken it off with K, made a great home, and loved my work, life was about to get really bad.

When my ex-husband, Leo, went in front of the grand jury in 2000, he didn't just snitch on his drug dealer buddies; he also told on me. We weren't married anymore, so I wasn't protected by the law. Junior heard from his brother Adrian that Leo was planning to snitch on me as soon as our divorce went through, and he tried warning me.

He's just threatening me and trying to control me, I thought. *He won't actually go through with it.*

Unfortunately, I was wrong. The feds raided my salon in front of all my workers, then hauled my ass down to the federal building for questioning. Leo accused me of laundering the money he'd made from his drug deals, which wasn't true. The feds' proof was a $76,000 deposit I'd put in the bank, but that was money I'd made playing blackjack in Vegas. It was clean—I was clean—and I was going to prove it.

"We won't charge you if you wear a wire on K," the investigator said as he questioned me. "We've wanted him for a very long time, and you're going to help us get him."

"You're saying you want *me* to tell on K because my ex-husband is telling on me?" I was not a snitch bitch. Snitching was something Leo did, not me.

"Yes. And if you don't, we'll indict you. You're facing seven years in federal prison."

Fuck that. I wasn't a rat, and I was never going to be one. I decided that I was going to stay loyal to K, so I told the feds to go to hell. Because I wouldn't cooperate, they indicted me. I hired a defense attorney to represent me because there was no way I was pleading guilty to seven fucking years. I was determined to take it to trial. The feds knew I wasn't backing down, so they offered me a plea agreement for what they call a split sentence, which is five months in prison and five months of house arrest. My mom is my number one supporter, and she begged me to keep fighting.

But seven years in prison wasn't a chance I was willing to take. I took the plea agreement and signed on the dotted line.

K stood by me the whole time, and he promised to do the same forever. So in November, 2001, we flew to Vegas, me and the ghetto superstar got married in this little chapel with no one else around, and I told myself that would be my second, best, and last marriage.

When I said my vows, I knew I was making a mistake. I didn't even call my mother to tell her the good news. I loved K desperately, but it was a toxic relationship. Up and down and back up again; a cycle of fights and passionate make-up sex. K was more controlling than my first husband and my son's father put together. He beat me—hard and often. One time I was driving in my car with my girlfriend, after I'd fled the house, deciding once and for all that I didn't want to be with him. As I was driving as fast as I could, I felt something ram into the back of the car, like a train had crashed into me. It was K. He did it again and again, trying to throw me into oncoming traffic, till the trunk of my car was in my backseat.

The police came, but I refused to press charges. They were furious, but I was not a snitch.

I *always* believed K would change, even when he shot five bullets through my front windshield. I *always* loved him, even when he put a gun to my head, then turned it on himself and threatened to pull the trigger if I walked out.

Junior came by our house after I got back from Vegas. I was in the kitchen, washing dishes, and K called him inside.

"Hey, little brother!" he said. "Olivia, show Junior your ring."

I picked up my finger, but not my head. I just couldn't look at Junior.

"Oh, you got married?" he asked. He didn't sound upset, just shocked.

I was so embarrassed. It wasn't that I wanted to be with Junior; I was faithful to K, and Junior was a gentleman. I just knew that he suspected what I felt deep down: I'd gotten married because I didn't want to be alone when I went to prison. K was a convicted felon, so he couldn't have visited me if we weren't legally married.

I tried to love K the five months I was behind bars. In prison, you have all the time in the world to think about nothing or everything, and I chose to think about myself mostly.

Mom and Dad visited me with Xavier, who'd been asking about me nonstop. While it was painful to see his little face as he walked into the visiting room, it was almost worse to see my dad. Dressed in my prison garb, I could hardly look him in the eyes. Then, there was my mom, who'd lost her mom the day before—my sweet, pretty grandma—and I hadn't even had a chance to kiss her goodbye. My mom was broken, yet, there she was, trying to make sure I was okay. I thought, *My whole life, all she did was put me in front of everyone, even herself, and all I did in return was push her away.*

I really believe in karma, and I decided bad things would keep happening to me if I didn't do better. I didn't come from a broken home. I'd had a great childhood; I'd just chosen to run wild. I needed to make better decisions, and that meant surrounding myself with better people.

I realized K wasn't among them.

I started calling him more and more infrequently, and I asked him to visit me once a week rather than twice. For the first time in my life, I began loving myself and feeling like I didn't need a man to make me happy. I could take care of myself.

When K picked me up in June 2002, at the end of my time, he was like a different person. He'd always hung out with rappers and music producers, but he'd founded his own record label called Dinero Records and had started working with DMX, Fat Joe, Busta Rhymes, and this up-and-coming artist from Chicago named Kanye West. He went from flashy dude on the street to some kind of rap mogul in a matter of months. His ego had grown right along with his business. I'd changed, too; I'd grown away from him.

I knew I was never going to leave K, though. I loved him too much, so I tried to adapt. I'd go to his studio every evening wearing my court-ordered ankle monitor, and we'd record till dawn. I figured, *If you can't beat 'em, join 'em,* so I worked my butt off, and sure enough, I discovered I was great at running the record label. I set up an office, hired a publicist, met amazing people, networked, and built up strong business relationships. I was constantly on the phone with record labels, entertainment attorneys, and even famous artists, getting clearance for the records we were recording. We even stayed on the Hollywood set of the movie *Never Die Alone*, starring DMX, for a few months because K was an executive producer. It was a whole new world for me, and I really, truly loved it.

K threw a big party at Chocolate Factory, R. Kelly's recording studio, on the Fourth of July, just a little bit after I got out of jail. Junior was there along with hundreds of people, and when I saw him, I can't explain it; I just got so overwhelmingly happy. I thought, *Oh my God, a familiar face!* We caught up, and it felt organic, not awkward like the last time. I missed his friendship and the connection we'd always had.

I'd lost that connection with K, though. During my five months of house arrest, even though I was so happy running three companies, nothing got better between us. I knew he was still up to no good. Every morning I'd wake up and cook him breakfast, trying to get him up and moving, just so I could get him out the door. "I don't think I'm going to the studio tonight," I'd say. All I wanted to do was be alone, and I normally *never* want to be alone.

Then, in 2003, I found out I was pregnant.

"K, I don't want to have this baby," I told him. He knew we'd become two different people and that things were just bad between us. I didn't want to bring a child into that kind of situation. I'd done that with Xavier, and while he was my world, I'd been unfair to him. Sure, he went to great schools and had a mom and grandparents who loved him, but he'd had a hard life. I regretted the heartaches I'd put him through, and I didn't want to bring a baby into another single family home or unstable relationship.

"If you kill my child, I'll kill you," K said.

I knew he wasn't kidding.

Day after day, I accepted my life. I thought, *Okay, I'm going to make this work. For my marriage, for my son, for my husband, and most importantly, for my baby.* Where was I in all of that? Nowhere. I became passive and distant. I didn't fight back when he insulted me. I refused to do anything that would make me crazy, like going through his phone. Little by little, the drama went away, and I just disappeared.

When I was about four months pregnant, standing outside in front of his mom's house, I saw his closest friend flying down the street toward me. From the look in his eyes, I knew something serious had happened.

"What's wrong?" I asked.

"K's been shot," he said.

I don't think I even had time to process what he said. I just sprang into action and started to walk toward my car. *K's been shot before,* I told myself. *We've been through this. It's no biggie.*

"Which hospital is he at?" I asked.

The answer was drowned out by screams.

"They killed my son! They killed my son!" I looked up and saw K's mom running out of the house, her arms extended in front of her like she was begging God to give back her boy.

I fell to the ground, my belly in front of me. *I want to die,* I thought.

K had walked into a barbershop just north of Little Village, right near Douglas Park, and he'd been shot in the head four times. A rival gang, the Vice Lords, controlled that part of town, but K thought he was untouchable, that he ran the city. In reality, he had so many enemies that he couldn't trust anyone.

The funeral was a circus, and it was devastating for me. I just wanted to mourn my husband in peace, but there were probably a thousand people there, including DMX, Fat Joe's wife, and every Latin King in Chicago. The crowd was a sea of black and gold, and even the roses that were draped over his casket were spray-painted the gang's colors.

My dad, a dedicated police officer all his life, stood at my side along with my family, almost all of whom were Chicago cops. Their mouths were wide open the entire time; not only did they think K had left the gang life behind for the music business, they couldn't understand why anyone wanted to be remembered that way. The feds had also come, and they circled the outside, taking pictures, trying to scope out who they might be able to haul in. They knew all the heavy hitters would be there.

Everybody kept walking up to me and saying, "Oh my God, you're pregnant," and all I could say was, "It's okay. I'm fine." It sounds strange to say now, but with his baby in my belly, I felt like K was still with me. I didn't have to process his death if there was a part of him growing inside me, and I wasn't willing to let him go.

The twins were there, too. Junior approached me, reaching out to hug me. I fell into his arms like a baby.

"I'm so sorry, Liv," he said, "If you need me, please call me. I'm here for you."

A few weeks later, he called and said he knew I wasn't doing well. It was true; I was so sick I couldn't move, and my strength was gone.

"You need to get some fresh air," he said. "You're going to make yourself sick, and it's not good for the baby. Can I please take you to lunch?"

Junior had two little girls named Sasha and Samantha, and being a devoted dad, he understood my pain. He knew it wasn't just me that was hurting; it was my baby, too.

I quietly agreed to see him, and Junior picked me up in one of his fancy cars, I think the red Ferrari. But I was so out of it, it could have been a beater for all I cared. I must have seemed so out of place getting into it because I'd stopped putting on makeup and would only wear jogging suits. I looked exactly how I felt—like shit—but the sight of Junior sparked something inside me.

"Hey, where are we going?" I asked.

"Just up the street. It's nothing fancy."

We went to some totally normal diner that I'd passed by a thousand times; the kind of place where you can sit all afternoon and they'll refill your cup of coffee a hundred times. We just talked and talked and talked. He told me about everything that Samantha and Sasha were up to. I talked about Xavier, my pregnancy, and the fact that, because K hadn't had a will, I'd decided to give up my rights to Dinero Records in probate court. I wanted to avoid drama with his family. He asked me if I'd miss the music industry, and I said that someday I wanted to start my own label. For the first time in years, I felt happy and hopeful in the most innocent, simple way. All I needed was someone to feed me and make me smile, to treat me like a normal person and not the Million-Dollar Bitch. Inside that diner, that's exactly what Junior did.

We started going out to eat every few weeks, first lunch, then dinner. Every time, he reminded me how strong I was, and as my confidence grew, I put away my joggers and started to put on makeup. When I'd see him, my face would light up. I wanted to look pretty again, but not in a sexual way. I was a pregnant widow, and hooking up was the last thing on my mind. With Junior, it was different. It was more like I was falling in love with all of him, the whole *person*.

He motivated me to get working again, and within a month or so, I signed an R&B artist and hit the studio again. Staying busy helped clear my mind, and I didn't have time to feel anything negative. Junior and I went to New York City to record with Swizz Beatz and Kanye West, and we shot a video DMX made in honor of K. Everyone came out, including Fat Joe and Busta Rhymes.

Junior and I didn't care about being around famous people and living that life. When everyone would head out, we'd go to the grocery store, then go back to the hotel, chill out in our PJs, and eat cereal. When it was only us, there was no makeup, designer clothes, or jewelry. We just talked and laughed. It was the simple times that made us fall madly in love.

When he asked me what I dreamed of for my life, I was honest.

"I want my parents' life. I can't be with another bad boy or drug dealer. I need to grow old with someone who can give me stability."

Junior wasn't expecting I'd say that. But I could tell it got him thinking, so I continued.

"I have no idea why you're in this life, Junior. You can do better. With your intelligence, you'd be successful at anything." Then I paused, knowing that I couldn't live with myself if I didn't keep pushing. "You should change your life before it's too late. You don't want to go to prison with Leo or end up dead like K."

He just sat there, quiet, in deep thought.

A few weeks later, Junior took to me to see a show in downtown Chicago, and afterward he led me down a block toward Capital Grille, a restaurant right off the Magnificent Mile, where everyone knew him on a first-name basis. When we got close, I noticed all the lights inside were turned off.

"Junior, it's closed!" I said.

"Just wait," he answered.

When we got to the entrance, the lights came on, and the hostess welcomed us inside. Junior had filled the whole restaurant with flowers.

Everywhere I looked there were long-stemmed red roses, from the front door all the way to our private table in the back. They were beautiful.

I can't believe he rented out the whole restaurant for me, I thought.

Over dinner that night, Junior took my hands, looked at me and said, "I want to take care of you and your baby. I'll raise your baby like my own."

I gazed into his eyes and really considered what he said. *This man is as caring and compassionate as my own dad,* I thought. *I feel truly safe with him, like I'm finally myself, at home. I hate what he does for a living, but this is the person I've been looking for my whole life.*

I squeezed his hands. Just like that, I knew my baby was going to have a father, and I was going to have a new life.

CHAPTER 4

Peter

Mia

Even though we'd moved to West Lawn, I still went back to Little
Village to see my grandparents and my good friend Ana. My mom and
dad would let me spend the night at her house, but both they and Ana's
parents forbade us from going past their front yard since 26th Street,
where she lived, was so infested with gangs.

Ana had grown up just down the block from these identical twins
named Peter and Junior. She always talked about them, how cute and
nice they were, and how they weren't in a gang, but they were always
hanging around the neighborhood. I didn't get a chance to meet them all
the years Ana lived there, though. My dad was in the gang unit, patrol-
ling that area, and getting caught disobeying was *not* my idea of fun.

But in 1996, the twins moved to 72nd Street, which was only a few
blocks from my house.

"Pete and Junior are your neighbors now!" Ana said when she came over
one day early on in high school. "Let's call them. I want to introduce you."

Finally, I was going to meet the legendary Flores twins.

I knew Peter and Junior had moved into one of the nicer houses in
our area. It was two stories, and if you had stairs leading up to your bedroom, you had money. I'd seen them walking around, and even though I
couldn't tell them apart, they seemed like they could be cool. They were
handsome and wore nice clothes, and Ana liked them, so I supposed that
was good enough for me.

I was petite for my age, with blond hair, but being Brazilian I was blessed with natural curves and exotic features. I didn't look like your average sixteen-year-old girl, and boys in my high school were always gross, making comments about my body or my looks. When I'd meet a new guy, it would always go something like this: he'd look me up and down, throw his head back a little, and say, "Hey, babe, what's up?" It was the total opposite of charming.

The Flores brothers couldn't have been more different. When Ana introduced me to them, Peter shook my hand, looked me in the eyes, and said, "Hi, Mia, how are you? It's nice to meet you." It was like his mom had drilled those exact words into his head and made him say them, over and over.

Who the heck talks like that and shakes your hand? I thought. *Especially a fifteen-year-old?*

Soon, I started hanging out with them, and it was all innocent. We'd go to the lake, head downtown, or hit some parties. When the weather was nice, kids in West Lawn roamed around looking for something to do, but we were never up to anything. Not the Flores twins, though. The more I spent time with them, the more I realized that behind closed doors, something was just off with them. They were not normal teenagers. They were always wearing brand new clothes and shoes, which was strange to me. I'd ask myself, *What fifteen-year-old doesn't wear the same sneakers twice?* Their older brother Adrian drove luxury cars, had tattoos all over his body, and wore jewelry that shined so bright I could see it from down the block. When I'd pass by their house I'd see random people detailing Adrian's fleet of cars and motorcycles. He *screamed* drug dealer. I was no dummy, and I put two and two together and realized that it wasn't just Adrian; their family was making money some way, and it wasn't legal.

Pretty quickly, I stopped wanting to hang out with them so regularly. They were super cool, but their life was foreign to me, and I didn't want to be around people like that. I'll admit I was pretty stuck up and prissy then, but now that I think about it, I really *was* too good to hang out with them.

Plus, my dad told me they were bad news. "I raided their house when they lived on 26th Street," he told me. "And their brother Adrian went to prison 'cause he's a big kingpin."

As time went on, though, something about them kept calling to me, especially Peter. He was so much fun to hang out with, but at the same time, such a gentleman. He was mature, not rude and obnoxious like the other guys my age. Sure, his family was up to no good, but he seemed good on the inside. He'd already gone through things in his life, and it showed. He was like this little grownup.

One day when I was sixteen, I decided to have a party at my house, with my parents' permission, of course. I told my dad I'd invited Peter, and he was not too happy.

"I've told you before and I'll tell you again: that family is trouble."

"But, Dad, he's different. And besides, he's bringing his girlfriend and I'm bringing my boyfriend. Peter's just a friend."

When Peter arrived, my dad immediately had him cornered.

"I don't know what you're doing hanging out with my daughter," he said, "but stay away from her. She's a good girl." Then, realizing the risk I'd put us all in, he added, "Don't tell any of your little friends from 26th Street where I live."

Honestly, having a relationship with Peter was the last thing on my mind. Sure, I was with my boyfriend, Mark, but it was more than that. I just couldn't see myself with Peter. I liked his maturity, his whole demeanor, but sometimes, it intimidated me. I'd always dated selfish little boys, and now I was with a cocky cop-to-be. Maybe I wasn't too good for Peter; maybe *he* was too good for *me*?

Still, I identified with him. I spent every afternoon and school vacation cleaning the house and babysitting my brother and sister, so both of us, in different ways, were already living adult lives.

While being grown up for me meant discipline and responsibility, Peter's version meant making real money for his family. And for him, money came from drugs. I'd heard friends talk about the fact that he was dealing, but I shoved it to the back of my mind or denied it entirely. Growing up in the city, drugs were just accepted sometimes, especially if they weren't out in the open. If you had to deal to get by, that's just the way it was, as long as it didn't spill out onto the streets and make a big mess. I imagined Peter's dealing was small, something to put food on the table, not a lifestyle.

I soon found out that wasn't the case at all. Ana called me up and told me that something terrible had happened to his family.

"Someone broke into Pete and Junior's house, Mia. They tied up their whole family with masking tape, put guns to their heads, and stole a bunch of money they made from their business."

I held the phone tight and thought for a second. "A bunch of money? What do you mean by that?" I didn't even know they'd had a business.

What scared me even more was that a home invasion had happened right down the road from me. Stuff like that only happened on 26th Street. *Who and what are they bringing into my neighborhood?* I worried.

Peter and I didn't grow closer or grow further apart after that. We just stayed friends and neighbors, and I tried not to let on what I knew about his and his brother's true colors. They could do what they needed to do to make a living, as long as it was discreet, and I'd do what I had to do. For me, that meant making good grades in school, getting into college, and marrying the right man at the right time. So many of the guys I'd been dating had turned out to be jerks, so I was willing to be cautious and wait. I'd make sure that whoever it was, my parents would be happy with him, and until then, I'd live at home.

I went to college for court reporting and did well. But despite that, I decided to take a year off because Mom and Dad just couldn't afford my school bills and support my brother and sister. I wanted to help out, and luckily, Mom was in such a good position at her job that she could hire me. She and Dad had instilled confidence and a great work ethic in me, so I started working with her and earned good money. I made real goals: finish college, become a stenographer, and later on go to law school. I bought my own Mercedes and paid for the insurance myself, went to clubs on the weekend, and enjoyed mini vacations with my girlfriends. I just wanted to have fun, and I loved the fact that I wasn't tied down and didn't have to depend on anyone. A lot of my girlfriends were in serious relationships, and they weren't living life to the fullest, so I figured it was my time to be selfish. I was so giving at home that it was okay, out of the house, not to have a care in the world.

I never took my eye off the ball at work, though. Sometimes, I'd get home at six in the morning after a night out, just in time to take a shower and get lunches ready for my brother and sister. My mom would say, "You better not be late!" But I'd get ready fast and wave to her as I passed her on the highway, arriving at work before she did. When she'd walk in and spot me, she'd smile and say, "Mia, you're crazy!"

It was the middle of 2002, and I was seeing Peter a lot, but just as friends. Even if we were dating other people, we always made time to call each other or go out to dinner. In fact, I rang up Peter as much as he called me. He'd always laugh and say, "Hey! I'm supposed to be calling you!"

Every time we saw each other, the chemistry between us grew. But still, nothing happened.

On one of his visits, he invited me to take a ride with him to talk.

"Mia, why are you always picking the same type of guys?" he asked while he was stopped at a red light. "You need to choose someone totally different than what you're used to."

What he said or how he said it didn't feel too forward to me. I'd always felt comfortable venting to him, and giving each other advice was what we'd always done. But it got me thinking. *Maybe he's right. Maybe I have been looking in all the wrong places.*

Peter and I made plans to go out the following weekend, and all that week, I couldn't get him or what he'd said to me out of my mind. I thought to myself, *Why am I ignoring my feelings for him? Is it because we're "just friends"?* By the time the weekend arrived, I'd decided to stop being so careful and just go for it. I went to the mall and bought the prettiest dress and heels I could find. I knew exactly what would drive him crazy. That night, I put on full makeup and did my hair, and when Peter picked me up—looking incredibly handsome—and opened the car door like a perfect gentleman, I thought I was going to die from nervousness.

We went to dinner at a beautiful restaurant downtown with some of his associates and friends, and I couldn't believe I was so jittery. We'd been friends for so long and hung out so many times that not feeling comfortable was a strange feeling to me. Something was different that night. We just couldn't hide the fact that we had feelings for each other.

After dinner we went to a club and laughed, danced, and drank until the wee hours. When we finally left, my feet hurt so bad from my heels that he had his bodyguard carry me to his car. We went to an after-party at his house, and Peter called me into the bathroom. When I walked in, I saw he'd filled the bath with water so I could soak my feet. I sat at the edge of the bathtub, he took my heels off, and before he got up and I stepped into the water I looked right at him and kissed him on the lips. You got it: I kissed him first.

A few weeks later, we were sitting around daydreaming, and I blurted out, "I love California so much. I went there once, and I'd love to go back."

"Let's go. Right now," Peter said.

I looked at him like he was crazy. I was working full-time and I was so responsible when it came to work—I couldn't just leave my job like that. I'd never been impulsive, but the idea suddenly felt good. I thought about it for a few minutes, then blurted out, "Okay! Let's go!"

I didn't tell my parents I was going with Peter. I lied and said the trip was with some girlfriends, and I'd be back in a few days. Because I'd been working so much, my parents were thrilled I was leaving on vacation.

Peter had booked a penthouse suite in Santa Monica, and it was like something out of the movies. When you walked into it through double doors, all you could see in front of you was the ocean. The windows ran floor to ceiling and wrapped around the whole penthouse. Our first night there, we ordered room service, had unforgettable sex, talked and laughed until dawn, and went shopping the next day. He took me to all the high-end boutiques, and I felt like Julia Roberts in *Pretty Woman*. I was sure I must be dreaming, and days later, when Peter said he had to leave early to fly to Mexico for a business trip, I was crushed.

"I'll call you when I'm back, Mia," he said.

Not ten minutes after he walked out, the concierge called and said I had a delivery. When the valet showed up, he wheeled in ten dozen red roses, courtesy of Peter.

When he and I both got back to Chicago, we spent the next two weeks solid together. Then one night, he showed up, unannounced, and we sat down together in front of my parents' house. He looked miserable.

"Mia, I need to tell you something."

"What is it?"

He paused, just a little too long. "Angela's pregnant," he said. Angela was his ex-girlfriend. "She got pregnant when she and I were still together, before you first kissed me, and she's due in May. I'm getting back together with her. I'm going to make it work for the baby. I have to be a good father. But I'd like to stay friends; you're too important to me, and I don't want to lose you."

I think I went white. I knew he hadn't cheated on me—we weren't serious yet, or even exclusive—but I still felt betrayed. I'd worked so hard to really *be* someone, only to fall for a guy who got another girl pregnant. That wasn't who I wanted to be. It wasn't who I *was*. My Mom used to say, "You're a diamond in the rough!" and I took that to heart. Always. Everyone I knew who was my age had kids from different people, and to my parents—to me—I was this prized package. At twenty-one years old, I made a firm decision that there wasn't going to be any baby mama drama in my life. I was ready to say goodbye to Peter Flores forever, and right then and there on my parents' front steps, I did.

CHAPTER 5

The Heat Is On

Olivia

When K died, I didn't fully mourn. Even though I'd watched his body lowered into the ground, having his baby kept him with me or, rather, prevented me from really believing he was dead. My mom knew I was running myself into the ground trying to stay busy, so she kept saying, "You need to stop and mourn. This is not healthy for you or the baby." But my heart just wouldn't let go.

I went to have an ultrasound almost five months into my pregnancy. It was the day I was going to find out if I was having a boy or a girl, and while I was lying on the table with goo on my belly, the tech rubbing the ultrasound wand all around for what felt like ten minutes, she stopped.

"Hold on," she said, looking kind of pale.

"What's wrong?" I asked. "Please tell me."

"Let me get the doctor," she said and walked out of the room, leaving me all alone.

I knew something was wrong even before the doctor came in.

"I'm so sorry," he said. "There's no visible heartbeat. I think the stress from your husband's murder was a major factor here," he said.

He sent me to the hospital, and there I said goodbye to my baby, a child I'd never had a chance to get to know. When I gathered myself together and wiped away the tears that had been pouring from my eyes for hours, I realized, *It's not just my baby who's gone. So is K. I've lost them both.*

Right then, my whole world caved in. I was in so much agony I didn't even want to find out my child's gender; knowing it would have made the death way too real. I probably should have been feeling this kind of deep pain during K's funeral, but I suppose it didn't matter now. I felt *all of it* that afternoon. When my baby died, K died with him.

After I came home from the hospital, Junior was by my side through the whole ordeal, never saying one thing about himself. It was all about me and making me feel better. But that night he ended up coming back, and he looked distraught.

"What is it? What's wrong?" I asked.

He started crying. "Peter's been kidnapped. Somebody got my brother. We think the cops are involved, but I've got a really bad feeling it's worse than that, Liv." He paused. "I don't think I'm ever going to see him again."

"Shut up," I said. "Don't say that. Never say that. You've got to fight." I felt so close to giving up, but that was not something I was going to let Junior do. My baby was gone, but Peter deserved to live, and Junior had to fight to get him back.

"There are these killers who've been kidnapping guys in the city," Junior said. "They rob them for work and shake them down for money. But they're not alone. They have these crooked cops doing surveillance and the dirty work for them."

Whoever was behind this had gone after Peter because he and Junior were major players. By the middle of 2003, they'd become the most prominent drug traffickers in Chicago, selling up to two tons of narcotics a month. Their enterprise had Mexican-based suppliers, stash houses in and around Chicago, and dozens of workers, many of whom they'd known their entire lives. They were the highest link in the drug trade's chain of command, with access to the highest-quality narcotics that could be found in the Midwest.

That meant they had loads of money, and a kidnapper and some dirty cops wanted it.

"So what are you going to do?" I asked.

"All we can do right now is wait."

We sat there in my parents' house, just holding each other's hands and feeling helpless. We knew next to nothing, and there wasn't a fucking thing we could do. For that moment, I put my pain aside. I needed to be there for Junior. He wanted to do something—anything—to get his brother home, and I just wished I could help him.

I was so worried about Peter, too. Not just for Junior, but because I really loved his brother. Peter's outspoken and forceful like me, and I always identified with him. Sometimes I even thought that Junior wanted to be with me because I was so much like his brother.

Junior's phone rang, and he answered.

"Hello? Oh, God, it's you, thank God. Are you okay?"

"Is it Peter?" I asked.

Junior waved his arms at me to be quiet, then started to nod his head. *Peter was alive.*

"Okay, okay. I'll give them whatever they want. I just want you out of there." He snapped his phone shut as he reached for his coat.

"I have to hand over $500,000 and one hundred kilos," he said. "They've got Peter, and I think Saul Rodriguez is behind it. Saul has to be the one who kidnapped him; word on the street is that he's got a crew of cops, and they've been kidnapping guys for work. Saul's been reselling it all back on the streets. They're all in it together, Liv."

He kissed me on the forehead and walked out the door.

Saul Rodriguez, I thought. *Goddamn Saul and some dirty cops.*

Mia

I didn't see Peter from the time he found out about the pregnancy till after his daughter, Sophia, was born in mid-2003. I was proud he wanted to be a good dad. My biological father hadn't been present in my life, so I knew that Peter being there was the best thing he could have done. The last thing he needed was to live with regret.

I was devastated about us going our separate ways, though. It would have been easy to say goodbye to him if he wasn't this perfect person to me, but I missed him so much my stomach was in knots all the time. It didn't matter what I was doing or where I was, my thoughts always came back to him. On my way home from work I would drive down the street near his house hoping I'd see him. He and Junior owned this really successful barbershop called Millennium Cuts, where people would stand in line for two hours waiting to get in, and I'd always pass by, expecting to catch him mingling outside.

After Sophia was born, he called me from time to time. He told me things weren't great with his girlfriend, and they weren't even that serious, but he was head-over-heels in love with Sophia. I was happy for him, like genuinely, sincerely happy. We talked about how much we missed each other, and how difficult it was to be away from each other. I accepted that situation because it's what I wanted.

We even saw each other a few times, once at a dinner where I met Junior's girlfriend, Olivia. She was older than me, and she'd had a lot more experience in pretty much everything, which showed. I remember thinking, *Who is this girl? She is so unlike me.* The thought passed quickly, though; I was more focused on Peter, and I couldn't stop asking myself: *Why am I not with him? I've stayed in relationships for all the wrong reasons, but being a father isn't wrong.*

But I just couldn't do it. I'd made up my mind.

We had many of the same friends, and I often heard about him through them. One night, I went to dinner with one of them, somebody who worked for him. Her face was practically white when she sat down at our table.

"Mia, I don't want you to be scared, but I need to tell you something. Peter's been kidnapped."

I think I stopped breathing. *Kidnapped?* I saw that shit on movies and TV, but it didn't happen where I came from. I'm not even sure what I said next.

"We think it was the cops," she added.

My dad is a cop, and he's the most honest man I know. I grew up with the CPD. I saw what they went through, going into war zones every day just to put food on the table for their kids. They were constantly disrespected by the people they were trying to protect. Why? Because Chicago police had been getting themselves into corruption scandals since the days of Al Capone. Right then, the bigger part of me was terrified for Peter, but another part was just pissed off.

"You've got to be kidding me," I said. "What's happening? Where is he?"

"His brother is working it out. He'll be home soon."

After dinner, all I could do was think about Peter. If something were to happen to him, I wouldn't be able to live with myself. I worried about him all night, thinking, *I'll never get the chance to tell him how I really feel about him and how much I know we belong together.*

Peter's worst nightmare—and mine—had come true.

Olivia

I'd known Saul Rodriguez since I was a kid, and he'd always been bad news. Once K had caught him creeping through our alley and circling the block. When he'd stopped him and dragged him out of the car, the only thing that saved Saul was the fact that a cop passed by. I knew what he was up to, though. He was staking our house out, plotting to kidnap K and hold him for ransom, just like he'd been doing to other drug dealers all over the city.

Now he'd gotten Peter.

But where did the cops fit in? After Junior had paid the ransom, which was money and drugs totaling $3 million, and they'd let Peter go, Junior told me the whole story. It was just about the worst thing I'd heard in my life up to that point.

Peter was behind their building, just a few blocks from Midway Airport, when he saw an unmarked police car. *Oh, shit,* he thought when two cops jumped out and started moving toward him. He'd never been arrested in his life. He didn't have anything on him, but when you're a drug dealer, cops freak you out.

One of the police officers told him to turn around. He did, and the officer handcuffed him, read him his rights, and shoved him in the backseat of the car.

"What am I being charged with?" he asked, but neither answered. Instead, the other cop jumped in the back with him, tied his feet together, and put a bag over his face. When they got to the Park & Go by Midway, they took him out and threw him in the back of a white van.

That's when he knew he was in deep shit.

They took him to a tri-level house and tossed him into the basement. When they lifted the blindfold, he saw someone who looked like a fireman standing in front of him. Except this was no fireman. He was wearing a Hazmat suit, a facemask, and rubber boots. The walls and the floor were completely covered in plastic, with duct tape holding the sides down.

The guy in the suit started beating him, and he didn't fucking stop till the phone rang.

Mia

Peter told me later that it was Saul Rodriguez on the other end of the line. And even though Saul was known for torturing people, he told the guy in the Hazmat suit to take mercy on him.

"Peter's not a violent guy," Saul said, "so take it easy on him."

The "fireman" then tied Peter to a chair and left him there for twenty-four hours without food or water. His only company was a parrot who'd been trained by one of the kidnappers. He squawked, "Fuck you!" all night long.

Olivia

Junior came through with the ransom, over one hundred kilos of cocaine and some cash, as quickly as possible. But it was shitty cocaine, and Saul was furious. After teaching Peter a lesson, he had him call Junior.

"Junior, you pissed them off by giving them that garbage," Peter said, sounding frantic. "Just give them whatever the fuck they want, or they're going to kill me."

Junior came through with another hundred kilos, this time the good stuff.

The kidnappers then gave Peter a cell phone and kicked him out at the Home Depot by Riverside, a suburb of Chicago. He called his brother, and when Junior showed up to get him, he said Peter just looked different. He was pale, tired, and dirty. He didn't want to be around anybody.

He'd been in the back of a van or in a basement, bloody and beaten, for three long days, and part of him had changed forever.

Mia

Peter left Chicago and went to Mexico for a month, just to get away from everything. I was so worried about him, but I figured he had to do what he had to do. He needed room to breathe and space to recover.

Then he decided he wasn't going to go after the guys who kidnapped him. Junior had paid the ransom, and Peter was safe. Besides, he was a drug trafficker, so what was he going to do, go to the police to say that one of their own had arranged his kidnapping? He also knew that Saul was a paid informant and was always looking for a quick come up. Peter had no choice; he had to move on.

But given what he did for a living, and given what people were capable of doing to him, I started to wonder: *Should* I *move on?*

Olivia

I was having misgivings about being with Junior, too. When he handed over almost $3 million in drugs and cash like it was nothing, it stopped me in my tracks. I remember thinking, *Oh, shit. This guy is in it bigger than I ever thought.* I knew Junior had supplied K, and I knew he had the money to afford the kinds of fancy cars he drove. Taking losses was the cost of doing business. But losing $3 million? That put him on a whole different level.

I started to feel really conflicted. I thought, *This is not what I want. I don't want to go back to this life again.* I've never been one to hold anything back, so I told him.

"Junior, I'm scared for you. I don't want to lose you to jail or see you get hurt. I'm afraid you're going to get kidnapped like Peter or murdered like K. You're better than this. If you want to change your life, we can do this together. I love you, and I don't want to lose you."

"I love you, Liv," he answered calmly, but firmly. "I know you've been through so much. I promise I'll make it right, so please just be patient."

I paused and starting thinking. *If I've changed so much over the last few years, he can, too.*

With all my heart, I believed him, and I believed *in* him, so I stayed.

Mia

Peter came back from Mexico after a month, and I was the first person he got in touch with. *Oh, thank God,* I said to myself when he called and said he wanted to come over to my parents' house. I was *so* relieved to hear from him. We hadn't talked when he was gone, and I'd missed him terribly.

"Mia," he said when he showed up that night, "I'm so sorry, I just couldn't stay away. I can't stop thinking about you. Every thought just comes back to you and me. My happiest moments are when we're together, and I need you in my life." He paused and held both my hands tight. "You can trust me; your heart's safe with me."

Oh, man, I thought. *It's decision time. Either I say goodbye to him forever, or I jump right in.*

I'd spent hours and hours going through our situation while he was gone, and I'd realized I could live with being a stepmom. But could I be in a relationship with a drug dealer? And could I—the daughter of a cop—willingly enter a life built on crime?

Peter was everything I'd wanted in a person and everything I thought a man should be—minus what he did for a living. But life without him felt hollow. I hurt without him around. I took about thirty seconds to remember how I'd ached when he'd been away, experienced it all over again, and made my decision: I wanted to be with the drug dealer with a heart of gold. I loved Peter for all the goodness and kindness I saw inside him, and I'd choose to let the rest slide.

"Peter, I trust you," I said. "Just, please, don't break my heart."

"I promise I won't," he answered.

From that moment on, I was a part of his world. I didn't see everything—in fact, he wanted to protect me, so most of what he and Junior did was out of earshot or behind closed doors—but I knew it was there. I justified it, too. I'd think, *He's never known another life, and he's doing this because he needs to take care of his family.* He had dozens and dozens of hardworking people under him—mothers and fathers who depend on him to help put food on the table. *These people would be working at McDonald's if it wasn't for him and Junior.* It was true; his employees made more in a week than people working minimum wage made in a year, and they were decent people just trying to give their families a better life.

Olivia

In Chicago, Peter and Junior were constantly busy. They had dozens of customers, and every time a shipment came in they had to know exactly which warehouse it was going to and who was unloading it. Then someone had to deliver the goods, collect the money, and count it. There was an unbelievable amount of money coming in, too: tens of millions, all stacked up in their stash houses.

Mia

Peter took me to a stash house once. We were driving through the West Loop, right near Oprah's Harpo Studios, when he coasted his car toward the garage of a townhouse.

"Mia, this will only take a minute, I promise."

"It's beautiful over here," I said, looking out my window.

"I know. That's the whole point. Our stash houses are in upscale neighborhoods, where the cops won't look."

There were no cars around, and definitely no cops. Somebody could step out of a car and give somebody a bag, and it wouldn't look suspicious. Back in Little Village there was a cop on every corner; if someone handed you a bag, you'd be cuffed in seconds.

The townhouse had to be worth at least $1 million, maybe $2 million. As we walked inside from the garage, I could see beautiful furniture—really high-end stuff that you'd never picture in a drug den. Peter moved toward a wall and pulled a handle, which popped the wall right open. It made that *whoosh* sound that hydraulics make and opened really smoothly, like it was floating. I took a peek and gazed upon more money than I'd ever seen in my life. When I walked into the room, I saw stacks of it. It was all banded together and scattered around, with two workers running the bills through several money counters. *They're going to be counting for a long time,* I thought.

Olivia

One night, Junior left Hoops early to meet up with someone. I was with him, and on the way out, we bumped into R. Kelly, who he balled with practically every night.

"We'll meet up tomorrow," Junior hollered as we walked out. "Something came up."

We got in Junior's car and drove to one of his and Peter's stash houses.

"Can you get the garage door opener?" Junior asked.

"Sure," I said, grabbing a labeled opener from his bag. It was hard to figure out which one to pick since there were so many, and they all had code names. *This looks pretty damn sophisticated,* I thought to myself.

We couldn't park in front. We had to go through the garage, so no one would see us or our car. Once I was inside, I met all the workers. They were dressed up, business casual. They weren't allowed to wear flashy jewelry; they had to be clean-cut. You'd never know they were drug dealers or that they were carrying money. They were well spoken and didn't look like they were from the streets.

Behind closed doors, I met their personal property manager, who they paid to secure all their stash houses and warehouses. She used to come up with fake papers—everything from credit reports to bank statements to IDs—and get condos at $7,000 or $8,000 a month in rent. She'd say something like, "I'm dating a politician, and I don't want anyone to know, so I'll just pay for the year upfront." The landlords wouldn't do background checks with that kind of money in their hands.

Mia

I didn't ask any questions that day, but later on, I learned how the stash houses worked.

When money came into a house, workers would count it immediately. Each house never had more than $7 million in it, and counting a million dollars took each worker probably two hours. The stash houses that only held money were equipped with soundproof rooms, just like in a recording studio, because there were several counting machines going at the same time. The workers counted and packaged money in three shifts a day, each eight hours long.

Olivia

Different workers would pack up the drugs, and they'd do it really carefully, with cling wrap, vacuum bags, duct tape, and fabric softener sheets to minimize the scent so the cops and K-9 unit wouldn't be able to detect it if one of their workers got pulled over.

Never, under any circumstances, did a crew member go to a house other than the one where he was stationed. If someone was working at a house, they stayed there; going in and out too often looked bad, and Peter and Junior trained their workers never to draw attention to themselves or what they were doing.

Their workers always kept the same responsibilities, too, never switching out. Peter and Junior's first job had been at McDonald's, where they'd learned this "every worker to one task" system. Every employee there did the same thing every single day: The fry guy dipped his basket into the bubbling oil. The girl at the drive-through handed you your order. Some other girl took your money. If you were only doing one task rather than ten different ones, it was harder to fuck something up. They built their whole infrastructure around this system. It was genius.

Mia

Peter had so many burner phones, one for each customer. At any given time, you could expect him to be hauling probably twenty phones around with him, and they rang constantly. He'd answer *every single call*. Then a few weeks later he'd toss the phone, get a new number, and start all over. I've never seen anyone multitask like that.

Olivia

Junior and Peter had dozens of cars and trucks and were constantly inventing new ways to move drugs around Chicago and beyond. They switched up vehicles like they switched up phones, buying the same model and same color cars so that neighbors wouldn't realize that there were different workers coming in and out of the stash houses.

They also outfitted these cars with secret compartments; One could be opened with a foot pedal that you could activate only when you turned on the defroster and rolled down the windows. They'd moved way past hiding pot in gas tanks—that was the stuff they'd done for their dad when they were seven.

Mia

Most of the time, Peter and Junior thought they were flying under the radar. And except for Peter's kidnapping, they were, at least initially.

By the middle of 2003, though, the Drug Enforcement Administration was on to them, and they had people on the ground in Milwaukee investigating them. Why Milwaukee? Because it was a major distribution area for them; they constantly sent drugs there through one of their many couriers.

Olivia

In fact, Milwaukee was one of the first cities they expanded out to as their empire began to grow. When Adrian was in prison for drug conspiracy in the early 2000s, one of his associates named Tommy Arevalo introduced Junior and Peter to a couple of connects from Mexico, and they began shipping cocaine right up interstate 94 to Milwaukee.

Mia

By the time Peter was kidnapped three years later, DEA agents in Wisconsin had started to question street-level dealers, who spoke in hushed tones about "Peter" and "Junior." The investigation led back to Chicago, where the feds were trying to build their case and had started sniffing around.

Olivia

All that time, though, they felt they had to keep working. But Peter thought he was putting in more time than Junior, and he was on his brother's ass because of it.

"You're slipping, Junior," he said. "You care more about your girl than your business."

Junior didn't care; that was just Peter being controlling. Junior *always* handled his business.

In September 2003, we got a beautiful condo together in Lincoln Park. Some people were mad that I hadn't waited a year to find someone new after K died, but I couldn't help what had happened. You can't dictate when you fall in love. We moved together with Xavier, who was in middle school and was growing up to be this wonderful little man. After all that my son had been through with the men in my life, I was initially reluctant to have him get to know Junior. I'd told myself that if I ever moved on from K, it would be with someone who worked a nine-to-five job. But I fell for Junior when I saw the good in him and the great father he was to Samantha and Sasha. I knew I could trust him.

Xavier absolutely adored Junior, and Junior felt the same. He'd drop my son and his friends at Dave & Buster's, or spoil him by buying the new Jordans that were always so hard to get. To Xavier, Junior was this hip, cool guy, like his buddy, and when I saw them together, I'd tell myself, *It's okay. Relax. You're being a good mom by surrounding your son with good people who love him.*

I think that North Side condo is where we really became a family. Junior had Samantha and Sasha every other weekend, and I babied them like they were my own. I'd always wanted a daughter, so I secretly wished they were mine, and I'd change their Pampers, shower them, cook for them, and comb their hair. They would tell me, "I want to be pretty, too!" so I'd let them put on my makeup and play dress-up with my clothes.

We did everything together, me and Junior and the kids. And when they weren't with us, we were traveling and living it up. We sat ringside at the De La Hoya–Mosley fight in Las Vegas. Junior invited all his friends, who happened to be his workers, and he rented out sixty rooms at Mandalay Bay for them. We all went out and shopped all day, ate steak and lobster at night, partied in the VIP sections of clubs at night, and had drunken sex till the morning. It was exactly what Vegas should be.

That Christmas, Junior gave me a ring. It was this big, beautiful yellow diamond ring, around seven carats. *Is this an engagement ring?* I thought. But Junior didn't say anything, and I didn't ask. I knew I wanted to marry him someday, but it could wait.

"Let's go to Mexico for New Year's, baby," he said that night. Without any hesitation, I agreed.

We drove thirty-six hours to Mexico and talked the whole way about everything—our kids, our families, and how we wanted them to come together in the future. I didn't care whether the ring on my finger meant anything or not. All that mattered is that I was with Junior.

We went to his family's ranch in San Juan, a few hours away from Guadalajara. Within days, I think I'd made up my mind. On that gorgeous plot of land in the middle of nowhere with more horses than people, I thought, *I'm safe. Nothing is going to happen to us here. We don't have to worry about someone coming to kidnap us or rob us or the feds taking Junior away. Simplicity, family, and love are all that matter, and we can have that here. I've changed, and here, Junior can, too.*

I broke the silence. "Junior, let's stay. Let's just stay in Mexico forever."

He looked me straight in the eyes and agreed.

All he needed with him was his brother.

Mia

If Peter was feeling the heat, he hid it from me. That winter, he got me a condo off of Michigan Avenue, and I moved in, all on my own. I was twenty-three years old, and I'd never lived away from my parents. I even quit my job to go back to school to become an aesthetician; Peter and I were planning to open up a spa together.

When we weren't holed up in that beautiful apartment falling in love with each other all over again, we were going out to eat, making plans for our future business, or shopping at Chanel or Cartier right down the block.

Unfortunately, that January, bad things started happening in the midst of what should have been the happiest time in Peter and Junior's lives. In January 2004, one of their employees, a guy named Stubby, ratted on him and Junior. The feds raided one of their stash houses, then another.

In late February 2004, Peter and I were together at my condo. We were relaxing and talking, like we always did. We decided to watch a movie, cuddle, and go to sleep early. While we lay in bed, he made me laugh so hard and so much that I suddenly became exhausted. Before I passed out cold, he told me he had to work the next morning. That wasn't unusual; I'd begun to understand his life, but I didn't ask questions. When you're so young and feel carefree and happy, you just go with it. At least, I did.

The next morning, Peter woke up, rolled over, and looked at one of his twenty-some phones.

"Oh, shit, I have twenty missed calls. Did I turn the volume off?"

Having missed calls was basically a drug dealer's worst nightmare. Something was wrong. Really wrong. Peter switched on the volume, and the phone rang immediately.

"Alicia, I'm so sorry I missed you. What's up?" Alicia was his sister. He paused while he listened to her. "Oh my God. Call the lawyer and don't say anything."

I was terrified. "What is it? Is everything okay?" Peter didn't answer; instead he moved toward the window and pressed his face against it.

"What are you looking for?" I asked.

"The feds. They raided my house. They also hit the barbershop and Junior's house. They're looking everywhere for me and Junior. I've got to go."

He was pulling on his shoes when another phone rang not three minutes later.

"Silvia," he said. That was another sister. "Oh my God. Get out of there and don't say a thing. Call me later." Peter moved back to the window to scan. "Mia, I need you to drive me somewhere. The feds raided my sister's house."

I didn't even ask who he was supposed to meet. I just pulled on some clothes, got my keys, walked to my car, and started it up, bawling the whole time.

As I drove, I was crying so hard I was worried I was going to hit something. The only thing I kept thinking was, *I can't drive through a red light. They'll catch Peter if I do.*

When we finally got to a parking lot a few miles downtown, I looked at Peter and said, "Am I ever going to see you again?"

He smiled, took my face in his hands, and kissed me, hard. "Of course you're going to see me again."

And with that, Peter Flores walked away from me, left the country, and didn't return to the United States for almost five years.

PART TWO

MIDDLE MEN

CHAPTER 6

San Juan

Olivia

In January 2004, Junior and I decided to move to San Juan to be close to his family. That's where his parents were from and now lived, and it was where Adrian had settled with his girlfriend, Daniela, after he'd been deported.

Mountains cut through San Juan—some of them really rugged and tall—and in other spots there are mesas, with steep cliffs and dry valleys. It's pretty much what you imagine rural Mexico to look like, and personally, I thought it was dramatic, gorgeous, and exactly the place I wanted to start a new beginning with Junior. For the first time in years, I didn't feel the weight of the past or fear for our future. Mexico was a place I could truly change my life. Where Junior could change *his* life.

The only concern weighing on me was Xavier, who was now a teenager.

"I don't think he'll want to move here," I said to Junior. We had always looked out for Xavier's best interests. I wanted to protect him, and so did Junior.

Junior responded, "We have to put Xavier's education first. He won't get a great education in a town like this, so let him finish out the school year, and then we'll move to Guadalajara, where there's an American school. It's an excellent school, and I'm sure he'll love living in the city. Plus, it'll give you enough time to make everything perfect."

When Junior said things like that, it melted my heart. Most men I knew were selfish and didn't really care about another man's son, but not Junior. He treated Xavier like his own.

Xavier had had a complicated life with all I'd put him through. He'd been there when the feds dragged my first husband to prison, and he was there when they lowered my second husband into the ground. The last thing I ever wanted was for my choices to affect my son, but I knew they had. I had a hard time forgiving myself for it. Xavier deserved better, and I worried that if I carted him off to a small town in Mexico he'd detach emotionally and resent me.

In my heart, I knew Chicago was the best place for him, and leaving would just *crush* him. He loved his school and his friends. He loved doing normal things like going to the movies, spending weekends at Dave and Buster's, hanging out at Millennium Park, bowling, or walking down Michigan Avenue. Before Christmas, he'd literally count the days till he could go see the big Christmas tree downtown—something my sister and I had always done with our parents. He adored my mom and dad, and living with them, he'd have the stability I wanted so much for him. He was enrolled at one of the best private schools in Chicago, had made the honor roll, played sports throughout the year, and truly made all of us proud.

I just couldn't make him leave all of that.

Besides, I didn't want him to be exposed to Junior's work. *I just need a little more time to convince Junior to change and get out of this business,* I told myself. *And it'll be easy now that we're here to stay. When that happens, I'll be the luckiest woman in the world, with the man of my dreams and my son.*

I knew I deserved to be happy, too. I was young, and I didn't want to grow old alone. I wanted to be happily married like my parents and grandparents, and I'd have that with Junior. We were destined to be together. It was like we shared the same heart.

Leaving Xavier was the hardest thing I've ever done in my life. I knew it wouldn't be easy living without him, so I made a plan. I was still producing records, so I decided to schedule work trips to Chicago every two weeks. It was a lot on me, but when I saw Xavier, it was like all my Christmases came at once, and I showered him with gifts and tons of affection. When I left, I felt so guilty, but I told myself this would only go on for six more months. Then I'd mark my calendar for his school breaks, when he'd fly to Mexico to spend holidays with us as a family.

In Chicago, though, he seemed happy, and that was all that mattered. He was at home, and now that I was in San Juan, I had to make it feel like home, too.

The town had practically nothing in it. About ten thousand people lived there, and there were only a few local restaurants and some taco stands situated on the corners in town. There was no supermarket, just a few little fruit stalls, and you'd have to drive two hours to get to Burger King or Costco. It was in the middle of nowhere, but it was beautiful. There was a mountain nearby with a statue of the Virgin Mary on top. In Spanish, they call that a *santuario*, and Junior and I would walk there every day and just sit and talk. At night, there was nowhere to go out, so we'd play charades or cards and tell stories with his family.

My future father-in-law, who we all called Señor, had moved back to San Juan in the early 1990s when he was on the run. He and my future mother-in-law lived in a pueblo just outside of town, and he was doing the day-to-day things retired guys do. He was so into betting on the cockfights that he flew in his own roosters, thinking they were stronger than the ones you could find locally. He went into town every single day to bet on the horses. And when he wasn't eating his wife's delicious cooking or hanging out with whatever kid or grandkid was there visiting, he was waiting for money from Peter and Junior to show up. They supported him because, in the old country, that's what you were supposed to do.

Señor was completely different than my sweet dad, but I clicked instantly with him. He was very macho, very Mexican, and thought that women should stay home, have kids, and never work. He'd sure found the right wife for that, too. I loved Junior's mother, but she was the polar opposite of my firecracker mom. She obeyed her husband, raised seven kids, and lived for him. I'd always take her places and spend quality time with her, and I think she liked going with me mainly because it got her out of the house. Plus, I was missing my mom, so I appreciated being with her.

"You should have as many wives as you can afford," Junior's dad used to say to his sons.

American girls are offended by statements like that, and I was no exception. I called him out. "Who do you think you are, treating a woman like that?"

He wasn't used to a strong, opinionated woman, so he'd smile and smirk. I entertained him and made him laugh. He enjoyed having *real* conversations, even though we'd get into these heated debates that I'd never back down from. He started to respect me because of it, and I felt the same.

He was such an authority figure in his family, always preaching about not doing drugs or drinking. He'd say, "Smoking will kill you!" if anyone around him dared to light up a cigarette. You'd think that would make him some kind of saint, but this was the man who introduced his kids to the drug trade. He was a bundle of contradictions.

Junior's older brother Adrian and his girlfriend, Daniela, were more my speed. They were funny and outgoing, and like me and Junior, inseparable. Adrian was a Latin King back in the day and ran with K, who'd been one of his best friends. In fact, he was a drug dealer, so he'd introduced K to hustling. I'd never met him, though, because in 1998 he'd gone to prison for drug conspiracy and was there the whole time K and I were married. Guess who was his cellmate in prison? My ex-husband, Leo. Chicago was a small town if you knew the money makers, like Adrian did.

Daniela became a sister to me almost immediately because she was sweet and protective, like my own sister. She and Adrian were instantly welcoming, making us feel right at home. They're a big reason I wanted to stay; I missed my family, and they stepped up and created one for me from the moment we got there.

Family really was everything to Adrian. He's fifteen years older than Peter and Junior, and when the twins were born, their dad was in prison. Adrian stepped in and basically raised them. He sold drugs to provide for the family, but he was insistent that his little brothers not get into the kind of trouble he was always in. He had them on a curfew when they were old enough to leave the house, and he did everything he could so they wouldn't join the Latin Kings. He'd constantly point to gang members and say, "Look at them. They're losers. You're better than that." He wanted the best for them, so he made sure they kept their grades up, taught them responsibility, and when they started working at McDonald's, Adrian matched their paychecks, dollar for dollar.

Like their dad, though, he was full of contradictions. One day he asked Junior to retrieve the keys from the trunk of his car. Junior walked out, came right back, and said, "Adrian, there are no keys there." His older brother's face dropped, and he ran outside with Junior, popped open the trunk, and grabbed ten kilos of cocaine from inside it.

"They're right here, Junior," he said. "Let this be a lesson to you. Not only do you have to be book smart, you need to be street smart, too."

Adrian honestly wanted to keep Peter and Junior away from the bullshit, but he couldn't; it was a family thing. When Adrian went to prison when they were seventeen, he'd made them too smart for the streets. Most drug dealers work in quarter kilos or ounces, but Junior and Pete's first deal at age seventeen was for thirty kilos. They made their first million at eighteen. By twenty, Junior was flying to Culiacán to negotiate prices.

In my mind, though, the past was the past, we were building a new future, and Junior was making me the happiest I'd ever been in my life. He wasn't that busy, so it was just him and me, with no distractions. Even though we spent every moment together, I still couldn't get enough of him. All I wanted to do was make love to him, and when I did, my love for him grew deeper.

Everything around me was new and exciting. When I arrived, the entire town was throwing a three-week festival called a *feria*. There were cockfights and carnival rides, and bands following us around, playing music. People partied every night for three weeks straight, and if your family lived in the United States, they'd flown back to enjoy it all. I remember thinking, *I can get used to this. This is my home now, and this is my family. I don't mind if we're in the middle of nowhere; we can live a simple life here.*

Mia

When I dropped Peter off that morning in February 2004, I had no idea he was planning to leave the country. At that moment, I don't think even *he* knew. But when the DEA agents ransacked his house, Junior's house, and his sisters' houses, all at the same damn time, he learned that he and Junior were officially under indictment. Fleeing was the only choice he had other than prison.

My first night alone, I didn't do anything. I just sat in my big, empty condo, staring way up at the ceiling, thinking to myself, *I've never been so lonely. I might as well just curl up and die here.* The next morning, I packed up my things and drove to my parents' house. When my mom saw me at the door looking like I'd been run over by a car, she let me in and wrapped her arms around me.

"Baby, what's wrong?"

"Peter and I broke up."

I didn't reveal why. I just couldn't. I was too scared to tell her.

For the next two weeks my mom sat with me probably five hours a day trying to console me. When she wasn't watching me sulk, she was cooking up one of my favorite dishes. At night, she got in the bed with me and didn't leave till I'd fallen asleep. Even though my mother is the toughest woman I've ever met, she had the softest heart for me. During those two weeks, she became more than just my mother; she started to speak to me like a friend.

"You're a strong, beautiful, smart woman. You'll get through this," she'd say.

"I don't know if I can."

My mom probably thought I was just being some dramatic twenty-something, but honestly, I felt like I was going to be swallowed up by worry and pain. Sure, I had a home and an amazing family, and Peter had left me some money so I could open up the spa we'd started planning. We'd even picked out flooring, fixtures, and color schemes. We were going to run it together, and I didn't know if I could do it without him. I felt totally, completely alone, and Peter could be dead, for all I knew.

On day 14, he finally called.

"Peter, where are you? Are you okay?" I was in shock.

"Mia, you saved my life. If I'd been at my house, the feds would have gotten me. I would have spent the rest of my life in prison. Thank you. I can't thank you enough."

"But where are you?"

"I'm almost to Mexico." I could tell he was driving. "I can't lose you again, Mia. I love you."

What Peter didn't tell me was that he and Junior were now officially under federal indictment, so he'd taken a huge risk by calling me. After he'd said goodbye to me, he'd gone into hiding at a friend's stash house in the projects. While he was there, he'd been so worried about the feds kicking in his door, and the neighborhood was known for home invasions. He'd switched out all his phones, paid his suppliers, and collected $15 million from his customers on the streets. The last thing he was going to do was leave business undone. He bought a brand new van with Indiana plates and cut up his IDs. Two weeks later, he got on the road to head to the border at Laredo. Worried that the feds had tapped his phones, he couldn't call me right away. He switched cars several times and looked in his rearview mirror every thirty seconds to be sure no one was tailing him.

"Mia," he added. "I have to stay in Mexico. I can't come back to Chicago."

I got really quiet. I didn't just think he was leaving me forever; I was also worried about him getting to Mexico safely. He was my best friend.

"I want you to come down here," he said. "I want to make a life with you."

I was half puzzled, half in shock. "Peter," I said, "I love you, but my parents aren't going to understand."

He was steady and firm. "I miss you, and I want to be with you. But the only way we can have a relationship is if you're with me because I can't go back."

I felt conflicted. I couldn't imagine leaving everything I'd ever known, but I also couldn't imagine letting the man of my dreams slip away.

"If you don't want to do this," Peter continued, "I understand. You can still go to school. I still want you to open your spa, too. I believe in you, and I know you can do it." Then he stopped and got super serious. "But if you want a relationship with me, I can't give you that from here."

The decision was all mine, it seemed, and it was a lot to ask of a twenty-two-year-old girl who'd just spent two weeks curled up in a ball in her childhood bedroom. But if I had to make up my mind, I would.

Just not yet.

Olivia

That February, Junior and I decided to go to Cancún to celebrate Valentine's Day. Adrian and Daniela came, too, and because Daniela's brother and his wife were in town, we said, "What the hell? Let's make it a family vacation."

I was completely happy there. I loved the freedom, and I loved the tranquil life Mexico brought. It was me, my man, the beach, and family, and none of us were looking over our shoulders worrying that someone was out to kill us. One night, I had a frozen margarita in my hand and was watching the sunset with Junior when his phone rang. It was Peter.

I can just hear him now, I thought. *"When are you going to stop honeymooning and start working?"*

"Hi, P, what's up?" Junior asked. There was a long pause, and he screwed on his worried face.

"What's going on?" I yelled. That look in his eyes was giving me the chills. Junior motioned for me to calm down, talked for about five minutes, then hung up.

"Pete's house got raided. Mine, too, and our sisters' places, all at the same damn time. They took everything: jewelry, cars, the whole bit. They're so petty they even took the damn TVs off the wall. If Peter hadn't been at Mia's place, they would have taken him, too."

"Jesus." I sat back in my beach chair and started to feel sick. I couldn't believe my dreams were crushed with just one phone call.

"The feds have a warrant out for our arrest, and Peter's hiding out. He's moving down here once he gets everything together and figures out a plan. We have to get the hell out of Cancún, too; too many people know we're here."

He hopped up, and I just sat there holding my melted drink. *My life is fucking cursed,* I thought. I'd told myself we'd gotten away, that we could actually start over, far from all the drama I was so tired of. But who was I kidding? I was in this relationship for the long haul. Junior was my world—he'd given up his life in Chicago to make me happy—and I couldn't forget that, even now, in the midst of all this bullshit.

When we got back to the hotel, Junior hopped on the phone immediately and paid someone to create two Mexican passports for him and Peter. When you're a fugitive, you have to get a new identity, and in Mexico, you can buy just about anything. Junior and Peter became Joel and Omar.

We left Cancún the next morning, expecting Peter would be calling any day now to ask us to pick him up at the border. We spent the trip to the airport getting our stories straight, in case we got stopped. We didn't want to attract attention at the airport, either, so we dressed down: muted colors, no fancy jewelry, and no expensive luggage. In fact, we'd gifted our Louis Vuitton bags to the bellboy at the hotel on the way out. He was thrilled, and so was Junior; he loved making people smile. As we approached airport security, my heart was pounding, but we made it through.

When we got on the plane, Junior ordered a drink, turned to me and said, "My brother's on his way to the border now, and I know he's thinking the same thing I am."

"What's that?" I asked, even though my stomach was in knots because I already knew the answer.

"I hope they don't grab us and put us in prison for the rest of our lives. We have to get to San Juan safely."

Peter called a few weeks later, and we met him at the border. The drive back was over twelve hours, through the sierra, and as I looked out the window I was nauseated the entire time. Whether that was from the long trip or from knowing Peter and Junior were now fugitives, I couldn't say, but Mexico didn't seem so peaceful anymore. The beautiful scenery now just looked dry. The long stretches of desert used to be pretty, and now they looked like shit. I kept thinking, *Now that his brother's here, there's no way he's giving up this life, even though we moved here to get away from the bullshit. It's going to take a miracle to make him stop dealing drugs with his partner in crime around. Every time I take a step in a new direction to get away from this craziness, I take two steps back.*

Peter interrupted my daydreaming. "This is the first time in weeks I haven't felt terrified," he said. "I want things to get even better, so I'm trying to get Mia to move here. I'm in love with her. She saved me."

"Go with your heart," Junior said. "You deserve to be happy."

I remembered meeting Mia in Chicago just once. She was this pretty Brazilian girl, with blond hair and green eyes. She was petite with a nice body, really soft spoken and sweet. She was a few years younger than me, and I could tell she was good people. She was different than me, though. I had never really cared to hang out with women, and she was such a girl's girl. So traditional, not that that's a bad thing. It was just not *me*.

If she came down, was I going to be able to get along with someone like that? Actually, was she going to be able to get along with someone like *me*?

Mia

I honestly didn't know what to decide about moving to Mexico, to a whole new country. My life had never been about having choices, not because I was a blind follower, but because I thought I had my life all figured out. Anything out of my narrow frame of reference felt really strange and scary.

What was there in Mexico for me other than Peter? I had no idea. I'd known Peter's mom, Amilia, since I was sixteen; he was absolutely wonderful to her. He'd take her everywhere, even to the movies or out to eat with us. I liked her. She was so sweet, had a smile that was contagious, and was always happy to be around her sons. I also knew his brother Adrian, who was a drug dealer and had that fleet of cars that he was always getting detailed. Every time I passed by the car wash, there was one of Adrian's cars sitting in front. And of course, there was Junior. I hardly knew Junior's girlfriend, though. We'd met once, and all I remember was that she was loud, with lots of diamond jewelry and this crazy body. She was pretty, but she looked like she was from a music video. I remember thinking, *This girl has seen a lot.* If I moved down there and started spending time with her, was she going to leave me in the dust?

My grandma Lola was really sick at the time, in and out of the hospital. She was my mom's mom, who'd taken care of me as a baby when Mom was working and my biological dad bailed. I was her first grandchild, and I'd always been her everything. When I was a baby I had huge, green eyes, so she nicknamed me Corujinha, which means "baby owl" in Portuguese. She loved to play bingo, listen to Julio Iglesias, and eat rice and beans every day. Not a day went by that she didn't tell me, "You're too skinny! Eat, eat, eat!" I loved touching her soft, wrinkly hands, and I loved that she was never embarrassed to speak English even though she had an accent so thick most people couldn't understand her.

I can't leave her, I kept telling myself. *I love her too much.*

But when Peter called a few days later to ask me what I wanted to do, the first thing out of my mouth was "yes." I didn't even hesitate. I think that's part of being young. You don't think things through before you act, and believe me, while I might have let questions enter my mind, I didn't seriously consider them. I just jumped.

My parents were so skeptical. That's a nice way to put it; they were in complete disbelief.

"His family owns a bunch of real estate down there," I told them. "And they're going to develop homes in gated communities."

"That family used to be bad news," Dad said.

"They aren't anymore," I pleaded. "People change, Dad."

Mom didn't believe me. "Two weeks ago I was practically spoon-feeding you because he left you, and now you're moving to Mexico with him?"

My dad didn't say much after that. He just looked depressed. His dream had always been for me to live next door to them when I got married, and he'd even talked about building an extension onto their house for me. Moving to Mexico had sure as hell never figured into that plan.

But they came around, finally. I suppose they just trusted me, thinking that I *must* know what was best for me since I'd never really gotten it wrong before.

"Call us every chance you get," they said when I started packing up. "And if you change your mind, just come back to us."

I went to see my grandma in the hospital the night before I left. She wasn't looking so good—skinny, with circles under her eyes, and a sense of resignation, maybe defeat, that I'd never seen come from a strong lady like her. It broke my heart.

"Grandma," I said. "I'm going to Mexico tomorrow, but I'll be back to see you soon."

"Have a nice time," she said and reached for me with her wrinkly hand. "I never go to Mexico, but I always want to."

"Oh, Grandma," I said through tears, "Don't worry. I'm going to take you there. Don't worry, Grandma."

I never saw her again. I got on a flight the next day, and four days later I got a call that she'd passed away. My grandma never made it out of the hospital, much less to Mexico.

Olivia

When Peter came to San Juan, we were together all the time because I was always with Junior. I think he thought I was like this Yoko Ono figure coming into his little world because he and I started bickering, constantly.

"My brother is such a good man. Why the hell are you so controlling?" Peter would yell.

I'd shoot back, "You knew me when I was K's doormat. I'm not the same girl anymore!" I'd vowed never to let anyone treat me like shit again. People treat you how you allow them to treat you, so I felt perfectly comfortable being as strong as I wanted to be. Junior appreciated that, and he loved the confident woman I'd become. He respected me and needed someone like me by his side.

So does Pete, I'd think. *For the love of God, please let that sweet little blond girl get down here soon so he'll get off my ass and leave me be.*

Mia

I was a mess flying down, but the second my plane touched down in Guadalajara, I told myself, *If it's the last thing you do, you're going to be happy in this new country with your new life and the man of your dreams.*

Peter met me in the terminal with a dozen roses, and he whisked me off to Puerto Vallarta. For the first few days, I'd wait until Peter had fallen asleep, and then I'd cry, missing my parents and my brother and sister. I'd force myself to stop, telling myself, *This is your new life. Get used to it.*

I called my parents almost every day, as promised, and my dad would say, "Baby, if you're not happy, I'll go down there and get you."

I'd pause and collect myself so he wouldn't hear my voice break. "Oh, Dad. Don't be so overprotective. I'm fine, don't worry about me."

I didn't feel like it, though. Another week went by, and I still felt terrible. But day-by-day, finally, I became happier. And soon, I was *so* happy. The happiest I'd ever been in my life. When we settled into Peter's parents' pueblo in San Juan after a month, I felt like I was home.

Olivia

Mia was like a butterfly who'd come out of her cocoon when she got to San Juan. When I first saw her, I was like, "Wow. You're so sweet and kind. You're exactly what P needs, and hopefully some of that sweetness rubs off on him." She just made such an impression on me. I finally had a woman besides Daniela and Junior's mom to talk to when Junior was working, and most important, she got Pete off my back. That man was *in loooove.* Like so in love that when he made her lunch, he'd cut hearts into her sandwich. I thought it was the cutest, sweetest gesture I'd ever seen.

Mia

San Juan made me feel like there was a bigger world out there, and I was ready to tackle it, head-on. In the morning, I'd get up, and a local fruit vendor would be by my front door, asking me what kind of fruit I'd like for breakfast. I'd take my pick, and he'd fix it. I remember thinking, *Wow, I actually know how to order something, all by myself, in Spanish!*

Since Peter was always so stressed out and busy because of work, I tried as hard as possible to bring out his fun side. I'd beg him to take me out partying.

"Only with you could I have the time of my life at a bar in the middle of nowhere," he'd laugh and say to me.

Peter tried to take care of my every need, all the time. He was so interested in protecting me; I honestly think he would have put me in a little bubble if he could have. But at the same time, he wanted to build me up and make me independent.

"Why don't you drive here?" he once asked, and sure enough, I got to be brave enough to get behind the wheel of a car on those crazy roads.

Olivia

Junior and Peter bought a ranch near their parents' place, and we all started to remodel it. It was sitting on top of the highest mountain outside of San Juan, so when you were winding down the road that went through town, you could look up and see this huge structure. It was a ten-bedroom, ten-bath house with a huge *palapa*, and it looked like a villa. We made an infinity pool that extended over the mountaintop, with shooting fountains that looked like the Bellagio in Vegas. The whole thing was lit up with LED lighting, too, so you'd get the full effect.

We were so far up that, one time, Junior and I decided to make love right on top of the mountain. We didn't think that anyone would ever be able to see us, but sure enough, a pickup full of men passed by and started honking and screaming, "Yeah! Yeah!" I jumped off Junior and squeezed in next to him, both of us laughing harder than we ever had in our lives.

"All they saw was a full moon with all that ass of yours," he said.

I was so embarrassed because everyone in town knew whose ass it was.

Mia

Junior and Pete built a basketball court they'd play on every night. Then they constructed this little zoo that had exotic animals like ostriches, monkeys, toucans, and other exotic birds. They even got a baby tiger at one point. In Mexico, that was just a thing you did if you have money. In the house, we had a rare blue mastiff named Kilo. He was huge and looked like a wrinkled up old sumo wrestler. Every time Olivia and I walked into the house and saw him lying there, it would scare the shit out of us.

Peter was so into horses that he built ten stables and filled them up. He bought a new horse every week, these gorgeous Thoroughbreds. On the weekends, we'd travel to different ranches to pick them out. A trainer exercised them every day and made their food from scratch. He'd dice up carrots perfectly and blend them with oats and vitamins to get them ready for the races.

When the horses weren't competing, we'd ride them into the mountains. One night, Peter and I sat in front of the stables to watch them sleeping. We grabbed a blanket and a bottle of tequila, sat under the stars, and stared at them for hours.

Olivia

The property was so big we had actual trails all over it, so when the horses weren't on them, we'd hop on our four wheelers.

People used to call us the Power Rangers because when we rode around, we all wore big helmets, with dark shades covering our eyes, and each person wearing a different colored suit. Just like the Power Rangers! Junior wore black, Mia wore pink, Peter wore green, I wore red, Daniela wore blue, and Adrian wore gold, of course. We'd suit up, drive down the mountain, miles and miles away into random towns nearby, and when we'd grab lunch people would look at us like we were from another planet.

Mia

There were so few times we weren't all together—Peter's parents, Olivia and Junior, Adrian and Daniela, me and Peter. We were one big, happy family. There was so little to do in that town, so some nights we'd just sit with my in-laws in the plaza and talk to everyone. People were always drawn into long discussions with Peter. He'd sit for hours in the plaza and let the old men in town tell him stories. He sure loved it.

Family was always visiting, too. Their sisters would come down and stay all summer, and Xavier, Samantha, and Sasha were down every single school break, including all summer.

About a month after I got to San Juan, a relative brought down Peter's daughter, Sophia, for a visit. She was about to turn one, and Peter had asked me to help surprise her with a big birthday party. I'd never met her before, and I was actually kind of terrified, even though I knew I could be a great stepmother someday. Being a nurturer and taking care of children had become second nature to me. Still, I remember thinking, *I've really got to prove myself here. This little girl may be my stepdaughter someday.*

I wanted everything to be perfect, so I got her dress custom made and mapped out every little detail weeks in advance. I might as well have been planning a wedding for all the stress I felt. When we picked her up, I thought she was just a perfect little girl. I smiled at her, hugged her, and said, "It's nice to meet you!" She just stared at me and then snuggled into her papa's arms. She came down every few months after that, and I'd drop everything for her. We'd do finger paints while Peter worked, or I'd let her toddle out to see the horses. I was always looking for her acceptance, and she became my number one priority when she was with us.

Olivia

Outside our four walls, though, it was a different world. San Juan wasn't exactly the most prosperous place I'd ever been. Most people in Junior's dad's generation had helped their parents farm sugar cane and guayaba, but a water table shortage in the 80s and 90s caused farmers to replace these crops with agave, which brought in less money.

In Mexico, there was no middle class. That meant there was us, the rich drug lords on the mountain, and them, the poor people in town.

That didn't cause jealousy, though. If anything, Peter and Junior were like royalty because they kept that town running. They had people walking their horses, cooking, cleaning, tending the grounds, waxing their cars, cleaning their pool, even taking care of the monkeys and the baby tiger. These people *needed* those jobs, and they were making good money. Everywhere else in Mexico you'd get paid maybe $120 a week. Junior and Pete were giving them four times that.

They had an open tab at the pharmacy for people who couldn't afford their medications. They kept a line of credit at the local furniture store, too, in case people needed a new bed or a crib for their new baby. They gave gifts to the poor kids on Christmas, and food to the elderly. There was this beautiful little girl in town who needed surgery. They paid for her operation in the United States, as well as her family's plane fare and hotel bills while she was in the hospital.

That generosity didn't go unnoticed, and sometimes it was taken all the wrong way. There aren't any factories in San Juan, so manufacturing jobs are nonexistent. Most men leave for America, looking for work, so the town is 60 percent female. Sometimes mothers and fathers would hike up to the ranch, knock on our door, and say, "Please marry my daughter." Then they'd present their daughter to Junior and Peter, right there on our doorstep. These girls were only teenagers, all of fifteen or sixteen.

Mia

The differences were even more stark when their wholesalers and couriers would come into town.

Peter and Junior had set up their Mexico-based operations after Peter crossed the border. In San Juan, they were closer to the source of the drugs they'd been trafficking, and because of that, they were growing. But since they couldn't be on the ground in the United States, they used Google Earth to help pick out new locations for warehouses and stash houses, then enlisted their legion of men and women on the ground in Chicago and throughout the Midwest to be their eyes and ears. They needed to see them frequently, though, so they'd fly them down to Mexico.

A lot of their wholesalers were black, and they'd travel down with their girlfriends. The townspeople would just stare at them, their mouths open and their eyes following them as they drove through town. Most of them had never seen a black person in their life.

I just took it all in and never asked any questions. I didn't think it was my business, and frankly, I didn't care. All I knew was I was becoming a different person in San Juan. I was seeing a world I'd never known. I loved going to the food stands in town and ordering things I'd never heard of, I couldn't wait to visit a new horse ranch on the weekend, and most of all I was totally infatuated with Peter, and he felt the same about me. I forgot about everyone and everything back home. *No one can touch us here in Mexico!* I thought. Unfortunately, I couldn't have been more wrong.

CHAPTER 7

Guadalajara

Olivia

There wasn't a year that went by that Peter and Junior didn't do it big for their birthday. For their twenty-third on June 12, 2004, they rented out a hundred rooms in Puerto Vallarta for a few days, and their wholesalers, couriers, workers, friends, and family from Chicago, Atlanta, LA, and New York all came in. Some brought their wives or girlfriends, and others brought their side chicks.

During the day we took over the hotel's pool and had one big pool party, and at night we rented out Mikado, which was the Benihana of Vallarta. The actual party on the day of was at Nikki Beach Club, right on the water, and it was an all-white private event. Everyone was dressed in white linen, completely iced out. It was beautifully decorated with white roses and white candles, white flowers draped over the cabanas, and bottles of Cristal on every table. The ambiance was breathtaking. There were almost two hundred people there, and even the famous mariachi singer Alejandro Fernández was hanging out at the beach.

We were having the time of our lives, dancing and drinking, without a care in the world. It felt like we never left Chicago, yet we didn't have to worry about the feds snapping pictures. That was the luxury of living in Mexico; you could enjoy things and blend right in. I was sprawled out in our private cabana sipping some Cristal, just taking it all in, when I heard Junior's voice over the speaker.

"Excuse me, excuse me." Junior was holding the mike with a big smile on his face. He loved making people feel welcome and always wanted to share his happiness with everyone. "Thank you for coming down and celebrating with me and P. It's so nice to see all of you. Now if I can take a moment, I'd like to ask my beautiful girlfriend to come up with me."

Now, I never mind having the spotlight on me, but something was different here. The DJ we'd flown in from New York had turned the music down when Junior got up, but he suddenly cut it off entirely. I was left sitting there in my tight white dress, holding a glass of Cristal, with every single eye on me. I put my drink down and walked up on stage, not even realizing what was happening.

Junior paused. "Olivia, you're the love of my life. You're the best thing that ever happened to me, and I want to spend the rest of my life with you." He got down on one knee, but I was still clueless, just standing there, in total shock. "Will you marry me?"

"Oh my God." He pulled out this massive rock. It was probably ten karats, absolutely heart-stopping.

"Olivia? Baby? Is that a yes?"

Obviously, this wasn't my first proposal, so I should have been used to this, but I wasn't. Standing up on that stage, it was like the world had come to a screeching halt right when the DJ stopped spinning. I felt like I'd been put on a pedestal, like I was the most special woman on Earth.

"Yes! Yes!" I started crying, happy tears, as I jumped up and hugged Junior. Everyone started clapping as he squeezed me right back. I realized, *I'm not dreaming. I'm finally going to have my happily ever after.*

After everyone went home and things settled down, I started to think about the actual wedding. I decided that because this wasn't my first trip down the aisle, I was going to stay engaged for at least a year to make sure we were ready. This was Junior's first marriage, and I wanted to make sure it was what he really wanted, too. Plus, I knew Junior needed time to change his life, and we also had to figure out where we wanted to live. San Juan was nice, but we needed to be around people other than Junior's family and find a place where we could build a future for our family.

We started looking for houses in Guadalajara pretty much immediately.

We'd been spending a lot time in Guadalajara. With over 4 million people, it's Mexico's second largest city, with six universities, a huge art scene, and a white-collar industrial center with companies like IBM, Intel, and GE. The culture felt European, not Latin American, and it was basically everything San Juan wasn't. I was in awe of its architecture and beauty. I felt like we were back in the states, it was so developed and clean. You would have never known that it wasn't all wholesome. But in the late 1970s, traffickers from Sinaloa had been pushed out by the military and decided to relocate there. They formed the Guadalajara Cartel, which was crushed in 1985. But given Guadalajara's location— close to drug routes and Pacific ports—a lot of drug lords stayed. They regrouped, joined or formed new cartels, and flourished. Today, Guadalajara is the money laundering capital of Mexico.

Now that we were flying under the radar, we wouldn't stick out like sore thumbs; in fact, our neighbors consisted of doctors, lawyers, and drug lords, all living side by side. In Guadalajara, a lot of people in the drug trade went to college in the States, so they're educated, proper. They look like they just stepped out of Barneys, dressed in Armani or Gucci. It wasn't like Chicago, where you could spot a drug dealer a mile away because of his blinding gold chains and spinning rims.

"Pick out any house you want," Junior said, and I went to town. We decided on a nice part of town called Zapopan, and we found a house that was absolutely stunning. It had a cobblestone driveway leading up to it, so even though we were in Mexico, when you drove up to the property you felt like you were in Miami. The door was freakin' enormous, but I didn't pay it any mind because I couldn't keep my eyes off the staircase. It was massive, like *Gone with the Wind* style, but modern. The master bathroom looked like the spa where Junior and I would go on the weekend, and I remember thinking, *I'll never have to pay for a sauna again*. I couldn't find a single detail I wanted to change besides adding color to the walls, but I still had somebody drive furniture, pillows, and sheets over the border from Restoration Hardware and Neiman Marcus because I wanted to make it feel like we were still in Chicago.

Junior and I had sex in every single room in that house, multiple times a day. I didn't care if we spent every second alone. He was all that I needed.

Junior and Pete's good fortune must have rubbed off on me, too, because my producing career took off. Being married to K had opened up a lot of doors in the hip hop world for me, and Junior had helped me maintain those relationships. Soon, I got a million-dollar deal with Universal Records, back when the labels weren't paying out like that. *This is my own million,* I thought, *like real, legit money. This is our winning ticket. If it all falls apart, this is my and Junior's way out.*

That first year in our new house, we built good relationships with Cool, Dre, and Scott Storch, and started recording an album. I began spending more time in LA, Miami, and New York working with A-list producers like Kanye West, Swizz Beatz, and the Trackmasters. I always stopped off in Chicago to see Xavier, who was doing so well in high school that we'd all decided he'd be happier staying in the States. If he wasn't in class, I'd take him with me because he thought it was exciting to meet rappers like Rick Ross, Akon, and Pusha T; he'd get totally starstruck.

I was traveling nonstop, and Junior and I missed each other deeply, but I felt like I was doing my part to build a great future for our family. We talked day and night on Skype and had phone sex to stay close. I loved him even more because he was so supportive of my work and my dreams; he was building me up, and he believed in me. He always told me, "I'm so turned on by how strong, smart, and wise you are. I'm with a real woman. It's why I fell so hard for you."

At home, I was still taking care of my man. I adored serving him food, color coordinating his closet, and laying out his underwear, socks, clothes, and jewelry on the bed. I was determined to be a good wife, and I couldn't wait for the wedding to make it even more real.

He was building a life, and I was, too. More than that, though, being in a new place, away from everyone, I felt like Junior was starting to change. He seemed to be seeing things my way about wanting something different, not continuing in the drug trade. Still, it would take time. Until then, we'd enjoy our life together in Guadalajara.

But, man, we sure did miss Mia and Peter.

Mia

I totally understood when Olivia and Junior said they wanted to move. Every day in San Juan felt like a romantic date, and being there helped my relationship blossom, but it was a *small* town. You had to leave to feel like you were anywhere. Peter and I were pouring every minute of our free time and money into our horses, and it was our whole world, but after a while, even that got lonely.

We visited Junior and Olivia right after they moved into their house in Guadalajara, and we loved it. It was so comfortable, so homey. Olivia and I would sit inside and gossip for hours while Junior and Peter went into another room and had meetings or talked about business.

I didn't know it, but that part of their lives was taking root in Mexico.

Olivia

Being in Guadalajara was going to take Peter and Junior's business to a whole new level. Junior was such a likable guy; he was always joking, laughing, and positive, and people warmed up to him quickly. In Mexico, men didn't really bring their wives around, but because I was always with him, they just got used to me being there. As Junior started networking, he'd meet new people every single day. And when he'd make one connection, it would lead to another. I'm telling you, the connections he formed there made Junior and Peter *millions*.

In the city, it's normal for people in the drug trade to mesh with legitimate businesspeople. Narcos are well educated and respectable, so it's just not a big thing for a regular guy to hang out with a drug dealer. Happens all the time, in fact. When we were buying our house, for example, the architect who was helping us out pulled Junior aside one day.

"Hey, I want to introduce you to someone. His name is Lic, and you have a ton in common. He's here from LA, so I'll hook you up."

There was no winking or nodding; it was just understood that Wedo was in the business, and so was Junior. My husband met Wedo a few days later, and sure enough, he was instrumental in helping Junior and Pete set up their trafficking route through LA.

Then Junior met a man named Cuate, who had a huge mansion like in *Scarface*. Everything was in red velvet and gold trim everywhere.

On another occasion, Junior and I were eating ribs at Tony Roma's. Junior left to use the restroom, was gone for what felt like forever, and came back with some random dude next to him. He introduced me to him, saying his name was Sobrino, and after some small talk this new friend went back to his own table.

"You just picked up some strange guy in the bathroom?" I joked. "What the hell was that all about?"

"He was wearing a Cubs hat, so we started talking. We have a lot in common. I picked up his tab."

I started thinking. *A lot in common. I've heard that before. Man, this whole city is connected.* It was such a small world in the drug trade; you meet someone in the bathroom, and sooner rather than later you're trafficking millions of dollars of drugs together.

Mia

Peter was in Guadalajara all the time, or on the phone, but actually being with his brother was something he really needed, personally and professionally.

I really missed Junior and Olivia, and I started to wonder whether we should move to Guadalajara, too.

"P, please," I said. "I need to be in a city again. We're both homesick here."

"Absolutely. Anything for you." True to form, he just wanted to make me happy, and even though he enjoyed the peaceful life, we started looking for houses that winter.

We never found anything that caught our eyes. But one day, Peter turned to me with this big, bright smile.

"What if we just buy the lot across the street from my brother's place? We can build our own house."

I didn't even pause to think about it. "Really? Okay!"

At the time, Peter and I were both totally obsessed with Jessica Simpson's house on her reality show with her then-husband, Nick Lachey. I thought it was perfectly simple and so cozy. We recorded every single episode and watched them over and over again, writing down every little detail we loved about the house. When we actually started the design and construction, Peter let me take the lead. He wanted to give me a perfect home.

It was going to take a while to build it to our specifications, so while we were waiting, we bought an unfinished house directly behind Junior and Liv's home. We even knocked down the wall that separated the properties and decided to build a massive pool and Jacuzzi sitting between them. When the plans were done, it looked like the ultimate retreat, and best of all, we were finally going to be all together.

Peter and I missed everything about the United States, though. We dreamed about American food so much that we searched and searched until we found a store that sold Lay's potato chips and candy you could only find in Chicago. We'd bring our bags of food into our bedroom, cuddle in bed, and have movie night. We loved Mexico, but it just wasn't home, so when we got the lot and started to make the plans for our house, we decided we wanted a secret room for just the two of us. This would be a place where we could get away and not feel like we were thousands of miles away from our real lives. We'd be free from meetings and phone calls and workers coming into town, and we could make love, talk all night, and get lost in each other. In that room, we'd never feel lonely. We'd always feel safe.

Unfortunately, we never got to enjoy it. We never even set foot in that room because we had to give up the house before we'd even moved in.

CHAPTER 8

The Ultimate Betrayal

Mia

In April 2005, Peter and I had finally finished construction on our new house and were waiting for our furniture to show up. Excited and nervous and impatient all at once, we spent pretty much all our time with Junior and Olivia at their house. Olivia and I would talk all night, complaining about silly things like construction or our housekeepers while the guys would sit in the next room, making big decisions and plans for their business. I remember thinking, *It feels so good to be with them. They're just like us. They can relate to everything we're going through.*

Olivia

We had everything in common except for one thing: I'd just found out I was pregnant, due at the end of the year.

Mia

Peter and I were so happy for Olivia and Junior. Every time that Xavier or Junior's girls came to visit, it was plain as day that they were meant to be a family. Having a baby was only going to make them closer. It was going to make *all* of us closer.

Olivia

I had this little pregnant belly, and I remember running around the house and all over town, trying to make Peter and Mia feel at home. We were so happy to be back together, and I was over the moon about having Junior's baby. It had only been a year since we'd left San Juan, but for twins as close as Peter and Junior were, that was a lifetime.

I thought it was the best time of our lives, full of promise and a new baby. How was I to know it wasn't? How were any of us?

Mia

Saul Rodriguez was the last thing on our minds. Sure, Peter's kidnapping still haunted him, but it always would. The bad memories were something he lived with, and Saul wasn't a present danger. Instead, he was like a bad nightmare you knew would return and keep you up all night, but was never going to kill you.

Olivia

In the middle of December 2004, we were all sitting at my house when Peter's phone rang. He was on the line for maybe five minutes, looking pissed off the entire time.

"Saul's on the prowl again," he said when he hung up. "He kidnapped one of our couriers and raided a couple of stash houses."

"Who? And how much?" Junior was yelling.

"Jerry. Saul grabbed him and got 290 kilos and $400,000."

Mia

Jerry? I thought, confused. The only Jerry I knew was the best barber in Chicago, and he cut my little brother's hair.

Peter must have seen the look on my face because he started talking.

"Jerry's a courier, but he also works at Millennium Cuts. He's one of the best there." *Of course,* I thought. Junior and Pete were close to him and trusted him. The idea that he'd been kidnapped made me sick.

"Is Jerry okay?" Olivia asked.

"He's fine," Peter said, "Saul released him. But we don't know where he is now."

Olivia

Two hundred ninety kilos was over $6 million. Add in $400,000, and you're up to almost $7 million. That was a lot of fucking money that Saul stole. To make matters worse, we found out that Jerry had been so terrified after Saul released him that he stole $600,000 and fled to Puerto Rico. And let's not forget the $3 million Saul got from Peter's kidnapping. All in all, that was over $10 million down the toilet, all because of Saul.

Mia

Later, we found out the whole horrible story of what happened to Jerry. After Saul and his crew grabbed him, they beat him practically senseless, tied him up, and began to search his house.

"Where are the openers?" they demanded, meaning the garage door openers for Peter and Junior's stash houses. Jerry was so out of it he couldn't even remember. Saul and the cops then completely ransacked his house, found what they were looking for, and dragged poor Jerry into a blacked-out van.

Olivia

The dirty cops had been doing surveillance for months, so they already knew the vicinity where the other stash houses were. They drove around, pressing each of the garage door openers again and again, hoping a door would open. One finally did. Then another courier walked out to see what was going on, and Saul and the cops kidnapped him, too.

With Jerry and the second courier in the back of the van, tied up, they kept driving, pushing the button on the garage door opener till they found a third stash house and robbed it.

Mia

Honestly, Junior and Pete were more upset about losing their three stash houses than they were about the drugs and cash they'd lost. It was easier for them to make the money up than it was to get new houses, cars, and workers.

"We're going to have to restructure," Peter said. "They know too much."

They moved 100 kilos to an emergency stash house. Unfortunately, the guy who managed it couldn't be trusted, either. We thought he was a friend, but he set up what looked like a home invasion and robbed them blind.

Olivia

When you lose $12 million, you can't just write it off. Peter and Junior had purchased the drugs from the cartels on credit, and they had to pay them back. No drug lord was going to feel sorry for them. Instead, they're like, "Tough shit. I'm sorry you got robbed, but you still owe us money."

For probably two weeks, Peter and Junior were stressed. Saul was still out there, and they weren't sure how much he knew. So they had to rebuild from the ground up. I'd wake up in the middle of the night, and Junior would be up, pacing around his office, on the phone nonstop. During the day he and Peter would sit together outside for hours, still rolling calls. When they weren't on the phone, they'd be having meetings or just walking around our connecting yards, talking to each other. They were always on the same page; it was like they shared two sides of the same brain, housed in two identical bodies.

"Our machine is up and running, and we're paying our debt back," Junior said to me one night at dinner. "We're not there yet, but we're close."

"I know, I just worry." I was just barely into my pregnancy, and stress was the last thing I needed. Junior knew it, too.

"Don't worry, Liv. Taking losses are part of our business."

That's just who Junior was; always staying positive and shielding me from this stressful life.

Mia

Pablo, who we all called Uncle Pablo, was the person collecting their payments and handing them over to the cartels. Pablo was an older man, probably in his late sixties, who lived near San Juan but had spent a lot of time in Chicago. He wasn't just a colleague, he was practically family.

Olivia

I'd met Pablo back when I was first with Junior. He was always with the two of us, going out to the clubs or to these big, private dinners we'd have. We even took Pablo and his son Tony to a fight in Vegas once, that time Junior rented out a few floors of the Mandalay Bay.

I'd been under the impression that he was Pete and Junior's uncle, but he wasn't. Instead, he was their supplier, which explained why they were inseparable. He was one of their main connections to the cartels since he got the drugs for them. Peter and Junior would accept the shipments at their warehouse, have their workers unload three or four hundred kilos, distribute them to their wholesalers, collect the money, run through it, package and vacuum seal it, then turn the money back to Pablo. The cartels sold on credit, and Pablo was the one responsible for paying them.

Mia

I met Pablo when Peter and I first started dating. When he came to the States, he'd stay with Peter. He was like an old grandpa, and he went *everywhere* with Peter. I remember we once went on a date to the movies, and Uncle Pablo came along.

At first, I thought their relationship was so strange. Pablo was completely dependent on Peter, but Peter just accepted it. One time I was sleeping over at Peter's house, and Pablo was in town, of course staying with him. We were lying in bed, and Peter heard Pablo down the hall, probably just waking up. Peter yelled to him, "Are you okay? What do you want for breakfast? Did you take your medicine?"

Is this how these people treat each other? I thought. The stereotype was that guys in the drug trade just looked after themselves, but Peter really seemed to want to take care of this man.

When I first went to Mexico, we'd go visit him all the time. It was so nice to see a familiar face, and I started to feel like he was family, too. He really liked me. We'd have dinner at his house and stay for hours and talk and laugh with his daughters. I thought, *Okay, this is pretty cool. I can get used to this.* I had Peter's family that I was getting so close to, and now his business associates. *Everybody's making money together, and they're happy, and everything's going great.*

That's why it was the ultimate betrayal when Pablo did what he did to Peter. We trusted him. The magic word in this game is *trust*. Yet you'd get close to someone and believe in them, and then suddenly you'd find out they weren't worthy of it, not even the slightest bit.

Olivia

Sometime that April, when Junior and Peter were still paying off their debt to Uncle Pablo, we were all invited to his house for dinner. Pablo lived maybe forty minutes from my future in-laws, so we were planning to stay overnight in San Juan with them. Pablo's wife had cooked up a delicious dinner, and we were all enjoying ourselves, laughing and catching up. Business was discussed, but it hadn't been a cause for concern. Everyone knew Peter and Junior were good for the money. That's why I thought it was so strange when Pablo suddenly got serious and started talking.

"I want to propose something to you," he said.

Junior was as confused as I was. "Is this about the debt?"

"Sort of. Hear me out." He sat up straight. "I've been good to you for so many years, and you're doing very well for yourselves. It takes people a lifetime to acquire what took you less than a year. You owe a lot to me." He paused and started to look upset. "Your loyalty should lie with me, and yet this is how you repay me?"

Junior stopped short. "What do you mean, *Tío?*"

"Even though you've been paying off your debt, your business that you've set up in Chicago is worth more to me than your money. You're in my country now, so I'll make the rules. I'll take over your business, and you can come work for me."

Pete looked furious. "Excuse me?" Then he added, *"A mi no me mandas,"* which means "You don't send for me," or just "I don't work for you."

"You can just sign over your warehouses, and let your employees know I'm the boss," Pablo said. "You'll still have big jobs, of course. Big responsibilities."

Junior and Peter looked at each other like Uncle Pablo had lost his fucking mind, which, of course, he had. They had put their blood, sweat, and tears into their business, and no one was taking that away from them. Junior slammed his fists on the table.

"You can go to hell, Pablo. We've worked too hard and too long for you to dictate what we can and can't do. We built this shit from the ground up without you. This is our business. We put this together, not you."

At the same time, Junior and Peter pushed back their chairs and motioned for us to get up. We didn't even finish our dinners. We just thanked his wife and walked out.

Mia

Maybe we should have known that when Pablo saw Junior and Peter buying properties, horses, and land, something in him changed, and he'd become envious of them. Maybe we should have realized that he was furious at Peter and Junior because they'd stopped receiving shipments from him. After all, once they'd arrived in Mexico, so many doors opened up for them that they decided to work with other connects. Or possibly we could have gotten into Pablo's head and figured out that he couldn't stand that Peter and Junior were younger, smarter, and more worldly than him, that they'd been in Mexico for less than a year and were already making more money than he ever would.

Olivia

But he was their uncle, so why would any of that matter? Why would he ever dream of betraying them?

Mia

We went back to San Juan that night and to Guadalajara just a few days later. Junior and Peter were still furious about what Pablo had proposed at dinner, but business was business, so I wasn't surprised when Peter told me one morning that he had to go meet with him.

"We have to do the *cuentas,*" he said. *Cuentas* were the accounts. "Junior and I have been arguing with Pablo about what we still owe. *Tío* says one thing, and Junior and I say another. *Tío* is totally off, so I need to go to his house to settle it."

The next day, we hopped into our car and drove through the mountains, two hours, to Pablo's house. We met Daniela and Adrian there, and I kissed Peter goodbye so I could drive to San Juan with them.

"I'll call you later, when I'm done here," Peter said. "It may take me all day, but I'll be back later tonight."

I wasn't worried. Peter was with his Uncle Pablo, and aside from that crazy fight at dinner the other night, I trusted him implicitly.

Olivia

The day after Peter and Mia had left to see Uncle Pablo, Junior and I were at home in Guadalajara, on the patio eating breakfast. They'd been staying with us while they were decorating their house, so it was our first morning alone together in weeks.

"How are you feeling, baby?" Junior said.

"Better than yesterday, but still not great. Eating helps." I was probably eight weeks pregnant, sick as a dog. I was trying not to vomit as I stared at the spread of food when Junior's phone started ringing.

"Hello?" He stopped, grabbed a cup of coffee, and walked into the other room. For the next five minutes, all I could hear was him talking under his breath in Spanish while he paced back and forth. When he came back into the kitchen, he was visibly in shock.

"Are you okay? What the hell's going on?" I asked.

"Somebody kidnapped my brother. They also took Pablo and Tony. Just grabbed them from Pablo's house. They're demanding $10 million, and they'll kill them all if they don't get it."

"Fuck," I said as I felt a pain in the pit of my stomach.

"I can't believe this is happening again to him," Junior said. "There are only so many times he can get out of a situation like this."

I held Junior tightly as we both stood there crying. I knew he was right. You just don't get kidnapped twice and make it out okay. Nobody's that lucky, even somebody as smart and strong as Peter.

Then I thought of Mia, and my heart sank. Had anyone told her yet?

Mia

Peter had said he'd be gone all day, so I hadn't expected to hear from him till at least five or so. When six o'clock rolled around and he hadn't been in touch, I got just the tiniest bit worried, so I called him. The phone went straight to voicemail.

"Adrian?" I yelled into the other room. "Have you heard from Peter?"

"Nope."

Peter always called me, even just to say he loved me. This wasn't normal. But I shrugged it off. *He's with Pablo. It's fine. Don't be stupid.*

I choked down dinner and called Peter twenty more times before I decided to go back to the guest room. I walked out to the balcony and sat down in a lounge chair, cell phone in hand. I probably dozed off three times before I got up and went to bed, leaving the sliding door open. Peter and I never spent a night away from each other, and I couldn't fall asleep without his arms around me. The thought of something happening to him made my heart hurt so badly that I cried myself to sleep. All night long, I'd wake up and hear sounds—a dog barking in the distance, the wind, or a car honking—and I'd jump up. But none of the noises were Peter coming back.

The next morning, I got up and walked to Adrian's kitchen to get coffee. I felt like I'd slept twenty minutes. I turned on the TV, sat down on the couch, got up, opened the blinds, called Peter's cell three times, and did anything and everything to keep myself busy. *Where is he?* I kept thinking. Honestly, I felt like my heart was shriveling up. Then Adrian walked into the room.

"Mia, I have some news. I really need to tell you something."

At that instant, I just *knew*.

"He's been kidnapped."

I fell to the floor and began crying hysterically.

Olivia

Adrian and Daniela drove Mia back to our house later that night. As soon as I saw her, I couldn't hold back my tears. I just held her tightly and tried to comfort her, even though I was just as scared as she was.

She was distraught. "What are we going to do?" she asked over and over. I tried to reassure her as best as I could, saying, "It's okay, Mia. Don't worry. They're going to let him go. Junior has a plan," but I was just making it up. Junior was just as confused as we all were.

Turns out, though, he did have a plan. It took him a few days to come up with it, but he sure as hell made things happen when he did.

CHAPTER 9

El Chapo

Mia

It had been a few days since Peter was kidnapped, and I was still a wreck. I couldn't sleep; I'd stay up all night worrying about him. I'd cry in the shower, and I didn't eat at all. I grew up in a religious family, so I got on my knees and prayed for hours a day. I kept thinking, *I could have been sweeter to him. I could have listened a little better.* I remembered all the times I shouldn't have been a brat, or selfish. I couldn't believe this was happening to me. To Peter.

But Junior said he had a plan, and I believed him.

Olivia

Unfortunately, Junior's plan was to meet with Joaquín Guzmán Loera, aka El Chapo, the head of the Sinaloa Cartel. It sounded like a freakin' suicide mission to me.

"The only reason Peter could have been kidnapped was because of our debt to El Chapo," Junior told me. "Peter and I have been repaying it. Pablo knows we're good for the money, and he should be telling El Chapo."

"So you're just going to march up to the world's biggest drug lord and tell him that?" I wasn't just skeptical; I was terrified for him.

"It's the only way to prove that we're on track, that there was no cause for Peter's kidnapping."

He was right. Junior loved P to death and was willing to do whatever it took to get him back, even if it meant jeopardizing his own life. Peter was worth every risk, and this was the only choice Junior had if he ever wanted to see his brother alive.

Mia

The Sinaloa Cartel is one of the most sophisticated, powerful, and dangerous criminal enterprises in the world. Its main function is procuring narcotics like cocaine, heroin, marijuana, and methamphetamines from their original source, shipping them into Mexico, then smuggling and distributing them into the United States and around the world.

Olivia

El Chapo was the most wanted man in the world. He was worth billions, all of it from his massive trafficking network, which was more sophisticated and extensive than Pablo Escobar's.

El Chapo wasn't that different from my father-in-law. He'd been born into poverty and had entered the drug trade in his youth, when he began growing opium poppies. By the time he was fifteen, he had his own marijuana plantation, and by his twenties, he'd started trafficking across the US border. But unlike my father-in-law, his special skill was violence, and he used it to increase his power until, in the mid-1980s, he gained control of the Sinaloa Cartel. El Chapo had airplanes, rocket launchers, submarines, and a vast army of dedicated workers at his disposal.

Mia

He was the most powerful man in Mexico, but he remained hidden.

The Sinaloa Cartel's base of operations was in Culiacán, a city of just under a million, the largest city in the state of Sinaloa. It's hard to run a criminal enterprise in the middle of an urban area, however, so much of El Chapo's business was conducted in the Sierra Madre just to the east of Culiacán. He could hide in the peaks, concealing drugs, prisoners, and millions in cash, and slip into a neighboring state if trouble seemed to be brewing.

Olivia

That's where Junior hoped to meet him, but the question was how to get to him. That April, Junior and Peter were just names on a piece of paper to El Chapo. They were American boys who seemed to be doing pretty well for themselves, distributing a lot of his cartel's drugs into the States. He hadn't met them, though; he had suppliers like Pablo do that for him.

Not just anyone could meet with Chapo. Being in the business wasn't enough; you had to have a personal connection, then they'd ask the boss himself. If Chapo liked the idea, you'd fly into the mountains to see him. If he didn't like what he was hearing, you might not make it back.

Luckily, Junior's best friend was a guy named Tomas Arevalo, who I'd met a few times through K back in the day. Tommy was K's connect after Adrian went to prison. He was from Sinaloa, and he knew a lot of the major players in the cartels. When I first started dating Junior, I remember seeing Tommy at a dinner party Junior and P were throwing at Ruth's Chris.

"What are you doing here, Tommy?" I said.

"I'm working for Junior and Peter now," he said.

I remember thinking. *If Tommy works for them, they're on another level.*

Apparently Tommy had a brother-in-law who knew a lot of the bosses in Culiacán. Junior's plan was to fly to Culiacán with Tommy, meet with the brother-in-law who had connections, and pay his way to meet with El Chapo.

Letting Junior go was torture, and I've never been more scared. But the decision was made, and we didn't even have to discuss it. We both loved Peter very much, and we knew that if he had to bring Peter back from the dead, he was going to find a way to do it.

The day he left, I stood in front of him, and with no idea if I'd ever see him alive again, I tried to reassure him.

"You're strong, and I believe in you. Just make sure you come back to me, okay?"

He looked at me, kissed me hard on the lips, and said, "I promise."

I just let the man of my dreams go, I thought. *I just let the father of my unborn baby head out the door to be killed. If something happens to him, I'll never forgive myself.*

Mia

I was so grateful to Junior, but like Olivia, I just didn't see how this was going to work. Cartel bosses don't do you favors. For all we knew, Junior was going to be tortured and shot in the head right beside Peter, and then Olivia and I would both be alone.

Olivia

When Junior got to Culiacán with Tommy, he started meeting with key players in the cartels immediately. Tommy's brother-in-law knew all of them, and pretty much everybody had some close connection to El Chapo. Junior was telling his story to anyone who'd listen, even offering a half mil to anyone who could just set up a meeting for him. Unfortunately, things didn't work like that, but he was desperate. He knew Peter was suffering; he could just feel it.

One day he was out with Tommy, and a familiar face approached him.

"Hey, *Cuate*!" That translated to "twin." "It's Omar. Remember we met at the bullfight in San Juan? I was with your cousin Tony. I was partying with you and your girlfriend, Liv."

Junior stopped short. "Yes, of course. I have bad news, though. Someone kidnapped my brother, Uncle Pablo, and Tony. That's why I'm here."

Omar didn't even pause. "I can help you."

Sure enough, Omar made some calls, and just like that, he set up a meeting with his boss, Alfredo Beltrán Leyva, aka Mochomo. This was a big deal. You didn't fuck around with Mochomo because he and his brother Arturo were the heads of the Beltrán Leyva Organization, and at the time, the BLO was part of the Sinaloa Cartel. Meeting with Mochomo was basically the next best thing to meeting with Chapo himself.

The next morning, a guy named Payo picked Junior and Tommy up in a bulletproof SUV and started driving. As they approached the plaza in Culiacán, in broad daylight, right in plain view, probably a hundred guys, all holding semiautomatic weapons, stood around the perimeter. They were protecting Mochomo, who was sitting in his pickup. One of the guards searched Junior for weapons, then nodded and let only him through. When Junior walked toward Mochomo, he introduced himself.

"It's a pleasure to meet you. My name is Margarito Flores."

Junior was intimidated by his army of men. Mochomo was big and serious looking, even though he was known to be the friendliest capo ever. "What's the reason for this meeting?" he asked.

"My brother's been kidnapped, and I'm here trying to get him back."

"Well, who do you owe?" Mochomo asked.

For the next few minutes, Junior talked big numbers and spoke his language. They discussed a shipment Junior had just received, and soon realized Junior was in debt to Mochomo because of it.

"I don't want you to use my money to pay for your brother," Mochomo said.

Junior then made it clear that his money was good, and that he could make payments fast. Mochomo liked what he heard and warmed up to him quickly.

"I'm impressed with how fast you move," he said.

Then he signaled for his radio and began making calls.

After he hung up, he looked Junior in the eyes and lowered his voice. "I know where your brother is. Don't worry, I'll make sure he doesn't die, and from now on, you'll work directly with me."

Junior's mouth dropped wide open, and it wasn't because the cartel boss had just handed him the key to expanding his business. Making deals was the last thing on his mind. All he cared about was getting Peter home safely, and Mochomo knew how to do that. But it wasn't just him he was concerned with. "What about my Uncle Pablo and my cousin?"

Mochomo looked straight at him, confused. "What are you talking about? I don't have them. Pablo's the one who's behind this."

"Pablo?" Junior stopped for a second and began considering what he'd just heard. *Of course Pablo's behind this,* he realized. *He's keeping the money for himself and telling Chapo we haven't made good. Now he's kidnapped Peter for the ransom, and that's what he's going to pay Chapo with. He put greed before us, his own family.*

Mochomo interrupted his thinking and motioned toward two men. "This is Juan and Chapillo Lomas. They'll pick you up tomorrow and take you to see Mi Papá."

In Mexico, everyone knows that Chapo's name is not to be said out loud. He's like the Lord Voldemort of Mexico, but everyone respects *and* fears him. There was no mistaking it; Mi Papá was El Chapo, and Junior was in.

The next day, a caravan of forty *sicarios* in eight armored SUVs picked up Junior. He'd never seen anything so crazy in his life. He called me from the hangar where they kept all of El Chapo's planes, including the one that would take him into the mountains, and told me he was terrified. Growing up, it was every drug dealer's ultimate dream to meet El Chapo, and here he was, about to meet the boss himself to plead for his brother's life.

"I don't want to lose you," I said. "Please be careful, Junior."

"Liv, I have to do this. I'm so sorry. It's the only chance Peter has."

He hung up the phone, and I burst into tears. Then Junior boarded a single-engine Cessna and flew deep into the heart of the Sierra Madre.

Mia

I'd never heard of El Chapo when I was growing up. When I watched the news or read anything pertaining to drugs, his name never came up. So it never dawned on me that there was a single person who controlled the flow of drugs. When I moved to Mexico, I'd hear Peter and Junior mention him every now and then, but I didn't really pay attention. He was a ghost, this guy who had a lot of power but may or may not have really existed. So when Olivia said, "Junior's getting on a plane to meet with El Chapo and to convince him to release Peter," all I heard was "release Peter."

"He's alive?" I asked.

"Yes. Junior's going to call us when he's back from the meeting. He has no idea how long it's going to take." I must have looked so out of it that it wasn't even clear that I'd heard her. Liv grabbed my shoulders. "Mia, Junior's not coming back without Peter. I promise you."

Olivia

When Junior boarded the Cessna in Chapo's hangar, he was greeted by the pilot, who couldn't have been more than seventeen and was wearing sandals and a T-shirt.

Junior looked at Chapillo Lomas and asked, "You sure he knows how to fly this thing?"

The pilot answered. "Don't worry. I know every single valley in these mountains. This is what I do all day. The military will never find us."

Junior was actually more worried about the kid crashing on take-off, but when he started to look around the plane, he realized he probably *should* be concerned about being taken down. Judging from the ten radios, dozen grenades, rocket launcher, and a military-grade M-50 that were lying in the seat next to him, it had happened before. But clearly, they were prepared to retaliate.

"Who's going to use these things if we're spotted?" Junior asked Chapillo.

"We are, of course."

They took off, and probably twenty minutes into the flight Junior started hearing a bunch of numbers being called out on the radios.

"There's a Black Hawk headed our way," said Chapillo. "Grab the M-50 and point it out the window."

Junior had never shot at anyone before, much less with an M-50. *What the hell have I gotten myself into?* he thought. But sure enough, when he heard the kid cut off the Cessna's engine and begin hovering as the whir of a chopper came toward him, he wasn't going to argue. He cracked the window, picked the weapon up, struggled to turn it because there was literally no room, and began praying his plane wouldn't go down that day.

Mia

Thankfully, within seconds the radio started bleeping out a bunch of other numbers, and the baby pilot started the engine back up. Feeling so much adrenaline he thought he was going to vomit, Junior put the gun down and tightened his seat belt as the plane began to descend.

"Where the fuck is the landing strip?" Junior yelled to the pilot.

The kid pointed out the window to a manmade strip that had been dug into the base of a mountain. "Right there." Then he cut off the engine again.

Junior was positive they were going to collide into the mountain. He thought, *This is it. It's all over.* But sure enough the plane touched down and rolled up that mountain just a bit, slowing down until it started to roll backward. Finally, it stopped completely. Chapillo opened the door, and Junior jumped out of the plane like it was about to catch fire. When his feet hit the ground he looked around and saw a crowd of men dressed in military-style garb. They were looking at him like he was from another planet. After all, he was young and American, and they weren't used to seeing his kind up in those mountains.

Olivia

A Hummer edged up to him, driven by yet another guy decked out in army gear. Surrounding it were dozens of armed dudes on ATVs all carrying grenades in their military-style jackets. They drove twenty minutes down bumpy trails that you'd be hard pressed to actually call roads, and as he looked out the window he noticed the bulldozers and excavators that must have been used to clear the mountains for Chapo's compound. Finally, they arrived at Chapo's *palapa*. It was open on all sides, with spectacular views of the surrounding mountains.

Chapo was wearing a black snapback hat with a military logo. He looked right at Junior and extended his hand. "I'm Joaquín Guzmán Loera."

"It's an honor to meet you," Junior said. "My name is Margarito Flores."

"*Mucho gusto*," Chapo replied in a powerful voice, meaning "Nice to meet you." Then he continued, "What do you want?"

Chapo's right eye doesn't move very much, so Junior felt like his stare was going right through his body. But he quickly pulled himself together and responded, "I'm here for my brother."

"You know people that come up here don't go back. I could kill you and your brother right now and go about my day."

Junior responded, "Yes, Señor. I'm very aware. But I am here because I only have my word."

Mia

Junior spent the next ten minutes explaining the deal he'd had with Uncle Pablo. But before going into the specifics, Junior brought up a valid point: Why would Pablo act like he'd been kidnapped, too, if Peter and Junior actually owed him money? Then Junior revealed that, yes, he had a $10 million debt to Chapo, but he'd been paying it back to Pablo in steady increments. In fact, he was right on schedule, only a few million shy, and he had the ledgers to prove it.

It was a miracle Junior had been smart enough to take his ledgers with him to Sinaloa. They didn't just save Peter's life; they saved his that day, too.

The ledgers were these thick, worn books, like big, old Bibles. For their entire career, he and Peter had been meticulous about keeping track of every single penny that had come in to them and every single payment they'd made to a supplier, and they'd marked it all in those books. It didn't matter if Peter was dead tired or coming home from a night of partying; he'd always walk into the kitchen, grab his binders, and sit there with his calculator adding and subtracting millions of dollars. You couldn't alter them—all the numbers were tiny, so there was no room to add anything, and absolutely nothing was scratched out. They were flawless.

Their notes and numbers indicated the debt payments they'd made to Pablo, with dates. When you added up the numbers, there was no question they'd made their payments, right on time. There was no way he couldn't prove to Chapo that Uncle Pablo was totally making it all up.

Olivia

"Show them to me," said Chapo.

Junior pulled the ledgers out his backpack, and together, they started flipping through the pages.

"You're moving a lot of work," Chapo said, and Junior nodded. "Chapillo, please go get my *cuentas*." He ran to fetch them, then handed them to his boss.

The drug lord spent the next few minutes comparing dates, pointing from Junior and Pete's ledgers to the notes he'd taken. He cross-checked numbers, nodded his head when he saw they lined up, and said, "Good, good," when he got to the bottom of a line item that showed a payment had been received on the correct date. It went on like this for probably fifteen minutes until Chapo slammed his notebook shut.

"Your numbers are good. You have been making the payments."

"Yes, Señor."

"I'm going to help you. But first, you need to settle things with Pablo. I'll send my people with you."

"Thank you, Señor."

"After you fix it with Pablo, I want you to come back to see me."

Junior extended his hand to Chapo. "Absolutely. It was an honor to meet you, and I won't let you down. You have my word."

Then Chapo turned his back, and Junior was escorted away by two armed guards.

Mia

Two days later, Junior drove up to our house. I'm not sure what I was expecting, maybe this romantic reunion between him and Olivia, or maybe that he'd walk right in the door with Peter. All I know is that I sure as hell wasn't expecting him to come back with a group of guys I'd never seen before.

"They're Chapo's people," he said. "They're going to be here a few days, staying in the back. I'll tell you the whole story soon, but right now I've got to take care of them."

Olivia

Chapo's associates were there to help Junior settle things with Pablo, but they'd also come to make sure that everything Junior had said at the *palapa* was true. In fact, they were going to put it on tape. It wasn't like Chapo was just going to send out his guys to rescue someone he couldn't truly believe in. He wasn't going to just say, "Okay, go get Peter!" Junior had to earn that trust.

For the next two weeks, that's all he did. They were constantly at the house, sitting around or talking to Junior and getting to know him. They couldn't have been more polite if they'd tried, but still, they were just *there*. Poor Mia was a miserable, worried wreck, and I was so sick I was living on saltines and Gatorade, but we put on our happy faces and made them feel at home. Our chefs cooked for them. Our housekeepers cleaned up after them. Soon, they warmed up to our family so much that they actually wanted to help us. Their hearts were in the right place, and being there stopped feeling like a job for them.

Then one day, Junior got the word that it was time to leave with them and go settle things with Pablo. If he was lucky, after that, Peter just might be freed.

CHAPTER 10

Rescuing Peter

Mia

The morning Junior left town with Chapo's workers, I was so tired I could hardly say goodbye. I'd been exhausted for weeks. Every time someone knocked on the door, I thought I was about to get a package with Peter's finger in it. I kept having nightmares that someone had sent Peter's head to our house, and when I woke up sweating, I'd lie in bed positive that he was dead. Olivia was the only person I could really talk to, and sometimes even that didn't feel great because I was so jealous of her. She had a fiancé and a baby on the way, and she was planning her wedding. She had a life ahead of her, and I had shit. She tried her best to reassure me and never talked about herself, but nothing she said could truly help.

Olivia

I practically pushed Junior and Chapo's guys out the door the morning they left to settle things with Uncle Pablo and, hopefully, free Peter. The days were passing, and I knew he was suffering.

But I'd watched Junior win El Chapo's people's trust all week, and I could see the hope on his face. He was determined to get his brother back, even if it was the last thing he did.

Mia and I were on pins and needles all day, waiting for him to call.

"Do you think something went wrong? Why hasn't he called?" Mia kept saying.

"It's fine. We gotta trust Junior." In my mind, though, I was just as scared as she was.

Finally, my phone rang late that night. It was Junior.

"Baby, what happened?" I asked and put it on speaker so Mia could hear, too.

"I'm okay. It's going to be okay. But, fucking Pablo. I don't even know who that man is anymore."

"Just tell us what happened."

For the next ten minutes, Mia and I didn't say a thing while he talked.

Mia

Junior had arrived at Pablo's house a few hours after he left home. He wasn't alone; he had four men with him: two of his own workers named Roly and Sosa, and Chapo and Mochomo's men, Juan and Payo. No one was armed. After all, they were convinced it wasn't going to turn violent.

Junior knocked on Pablo's door, and when it opened he was escorted in by someone from the state police, who apparently was protecting Pablo. When he stepped aside, there was Pablo, his hand extended toward Junior, like nothing had happened. When Junior refused to shake it, the police officer put a gun to his head.

"Motherfucker, I will have you killed if you disrespect me in my house," Pablo said as the police officer pushed Junior down to a seated position in a chair, jamming the gun into the back of his head.

Juan stepped in. "We have orders from Señor."

"I've been going up to those mountain tops for thirty years," Pablo answered. "You think I'm going to let you come and fuck it up?" Then Pablo grabbed his Classic 1911 Special 45, which he always carried, and pistol-whipped Junior.

Junior was not going to sit there and just take it, even if the truth was going to cost him his life. He only had his word, and he wasn't going to let some greedy, deranged man take that from him. The more Junior spoke, though, the more livid Pablo became. He realized he was looking like a liar.

But what he didn't know was that Chapo's people were getting it all on tape.

Olivia

Things suddenly shifted. One of the police officers who'd been protecting Pablo changed his mind and said, "Stop hitting him! Let him go!"

Pablo was stunned. "What the hell do you mean? You're on *his* side now?"

"Yes. They have orders from Señor."

Orders are orders, and if they're broken, they could cost you your life. But Pablo didn't care. Instead of dropping the gun, he just kept hitting Junior until Tony started yelling. "Pa! *Por favor!*" But his dad gave him a look of death, and Tony backed down.

"I want my money, Junior! Give me the money!" Pablo was out of his fucking mind, and Junior was sure he was going to pop him and his brother in the head just for making him look like a fool.

Junior turned to Tony and pleaded with him. "Tony, why are you doing this? How could you let your dad hurt us like this? We loved you all like family."

Tony paused. He knew his dad had to be stopped, so he said, firmly, "*Cálmate*, Pa."

Apparently, hearing that pissed off Pablo so much that he didn't just refuse to stop; he backhanded Junior across the face one last time. He couldn't believe his own son was siding with Junior.

Finally, Chapo's men intervened.

"Pablo, we have orders from Señor for you to end this. You will not kill *Los Cuates*. Señor will be contacting you once we get back to Culiacán."

Reluctantly, Pablo dropped the gun and nodded his head. He'd just agreed to negotiate Peter's release. Then, as Junior started to walk out of the house, the state police stopped him.

"Please tell Señor that this was all a misunderstanding," he said as he handed him his card. "I believe you, and I'm here *a su servicio* [at your service]."

Mia

Junior came back to Guadalajara right away, bruised but alive, but Peter didn't. His release was still going to take some time. El Chapo's people had to get the word back to him, then Señor had to call Pablo. I'm sure Pablo was scared for his life knowing he was caught in a lie and behind a kidnapping that never should have happened. His plan had backfired, and he never thought in a million years that Chapo would find out.

I was so relieved to see Junior. I'd been worried sick Pablo was going to kill him, and Junior had a baby on the way and loved Olivia so much. But still, I couldn't take the agony of Peter being gone anymore. I missed him so much my heart hurt.

Olivia

Junior headed back to the mountaintop with Juan and Chapillo Lomas. When he got there, Chapo was furious with Pablo.

"I just lost my brother, so I can imagine how you must be feeling," Chapo said. "I still want my ten million fully repaid, but remember: you can make up the money later, but you can never replace your brother." Then Chapo relaxed. "When your debt is settled, I want you and your brother to come back and see me. We need people like you."

"Yes, Señor," Junior responded.

Chapo waved for German Olivares, his accountant and right-hand man, to make arrangements for the payment with Junior. Then he was dismissed.

Mia

Peter's second kidnapping had begun much as the first had: with crooked cops.

When Peter went to his Uncle Pablo's house to settle things up with him, the first thing he did was walk up to his cousin Tony and hug him.

"Where's Uncle Pablo?" he asked, and Tony made an excuse. Minutes later, he heard a bang at the back door, and fifteen to twenty men in full SWAT gear and ski masks barged in, shouting *"Policía federal!"*

Upon entering, one of the policemen hit Peter in the mouth and stomach with a rifle, then beat him in the back till he fell to the floor. He could hear them struggling with Tony, too, and it sounded just as bad as what was happening to him. Then the cop pulled him to his knees, shoved his face into the sofa to suffocate him, and screamed, "You're fucking going back to the United States, you piece of shit!" Worrying about Pablo—wherever he might be—Peter yelled at the police, "Leave the old man alone!"

Next, the officer stripped Peter to his underwear, blindfolded him, wrapped his head with masking tape, and dragged him out the door to a police vehicle, where he threw him in the back. They drove him through the mountains to a remote town midway between San Juan and Guadalajara.

He sat outside, freezing cold, till the morning. The kidnappers returned and woke him up with a gun to his head.

"Get the fuck up!" they screamed.

Peter wasn't thinking about himself. "Is the old man okay?" he asked. But they wouldn't give him a straight answer.

They dragged Peter to a pickup truck and laid him in it, flat. One kidnapper pressed his boots into Peter's ribs, which was excruciating after all the beatings he'd endured. Then they drove to a shack, where they taped his feet and made him lie on the cold floor.

Olivia

Each morning, Peter's kidnappers woke him up by putting a gun to his head and cocking it. They asked the same question every day: "Who do you work for?" He never answered, so they'd hit him across the face and say, "You think you're slick. I've heard you sell tons of work in the United States, and you have all these fancy horses. Tell me who the fuck you work for. Do you work with Chapo and El Mayo?"

"No," Peter answered.

His captors laughed. "Listen, before the day's over I'm going to make you tell me who you fucking work for."

Peter didn't eat anything for several days and became disoriented from dehydration.

"You better eat," his torturers said, "I've seen people die because they won't drink a fucking drop of water."

He was forced to use a bucket as a toilet, while a gun was pointed at him. He began to look so bad that the kidnappers called someone on their radio and asked, "Should I kill him now? He's dying already."

Mia

Peter was so weak he didn't even ask the kidnappers to spare his life. The only strength that kept him going was the thought of me. *If they spare my life, if I make it through this,* Peter told himself, *I'll marry Mia.*

Four weeks into his kidnapping, it was Mexican Mother's Day, May 10. Peter could hear church bells ringing, calling all mothers to the service, and he thought about what his poor, sweet mom must be going through. Tied up in a bed and abandoned in a dark room for hours on end, he'd almost given up hope, not just because of how vicious his treatment had been, but also because he knew people don't usually come out alive from kidnappings in Mexico.

While he sat and prayed for his life, he also worried about his Uncle Pablo and Cousin Tony, who he assumed were in captivity just like him. For weeks, no one had told him otherwise. He hoped they'd been freed, but for all he knew, they were living some nightmare somewhere, too.

More significant than that, though, was the fact that he had no clue that his brother was already deep in negotiations to free him.

Olivia

A few days after Junior made his debt payment, Olivares contacted him.

"Pablo's not answering our calls," Chapo's accountant said. "But not to worry. We'll fix it."

Hearing this was reassuring, but it wasn't enough. Junior still hadn't gotten word about Peter's location, and he was so worried he wasn't sleeping. Then, he got a call from an unknown number.

"Hello?" he said. "Oh my God, Peter! Where are you?"

Junior yelled at me and Mia to run into the room. When we got there, he put the phone on speaker.

"I'm in the Sierra, but I don't know where. I'm going to try to find a road." Peter's voice was cracking. "I don't know how long my signal's going to last, but I just need to talk."

"Baby, I love you," said Mia.

"I love you, too. I can't wait to see you. It's the thought of you that kept me alive."

Oh, God, poor Peter, I thought as tears of joy flowed down my cheeks. Then I looked at Junior and realized, *He's been selfless. I'll admire him forever for doing the unbelievable, for saving Peter's life.*

"They drove me into the mountains for probably an hour," Peter said.

He's in the middle of fucking nowhere, I thought.

"They dragged me out of the car, kicked me in the back of my legs, and let me fall to my knees. I was expecting a bullet in my head, but the man leaned down and put something in my shoe. It was the key to my handcuffs. Then he grabbed my hand and put a piece of paper in it. Junior, it was your number. He put a phone in my pocket, then told me to count to one hundred and not move, or else he'd kill me. Then he just walked away."

"I'm coming to get you, Pete," said Junior.

"Wait. Did they release Uncle Pablo and Tony?" he asked.

Junior knew how fragile Peter was, and he didn't want to upset him. "They're fine, but it's a long story, Peter. I'll tell you everything when you're home."

Then he snapped the phone shut.

Mia

Junior knew Peter had to be north, in the mountains outside of Guadalajara, so he ran out the door with Sosa and got in his car. It was late, and they had to save Peter before the sun came up.

Olivia

Junior drove over two hours north, through the darkness. There was only one road from Guadalajara to where he was going, so he knew that if he kept driving and calling his brother, he'd find him. He was terrified the whole time that Peter's cell phone was going to die, but when he had service, he'd ring him up. "I'm getting close, Peter," he'd say. "Just hang on."

Mia

Peter was in the middle of the sierra, which was full of mountain lions and poisonous snakes that he knew might attack him at any moment. It was so dark most of the time he couldn't make out his hand in front of him, and when he could see, everything was blurry because he'd had a blindfold on for weeks. He was too weak to walk, so he began crawling toward the road, using the flashlight on his phone to guide him. He didn't have much of a voice, but when his brother would call, he'd always answer.

"I'm here. I'm okay. But I can't see, so I don't know where I am."

Olivia

The road through the mountains was windy, but Junior knew it so well that he didn't slow down. It was pitch black, and he realized that if he flashed his brights, Peter would see them from miles away, know it was him, and call him.

"I see you," Peter said. "You're getting closer."

"But I don't know how far you are," said Junior. "Do you have a light?"

"Yeah, but it's not great. Do you hear those coyotes?"

"I do."

"Drive toward them."

Sure enough, Peter was right near some coyotes, and as he held his phone out, Junior could hear them barking and howling through the phone. He drove toward them, listening to their wails grow louder and louder.

Finally, Junior saw Pete's little flashlight up ahead in the distance. He got closer and stopped in the middle of the road. He couldn't pull over because he was on the edge of a cliff. Junior opened the door, and Peter crawled into the car, so skinny that he looked like a little old man. He burst into tears and grabbed Junior's head because he had to see his brother's face. Peter was in disbelief; he was still convinced he was about to die.

"Nothing is more important to me than you," Peter said.

"I'm just so happy to see you," Junior said as he hugged him.

"I can't believe they let me go, Junior. I thought they were going to kill me."

"You're safe now," his brother reassured him, but it wasn't enough. Peter was dying to know something else.

"Where's Mia?" he asked.

"She's at home," Junior answered. "And that's where we're going right now."

Mia

The sun had just come up when Peter and Junior walked into the house.

I saw Peter from the top of the stairs, but I had to look twice to realize it was him. He looked like a ten-year-old boy. After I ran down and pulled him close to me, I felt him start to heave. He was frail, his eyes were sunken, and he was so cold it was almost like he'd died. We stood together like that for probably ten minutes, and I knew he was never going to be the same again.

I led him back up the stairs, and we walked into the bathroom. I started to turn on the light, but he stopped me. "Don't, please. It hurts my eyes," he said. When we took off our clothes and got in the shower together, a smell like sweat, garbage, and death overcame me. Then I began to wash him gently so I wouldn't hurt his wounds.

"You're home," I said. "And I'm going to make sure you never leave again."

When we finally got out of the shower, Peter started talking.

"The whole time I was gone, I prayed. I asked God to protect my brother for the rest of his life, and I prayed for Olivia, that she would stay strong and love Junior forever. I thanked God for causing her to be so good to him, and I apologized for always giving her a hard time. I prayed that my daughter would live a long, healthy, and happy life and find someone great to love her, as much as I do. And I asked God for your forgiveness."

"For what?"

"For leaving you like I did."

"Don't be silly."

"And I said to God that if he brought me home, I'd marry you and be a devoted husband and father. Mia, you saved my life again."

We didn't exactly get engaged then, but it was coming. Something fundamental had changed in Peter—something that was rooting him to me and to life in Mexico—and I felt deep in my bones that life was about to get a lot more complex.

I was ready for it. Sure, I was terrified that the man I loved had stared death in the face, but I was prepared for life with a man who I loved without question, despite the job he did every day.

But was I ready to risk my life for that world? Were any of us?

It was a dilemma we'd be forced to figure out sooner rather than later.

PART THREE

IN TOO DEEP

CHAPTER 11

Sinaloa

Olivia

El Chapo had been expanding the Sinaloa Cartel's reach into the United States for years. But to keep his machine going, he needed trustworthy associates who knew the US drug trade inside and out. After Junior's meeting with him, El Chapo realized, without question, that those men were the Flores brothers.

Mia

Chapo liked Peter and Junior's neat, tidy ledgers, especially the way the numbers added up and kept getting bigger and bigger. He marveled at the fact that Junior and Peter complemented each other—while Junior was a natural at building business relationships, Peter excelled at handling logistics—and he was thrilled that the twins had repaid him more quickly than he'd expected.

Olivia

El Chapo knew he'd caught two big fish, and to reel them in, he summoned Junior and Peter to a meeting in the mountains not long after Peter came home in May 2005.

Mia

Peter was so skinny before he and Junior went to Sinaloa to meet with Chapo and El Mayo. He wasn't himself at all, still squinting when the light was too bright and waking up at all hours because of nightmares. I'd hear him cry in his sleep, and all I could do was hold him and tell him, "It's going to be okay. You're home, and you're with me."

I was scared for him, but I didn't try to change him. What he did for a living was hard to swallow, but quite frankly, I was so in love I didn't care. I knew being with him meant accepting every part of him.

Besides, I could have told him he'd just won the lottery and could move to Europe and be anyone he wanted to be, and it wasn't going to alter the course he was on. He was about to meet with the biggest drug lord in the world, and that was going to change everything.

Olivia

I don't think Mia realized that fully at the time, but I knew it. Once you were working with Chapo, you weren't going to say, "I changed my mind," because he owned you. You had to do whatever you could for the Sinaloa Cartel because, otherwise, you'd be shit out of luck. Chapo's people would break down your door and kill your whole family. That was Sinaloa.

That's why when Junior and P went to Culiacán for their meeting with Chapo, I was truly scared for them. I didn't want to leave Junior's side, but he insisted I wait at home.

"It's my job to protect you," he said. "So, please, stay here and just be my girl."

After three long days, he and Peter returned, and the first picture they painted wasn't pretty.

Mia

Junior had warned Peter about the Cessna landing uphill on that big-ass mountain's dusty airstrip, but even he had no idea they'd see what they did when they stepped out of the plane.

Probably thirty feet in the distance, there was a man tied to a scrubby tree. The sun was beating down, right on him, and he couldn't wipe the sweat off his face because his hands were shackled behind his back.

Honestly, Peter couldn't tell if he was dead or alive, and he couldn't really see his features because he had so much blood on his face.

"He looked about how I felt," Peter remembered.

Olivia

Just like on Junior's last trip, they were escorted to Chapo's *palapa* by a bunch of guys wearing military garb, carrying backpacks full of grenades and strapped with semiautomatic weapons. Junior and Pete were trying to shake off the image of the man they'd just seen, but it wasn't easy. You've got to be heartless not to feel affected when you see someone dying.

But once they got to Chapo, things couldn't have been more different. His *palapa* was clean, cozy, and ready for business. The roof was covered in moss, and the floor was concrete, so even though the sun was beating down, it was cool inside. El Chapo was wearing a military-style hat and a cotton button-down, not a silly silk shirt, like in that photo he took with Sean Penn. He never dressed like that. He looked simple, like a rancher, not a drug lord.

Instead of acting serious and skeptical, like he did when Junior had visited before, Chapo seemed happy. "It's so nice to see you," he said as he extended his hand. "Now on to business."

Mia

The mood of the meeting surprised Peter and Junior. Chapo made them feel welcome and relaxed, as if they had nothing to worry about. Chapo had the most amazing chefs—there were four of them who worked fifteen days on and fifteen days off—and they'd laid out a spread of fresh, homemade food. Sinaloa's on the coast, and most people from there love seafood, so there were grilled lobsters, shrimp, and oysters, plus *carne asadas*, filets, T-bones, and homemade tortillas. Chapo didn't really drink alcohol, so he passed Peter and Junior what he was sipping: ice-cold glasses of *agua fresca*, infused with watermelon, pineapple, and strawberry.

Olivia

"Eat, eat! You're so skinny, Pedro!" said Chapo. "We just want you to feel at home here."

Junior and Peter dug right in, then got to talking.

Mia

Peter started first. "My kidnapping really changed me, Señor. I almost died because of someone else's mistakes. Someone else's greed. I never want to put myself in that situation again."

Chapo said, "I can understand that."

"If my brother and I are going to do business here, we're only going to work with you. We want a direct line to you. No middlemen. We can only respond for ourselves."

Chapo stared at them both, and Peter couldn't stop looking at his lazy right eye. He felt like it was almost piercing right through him. There was dead silence for a minute, then Chapo spoke up.

"That's absolutely fine. I'll also offer you the same prices I give my other high-level associates." Then he stood up and shook Peter and Junior's hands—a gesture that meant *everything*. He didn't even have to think about it; they were in, right then and there.

Olivia

The drug trade is so cutthroat. People work for years and years to get the best suppliers, the best workers, and great connections. Pretty much everyone just tries to find somewhere they can fit in, and they stay in that same place forever, making a good living but never really reaching the top. During Junior and Pete's meeting with El Chapo, a handful of his associates were sitting in the room, all of whom had sweated blood and probably gotten on their hands and knees and crawled across the desert to work directly with El Chapo. Like Uncle Pablo, they probably sold out their own family just to sit in that comfy, cool *palapa* with its huge platters of gourmet food ready for the taking.

Then here come these two American boys, on their first and second meeting with the boss, and suddenly, they're working directly with him, no questions asked. When Chapo shook their hands, Peter and Junior looked around at the associates, and they could see their envy. They were standing in two lines next to Chapo, Junior, and Peter, literally on the sidelines, looking like they wanted to spit on them.

Mia

Peter wasn't done, though. After they went through their *cuentas* with El Chapo one more time, Peter spoke up.

"Señor, we've satisfied our debt to you."

Chapo nodded. "Yes, and you paid it fast."

"You charged us $10 million. As you can see from the *cuentas*, that's more than we owed you."

"True, but given the circumstances..."

"I'm not going to argue, especially here, in your beautiful home and with all you've done for us. I'm not going to be petty. But there's one thing you have that I want back."

Chapo paused. "We'll see. What's that?"

"I want my girl's ring. It's the only thing you have that's special to me. To her."

Chapo laughed. "You make enough money to buy her a hundred rings!" Then he motioned for one of his lieutenants, whispered in his ear, and nodded his head. "It's yours. You don't owe me anything for it. I'll arrange to get it back to you."

And with that, Peter and Junior were dismissed.

Olivia

The next day, they flew back to Culiacán, where they were set to meet El Mayo and his son, Vicente Zambada, who handled all of Sinaloa's logistics. Two of El Mayo's other sons, Mayito Gordo and Mayito Flaco, were also there. They were called narco juniors because they'd been given their power by their father. Vicente and his brothers were young and hip, in their early and midthirties, and they looked more like pop stars than drug lords, Vicente especially—his nickname was El Vicentillo, which translates roughly to "Pretty Boy Vicente," and he was always dressed in Armani or Tom Ford suits. He was handsome, with a movie star smile.

In Mexico, it was unheard of for someone to have made it to the top without being born the son of a cartel boss. Yet here were these two American boys, coming out of nowhere.

"Who have you been working with?" El Mayo asked. Apparently even in the drug world, everybody needed references.

"We have our own organization," Junior said. "We've been working with your associates for years distributing throughout the Midwest, but we'll be working directly with you now."

El Mayo paused. "You've got to be kidding. You moved this much work all alone?"

"Yes," Peter said. "We've done this all ourselves."

"Then, welcome, amigos." El Mayo shook their hands. "Welcome to my family."

Mia

At the same time that Peter and Junior made the relationship with El Chapo and El Mayo official, they also became associates with one of Mexico's other major drug syndicate: the Beltrán Leyva Organization. The BLO had worked alongside the Sinaloa Cartel for many years, and the two organizations gave each other work and connections. The BLO had a hierarchical structure; its founders were the five Beltrán Leyva brothers, and its leader was Arturo "The Boss of All Bosses" Beltrán. They had their lieutenants and employees below them, but they also worked with subcontractors, or associates.

When Junior first met with El Chapo, it was Alfredo Beltrán, aka Mochomo, who paved the way. Well before that, the Beltrán Leyvas helped El Chapo's brother run the business when Chapo went to prison in 1993, then they helped him escape in 2001. El Chapo's niece, Patricia, even married Arturo Beltrán. The two organizations were so closely intertwined that working for both wasn't a conflict for Peter and Junior.

In fact, it was good for everyone: more drugs into the United States meant more money all around.

Olivia

Peter and Junior needed more money, fast. After all, they'd suffered over $30 million in losses over the past year. Peter's ransom hadn't been paid with a handshake and a pat on the back; they'd forked over almost $10 million in cash, jewelry, and properties, including both Guadalajara houses; the San Juan ranch; Rolex, Chopard, and Cartier watches; several pairs of diamond earrings; a diamond necklace worth $100,000; diamond skull pendants; my jewelry from my past marriages; and Mia's promise ring from Peter.

Mia

Peter's Chicago kidnapping had put them in the red $3 million; a warehouse hit had cost $8.4 million when their worker Gustavo Campos was arrested; a theft by an associate named Pacman had chipped away $2 million, Saul Rodriquez had put them out $6.2 million; and Jerry had taken $600,000 when he left for Puerto Rico.

The losses were all part of business, though. We couldn't put a price tag on our lives.

Olivia

Now that they'd shaken hands with El Chapo and El Mayo, they were sure to make the money back. Not just that; they were ready to work their asses off to make their business grow beyond their wildest dreams. But it wasn't going to happen immediately. They'd spend most of 2005 and into 2006 pouring all their energy into their enterprise, preparing to see it explode.

I knew that moving up the ranks was going to change everything for them, but what I didn't fully realize was that it was going to turn our home life upside down, too. Believe me, it did, because after Peter and Junior came back from their meetings with Chapo and El Mayo, drug lords started appearing out of freakin' nowhere. We met hundreds of new names and faces who were just *so into* this cartel world. We hardly knew anyone in Guadalajara, and suddenly, there were guys driving up in Ferraris and Lamborghinis at all hours, then staying all day.

None of it felt normal. Junior, Mia, Peter, and I grew up in a different culture, and sure, the cartel people and our husbands were chasing the same thing, but we were Americans, not Mexican narcos.

More than that, it all freaked me out. I thought, *What is going on? What is our life coming to?* Yet I couldn't do anything. I'd pushed for years for Junior to leave the trade, but when the cartels started coming by, I stopped asking. I knew Junior and Peter were in so deep there was no way they could get out, and now that doors were opening up, word was spreading, and connections were being made, so much money began pouring in that it was clear they were becoming one of Sinaloa's biggest assets.

By the middle of 2005, Junior and Peter were already in too deep. And when bad things started to happen in our personal lives, it became clear there was no way in hell they were getting out.

CHAPTER 12

For Better or for Worse

Olivia

When I was in middle school I was always asking my mom permission to go out. I hung out with older girls who were allowed to go to parties all the time, but I wasn't, so I had to beg my mom anytime anything came up. I'd say, "But, pleeeaasse, Mom! Tonight's gonna be the biggest, baddest party!"

"Maybe next time," she'd respond.

Every weekend I'd get a new flyer advertising some huge event, wave it in front of her, and say, "But it's the biggest, baddest party!" Sometimes, she'd let me go and my dad would pick me up, but when she didn't, I'd act like it was the end of the world. I'd lock myself in my room and tell her, "I can't wait till I'm eighteen and can move out!" It pissed her off to no end then, but that's all in the past. Now, my family's favorite saying is "It's gonna be the biggest, baddest party!"

A memorable celebration was exactly what Junior and I wanted for our wedding on June 12, 2005, Junior and Peter's birthday and exactly one year after we'd gotten engaged. The theme was all-white, and I'd flown to New York City to pick out a Versace wedding dress and a Ferragamo suit for Junior. While I was shopping, I got so caught up in the moment that I bought an all-white Burberry suit for Peter, too. Junior and I planned to get married in Puerto Vallarta, right on the beach, near where we'd gotten engaged, and we'd hired an over-the-top wedding planner to put together all the details for the ceremony and reception.

We'd bought hundreds of white butterflies and white doves, and we were setting up a fireworks display that would last for almost an hour. We'd flown about a hundred family, friends, and associates down from Chicago, and we rented a block of rooms in the Four Seasons. We had an itinerary that lasted all weekend. We had dinner restaurants picked. We were going to go swimming with the dolphins one afternoon. There was the wedding, then the reception. It was going to be the biggest, baddest party anyone had ever seen!

Then, two days before it was set to start, with everyone checked into their hotel suites and me back in our beach house going over last minute details, Junior walked in with a look of dread on his face.

"What's wrong?" I asked.

"Peter wants us to cancel the wedding."

"What the hell do you mean?" At that point, he might as well have asked me to stop being pregnant. The train had left the station as far as I was concerned. I was sure Peter was just jealous because he was too much of a pussy to ask Mia to marry him, or maybe he was feeling so sorry for himself that he just couldn't stand to see his brother happy. I didn't mean any of this—I loved Peter—but I was still pissed.

"He just heard that a lot of guys on the street in Chicago have been talking about our wedding, and now he has a bad feeling in his gut," Junior said. "What if one of them decides to tell on us? We're fugitives, remember?" He took me in his arms. "I want nothing more than to marry you this weekend, Liv, but I can't just think of myself. I'll be jeopardizing my brother, too."

"He can go fuck himself."

I don't think I'd ever felt so hurt. Junior might as well have left me at the altar in my wedding dress, with my pregnant belly sticking out for everyone to see. I stood in front of him with my arms crossed, looking like I wanted to kill someone, and then I starting thinking. *What if I'm in the middle of saying my vows, and the feds bust in and drag Junior and Peter out in handcuffs? I wouldn't be able to forgive myself. What if my poor mom and dad, who've flown all the way from Chicago, and my teenage son, who's gone through so much in his life, are caught in the middle of a sting?*

As hard as we'd tried to swear our friends to secrecy, one of them might have let something slip. I realized right then I was being selfish. Junior and Peter's situation sucked, but it was a part of my life now.

But how was I going tell my family and friends? I still hadn't revealed to my parents what Junior did for a living. I wanted so badly for my dad to see what I saw in Junior, and if he knew Junior was a fugitive he'd never see past that.

I thought about it and decided I'd do what any woman in my shoes would do: I'd continue lying to all of them.

"Junior's dad got into a really bad car accident," I said in front of everyone at dinner the night before my wedding. "And we have to cancel our wedding. Junior had to go back to San Juan."

As I stood there, alone, with hundreds of eyes just staring at my little belly, I don't think I'd ever felt so ashamed and humiliated. I couldn't hold it together, and I started bawling my eyes out. I've never been one to feel sorry for myself, but at that moment, I didn't just pity myself, I felt bad for my baby, too. All I ever wanted was to be happily married, to have a family, and most importantly, to have stability for them. Yet here I was, canceling my wedding because my husband-to-be was a fugitive.

Our magical weekend came and went, and by Monday, everyone started leaving Mexico one by one. My immediate family stayed, though; they'd taken extra time off work and decided to make a vacation out of it. Suddenly, I had an idea, and I ran into our beach house, where Junior and Peter were hiding out.

"Guys! What if we have the wedding on Wednesday? My family's still here, and the wedding planner could make it happen. It'll just be smaller."

"It's brilliant," Junior said, and he broke out in this great big smile.

Peter wasn't convinced, though. "We're still not safe. They could still find us."

From the look on my face, anyone could see I was upset. I couldn't believe I still had to convince Peter. I'd even started doubting if he wanted me to marry his twin brother. Maybe he didn't think I was good enough for him? Maybe he wanted someone gentler and softer, someone more like Mia? I didn't know why he couldn't see that I loved Junior, that we wanted to be married more than anything, and that we weren't going to take no for an answer.

Luckily, I'd already thought through Peter's concerns.

"If the feds didn't show up yesterday," I said, "they're not coming."

"Yeah," he finally admitted. "I guess you're right."

Two days later, our wedding turned out even more beautiful than I imagined it would be. We moved everything to a twelve-bedroom luxury estate in Punta Mita, which was on an exclusive beach called Los Ranchos, on the outskirts of Puerto Vallarta. The house was right next door to the estate of Joe Francis, the guy who created *Girls Gone Wild* and where the Kardashians now vacation. The beach estate was completely draped with white orchids. The pool had floating candles in it, with white swans swimming all around. All the mariachis dressed in white, and Peter and Mia gifted us two white dancing horses, which we took pictures with on the beach in front of the breathtaking gazebo. Samantha and Sasha were the flower girls—dressed in white, of course—Xavier was the ring bearer, Peter was the best man, and my sister was the maid of honor. Junior wrote the most beautiful vows that melted my heart, and we released two white doves to represent eternal love. Our guests released hundreds of white butterflies, and it literally looked like it was snowing.

After dinner Peter asked for the mic, and I held my breath. Peter could be unpredictable, and after what we'd been through over the weekend, I wasn't sure how he even felt about me. But he called us over to him, then looked us both in the eyes and started talking.

"Today, I am not losing my brother, I am gaining a sister," he said as he turned to me. "Liv, thank you for being so good to Junior."

Hearing those words, I didn't just breathe a sigh of relief, I felt true joy. I realized he'd just been worried. *I'd be paranoid, too,* I thought, *if I'd gone through half the shit he has.*

That night, we had the time of our lives. We were so blessed to have our children there, both our families, and only our closest friends. I was so happy it was just the people we cared about. It was beautiful and intimate, and I realized it didn't have to be the biggest, baddest party. It was perfect just because I married Junior.

Mia

I'm not a twin, so I can't say exactly how it must be to be that close to someone, but when Peter toasted Junior and Olivia, I witnessed something really profound. Honestly, if Junior and Peter hadn't had me and Olivia in their lives, I think they would be just as happy with each other, alone. They aren't just identical; they're practically the same person.

It was hard for Peter to watch his brother get married, though. He was still paranoid and damaged from the kidnapping, and I think he was worried that Olivia was somehow taking his place. Sure, he and Junior had lived apart and had relationships and kids that took them away from each other, but this time it felt final. Still, Peter knew that Olivia was the most perfect woman in the world for Junior, and because of that, he was truly happy for him. Seeing Junior so lucky made *him* lucky.

I hoped I could make him feel half as good someday. With my promise ring back on my finger, Peter had made it clear it was what he wanted, too. I knew we'd be engaged soon, and it was what I wanted more than anything. I longed for the same happiness and commitment Olivia and Junior felt at their wedding.

Olivia

Peter and Mia were the most madly in love couple in the room that night, aside from me and Junior, of course. I remember seeing them dance all night, looking at each other like they were the only people on earth. Even if Peter was sad because he was giving his brother up, he was getting something, too, and that was Mia.

Mia

Peter had never promised me anything. Even when he gave me my promise ring, he didn't say, "We're going to be together forever." It didn't take me long to realize that he didn't want to lie to me because this life had no guarantees. Everyone I'd ever dated had sold me a pack of lies, but not Peter. He refused to even promise me a future, and to most girls, that would be depressing or ruin the fairy tale, but I needed that honesty.

That summer, in 2005, Peter got better day by day, even though he still had nightmares. He was terrified of being in Guadalajara, though, since Uncle Pablo knew where we lived. So Peter started pressing Olivia and Junior to move from there to be with us, and we took some time off to scout different cities to live in. Finally, the four of us decided to move into our beach house in Puerto Vallarta.

All through October, Peter and I walked on the beach every single night. It wasn't humid, so you could let the breeze blow past you and never get sticky. The sea turtles were laying their eggs, so we had to be careful not to step on them as we tiptoed through the sand.

One evening, we were strolling hand in hand, looking for eggs one minute and staring up at the stars the next. Suddenly, Peter fell to the ground.

"Are you okay?" I asked. Then I realized he was on one knee.

"Mia, I love you more than anything in this world," he said. "Will you marry me?"

Without pausing for one second to look at the massive ring he was holding, I screamed. "Yes!"

"I don't want to wait," he said. "I want to do it as soon as possible."

We didn't waste any time. We spent the next two months planning the wedding of our dreams, a black-tie beach ceremony. My parents hadn't visited us yet, and this was going to be their first time seeing my new world. Even though I talked to them all the time, I still hadn't told them the truth about what Peter did. But they had their suspicions. They just didn't want me to turn away from them, so they never pressed me on it. Instead, they'd say things to me like, "Just be safe. You have to be careful all the time." I wanted them to see me happy, to see how wonderful my life was going to be, so every detail of my wedding was important to me. To Peter, too; I'd never seen him so excited. We couldn't wait to be married, forever. On December 10, 2005, we were ready to say "I do."

Olivia

I was about to pop, scheduled to have a C-section in ten days, but that wasn't going to stop me from helping out as much as I could. Mia wanted to have a traditional wedding, you know, the whole big white

Cinderella dress thing, and it was going to be amazing. She ordered a ton of orchids from Colombia, and they were everywhere: on the tables in the ballroom where the reception would be, decorating the gazebo on the beach where they'd say their vows, and scattered on the high-tops where they'd have their cocktail hour. There was a violinist trying to figure out the best place on the beach to stand, and about three mariachi bands filing into the ballroom, which was draped top to bottom in satin sheets. I was waddling around, thinking to myself, *Holy shit. This makes our wedding look like a beach party.* Then I decided to go back to our house to see if Mia needed anything.

I made it into her bedroom after what felt like twenty minutes, and she was sitting on the bed in her wedding dress, sobbing. Peter was nowhere in sight.

"Oh my God! What's wrong?" I said.

"The wedding's off." She could hardly get the words out.

"What the fuck?"

Mia was a mess, crying and holding this balled-up tissue that she was dabbing her face with so she wouldn't ruin her makeup. "They're being extorted. Peter's off dealing with it now, and I don't know when he'll be back."

Mia

The whole situation was a fucking disaster, but, honestly, we should have seen it coming.

What happened? Let me start at the beginning with the players involved. We had a chef named Luis at our Puerto Vallarta house, and I'd never trusted him. When you're in the presence of a person who isn't wholesome or genuine, you feel it, and that was the case with this guy. He hadn't ever *done* anything to me, but I still hated him, and I realize that's a strong word. He was so proud, walking around all day in his Cordon Bleu smock, and I didn't want him cooking my food. I didn't even like looking at him. I'd been so close to begging Peter to fire him a hundred times, but I had no proof of anything, so I'd backed off. Peter had spoiled me so rotten that I had a tendency to be a brat sometimes, and I'd finally come to my senses and decided *I'm not going to be like that anymore. I'm a grown woman, and I'm going to act like one.*

We also had a property management company because that's what you do when you've got a huge beach house and you're not there all the time. They cut your grass, they water your trees, and apparently, they cozy up to your staff, including your backstabbing chef.

A few weeks before our wedding, Peter had to go to an immigration office to get the proper documentation necessary for our marriage license. While he was there, he noticed the customs agent sizing him up. Peter thought he recognized him, but he wasn't sure who it could be. He brushed it off and came home.

It turns out the customs agent's side job was working for our property management company, and he'd been tipped off by Luis that Peter was coming by for a permit. The chef knew that Peter wasn't clean, so he pressed the agent to do a little research, and sure enough, he discovered Junior and Peter were fugitives. What do you do with wanted men? You either call the United States and ship their asses back, or you extort money from them.

On the morning of our wedding, I was standing in my room in my wedding dress, looking at myself in the mirror. I was thinking, *This is absolutely the best day of my life. The man of my dreams, who treats me like a queen and loves me as much as I love him, is going to be my husband. I'm going to be by his side for the rest of my life.* Then, suddenly, I overheard men talking loudly right outside my door. They were angry, and their voices were getting really loud, like they were about to start fighting. I couldn't figure out what the hell could be going on, so I peeked out the door with my huge Cinderella dress wedged right in next to me.

I saw Peter standing there with two Mexican customs agents in full uniform. Right next to them was that piece-of-shit chef, Luis.

"Stay in the room!" Luis said, glaring at me. "Stay in there!" He slammed the door shut in my face.

I was too shocked even to be upset. I just knew that something bad was happening if two customs agents were there, so I had to think fast. I grabbed Peter's briefcases, which held all his ledgers, and scooped up all the phones that were sitting around the room. My dress probably weighed thirty pounds, but I moved fast. I ran into the bathroom, propped myself up on the vanity, and lifted up the window. There were a few huge bushes on the side of the house, right below me, and I opened up the briefcases and began dumping out all the ledgers, phones, and anything else that was in there.

Then I ran back to the door, my dress flopping all around me, opened it, and saw the customs agent holding a "wanted" photo that looked like it had been printed off the internet. Peter and Junior's faces were right there on it, one right next to the other.

I slammed the door and stood there in disbelief. *This is it*, I thought. *Peter's going to prison on our wedding day.*

Through my heaving and gasping, I could hear what was happening outside.

"Give us a million dollars, or the US Marshals are coming for both of you," said the customs agent.

"We'll take it in increments," added Luis.

Even though I was practically hysterical, I saw right through their bullshit. *Yeah, right,* I said to myself. *When they get a taste of even just a little bit of that money, they'll be back for more. And they'll keep coming back forever.*

Peter sounded furious, but he was measured. "Look," he said. "I'll give you $100,000 now and the rest when I get back to Guadalajara." He paused. "It's my wedding day, and I have to pay for everything. So just let me get married, and I'll give you the money later in the week."

When everything got really quiet, I knew a deal had been struck. Just like that, another million was gone, and so was Peter.

Olivia

While I was sitting on the bed with Mia, holding her and telling her everything was going to be okay, I really believed there was no way Peter would make it back in time. *They're getting married in an hour,* I thought. *This shit has to wrap up fast.*

I didn't tell Mia, but I wasn't sure Peter was really thinking things through, either. I mean, he'd canceled *my* wedding just by a thought, and now here he was, being extorted an hour before *his* wedding, and everything was just going to be okay? In my mind, he was putting himself and Junior at risk. Too big a risk. But remembering the nightmare I'd gone through, I couldn't stand to have Mia experience something similar. I just didn't have it in my heart to dash her hopes, so I kept my mouth shut.

Luckily, I was wrong. About half an hour later Junior walked into the room, looked at both of us sitting on the bed, and smiled. "It's settled," he said.

Mia let out a little gasp. "Where's Peter?"

"He's outside. Let's go. We have a wedding to attend."

Then he pulled Mia up to his right side, and me to his left side. All together, linking arms, we walked away.

Mia

Regardless of everything that happened, Peter and I had the wedding of our dreams. Our night was filled with nothing but love and happiness, and we partied into the morning hours. When my family talks about that weekend, they always say, "It was the most beautiful wedding we've ever been to."

As for me, I wasn't just happy because I had a fairytale wedding with my handsome prince; I was over the moon because I became Mrs. Flores.

CHAPTER 13

Margarito Senior

Olivia

My pregnancy had been totally healthy and uneventful, but in Mexico, doctors and hospitals will do anything to make more money, so they'd persuaded me to have a C-section.

Junior and I had scheduled the birth of our baby for December 19, 2005, and we were so excited that we went nuts getting ready for it. I bought Junior a Louis Vuitton backpack to use as a diaper bag, matching the man bag he used to carry all his cell phones. In my suitcase I packed a Burberry sleeper and matching hat, bib, and blankie. The night before we left for the hospital, Junior asked our housekeepers to wash all of my sheets and blankets so they smelled like Downy and to clean the baby's things with Dreft.

Everything surrounding Brandon's birth was our happiest time, and in the delivery room, I felt so close to Junior. He held my hand as he looked me in the eyes and reminded me how much he loved me. As the nurse laid our beautiful boy on my chest, we were overwhelmed. *He looks like an angel sent from God*, I thought, and when Junior picked up Brandon and held him in his arms, I realized: *Junior has the sweetest, gentlest soul, and he's given me my beautiful son. In return, I've given him the gift of knowing what a beautiful family is.*

Right at that moment, I finally let go. With Junior I didn't need to guard my heart. I trusted him, and I stopped caring about his job. I stopped wanting to give him a hard time. *He'll change when the time is right,* I thought. *He's given me his word, and I believe him.*

A few days later, we were home, and it was time to celebrate Christmas as a family.

Mia

Christmas Eve was five days after Brandon was born, but Olivia still wanted to host a big family dinner. She and Junior had put up a massive tree and placed white lights all over their house, which lit up the whole block. They'd wrapped all their presents and decorated every inch of their place with something Christmasy. It was my first Christmas as a newlywed, and, honestly, Peter and I would have stayed in bed all day if we could have. But Olivia had gone all out, and I knew she'd make it the best Christmas ever.

Olivia

Family gatherings are a huge deal in my family, especially to my mom. She has seven brothers and sisters, and every year, she cooks for all of them and invites them, their kids, and their grandkids over. Honestly, I don't remember a Thanksgiving without at least fifty people in our house. Mom still takes photos at all our get-togethers and creates albums from them, which she gives to each of us at Christmas. I sometimes tease her, saying, "You didn't pick the prettiest pictures of me!" But I'm kidding; I love and admire her so much for how she holds her family together—how she shows us what family is all about—and I've always wanted to do the same in my home.

Especially on my first Christmas with my brand new son.

I'd bought everything we needed for dinner, then lined up the ingredients in rows in the refrigerator and pantry. We were about to sit down to an American feast of turkey, ham, potato salad, yams, mashed potatoes and gravy, and six different desserts. After two weddings that year, this was our first official Christmas as the Flores family, and I wanted it to be the happiest we'd ever known. No one was in jail, no one had been kidnapped in months, and there was nothing to do but celebrate the season.

Mia

Peter and I were holding Brandon every second he wasn't eating, and Junior's girls, Samantha and Sasha, kept staring at him and saying, "He looks like a doll!"

Everyone was there: Xavier, Adrian and Daniela, Daniela's son and daughter, all of Junior and Peter's sisters and their families. And of course, there were my in-laws, who in many ways I was still learning to understand.

My father-in-law was *so* traditional. He thinks a wife should be home barefoot, pregnant, and cooking, so he was beyond happy Liv had been prepping dinner all night and cooking all day, even though she'd had a C-section less than a week before. He kept talking about it, and pretty quickly, it got irritating. I had to say something.

"She's done a lot more in her life than just cook, you know."

"But she's roasting a turkey when she can hardly stand!"

Olivia had produced records, had a kid when she was fifteen, and lived through a husband getting murdered, and yet cooking that damn dinner was the most impressive thing she'd ever done.

So much of the time, I thought my father-in-law was completely inappropriate, and he could drive anyone crazy. He wasn't at all like my dad, who was genuinely caring and always warm. I wasn't sure I'd ever really feel comfortable with him, but like everything in Peter's world, I was going to accept him because I loved my husband.

I'd started to realize my father-in-law *was* smart, though. I knew where Peter got his brains from. He didn't use his intelligence for the right things, but he could be impressive.

I remember meeting with a real estate agent in Guadalajara once, back when I first moved there. Señor had his little notebook out—something he always carried—writing down everything he wanted to know about real estate. He asked, "So, you might list this at a low price in order to start a bidding war?"

"Sí, señor." Then my father-in-law opened up his notebook and took notes.

He hadn't made it through middle school, but no matter who he was talking to, he wanted to learn from them. He wasn't affectionate, but he had a lot of good qualities. He just happened to be in the wrong business, and he never failed to make bad decisions.

Olivia

My father-in-law was never careful. He lived in this little town in the middle of nowhere, and he had a beautiful ranch with waterfalls, ten horses, and all kinds of roosters for cockfights. He was obviously the richest guy for miles, yet he refused to have security. "No one's going to touch me here!" he'd say. "I know everyone!"

Gambling was his thing—it made him feel alive—and he loved flashing his money around. In San Juan, there was this little place in the center of town where people would go play cards and dominoes, and he'd walk in with $50,000 in cash. Then on weekends he'd go to the horse races and bet $100,000–200,000, easy, and not care if he lost it.

"You can't do that," Peter and Junior would say. "And you can't go out alone. Take security. Take a friend. Just protect yourself."

But he didn't listen. He wanted to do what he wanted to do, and no one could tell him otherwise.

Mia

The day after Christmas, my father-in-law left Guadalajara to go home to San Juan. It was commonly known that he had another family there, a second wife and three little kids, but none of us ever talked about it openly. Not a single person in the family or town approved of it, but we all just didn't want to discuss it.

Sometimes before bed, though, Peter would begin to talk about it out of nowhere.

"Why does he do this to my mom?" he'd ask.

I had no answer. I wondered the same thing myself.

He and my mother-in-law, Amilia, had been married since she was just a teenager, and oh my God, did they fight about it when it came up. My father-in-law would be gone for a night or two, staying with his other family, and when he'd come shuffling in with his walker, my sweet mother-in-law would become another person and let him have it. She'd scream, "Where were you?"

"I was at the gambling hall."

She'd rail at him, he'd ignore her, and then an hour later, she'd come out of her room, make him breakfast, iron his clothes, and take him shopping. Every time I'd see them together I'd think, *Why does he do this shit? And why does she put up with it?*

Olivia

I hated that he hurt my mother-in-law. She was a wonderful woman; the kind of mother I wanted to be. Junior and Peter worked all night, so sometimes we'd all go to her house at three a.m., and she'd wake up with a smile on her face and cook us a full five-course meal like it was three in the afternoon. She was always so warm and loving. Watching her really helped me soften up, but not when it came to my father-in-law's other family, and especially not when he walked out the day after Christmas to be with them. I told him exactly how I felt, and trust me, I had no filter.

Mia

Not long after my father-in-law left, Olivia was resting, and Peter and I were sitting with Junior, who was doting on Brandon. I was amazed at what a great father he'd become instantly, effortlessly. Then, one of Peter's phones rang, and when he answered it and started talking, he looked grim.

"Oh, no," he said. "I can't believe it."

"What happened?" asked Junior.

"Dad's been kidnapped. He was walking through town with his three-year-old son, and someone grabbed them both."

"Fuck," Junior said. "It was only a matter of time. We told him not to go back to San Juan alone."

It was true. Walking around flashing money, with no security, you might as well have a target on your chest.

"We have to leave now," said Peter. "Whoever got them might be after us, too."

Olivia

It had taken me a month to make sure Brandon's nursery was perfect before he was born. And when we brought him home from the hospital our home felt so warm. But in our family, you couldn't have something happy occur without some sort of tragedy involved. In Mexico, we knew we might have to give up and leave at any given moment, so I'd taught myself to detach and stop caring about material things. Our safety was our number one priority, and our family always had to come first. When Peter and Junior said we had to leave the house right after Christmas, all I could think about was my father-in-law and his son tied up God knows where. It was devastating to me—to all of us—and I knew we had no other choice.

We decided we'd check into a hotel. Unfortunately, since it was Christmastime, everything was booked, so we ended up at this cheap motel a few miles away. The whole gang piled into a few rooms: my mother-in-law; Junior and Pete's sister; Xavier; Junior's girls; Peter's daughter, Sophia; Adrian, Daniela, and their kids; Peter and Mia; and me, Junior, and our less-than-one-week-old baby. I'm a germophobe, to the point that I used to make our housekeepers clean the bottom of our shoes with Clorox every day, and I remember looking around that nasty place thinking, *Oh my God, I can't be here. This hotel is not sterile enough for my newborn baby.*

Mia

We huddled up in that fleabag hotel for days, all crowded together. Peter was a wreck, mostly because he'd lived through two kidnappings and knew what these monsters were capable of. He'd pace around the room, wringing his hands, looking like he was putting his thoughts together, but going completely crazy at the same time. "What kind of people would kidnap a baby?" he'd say.

I'd just shake my head. "I don't know, Peter. But all we can do is wait."

Around the second day, one of the kidnappers called Peter. Peter had designated a particular phone for them, with a dedicated line. It was a silver flip phone with caller ID on it, pretty basic for 2005, and when that thing lit up that morning—and once every day after that—my stomach would start to hurt. We were convinced that the baby and my father-in-law were dead.

Peter was on the call for a few minutes, with a full-on serious look that I'd seen a million times before. He looked twenty-four going on sixty. When he finally got off, he didn't seem relieved, even though he had good news.

"They're alive," he said.

"Thank God!" I said, "Why don't you look happy?"

"The kidnapper wants $6.5 million. He sounds like he does this for a living."

I was confused. "Why does that matter?"

"Because this is not just about some random rich guy getting grabbed off the street for a ransom. The kidnapper's a professional; he knows what he's doing, and he wants me to be afraid of him. To tell you the truth, I am."

Junior was all business, basically ignoring his brother's feelings. "What else?"

"He wants me to refer to him as Comandante. He wants to be the boss, to be in total control. And he keeps calling whoever ordered the kidnapping 'the Old Man.'"

"'The Old Man'? What the fuck?" Junior kept pushing. "Anyway, anything else?"

Peter paused. "They say they're going to dismember the baby if we don't act fast."

I thought I was going to throw up right then and there. I didn't know that people actually *did* things like that. Torturing a child? In my world, that stuff didn't happen. In 2005, there weren't movies about cartels, so I hadn't heard of all the awful things they'd do before they'd kill people. I'd never considered that anyone, anywhere, would even think about cutting up a child.

Olivia

At that second, my world came crashing down again. I'd dreamed of stability, and I thought when I had Brandon everything *just might* be normal. Junior and I finally had it all: two daughters and two sons; it was like our little family was complete. But right then, hearing about that poor baby, my life just turned upside down.

Mia

From that moment on, Peter and Junior spent almost every day, all day, talking about the kidnapping. They quickly realized that the kidnapper was giving them clues. The nickname "Old Man" was strange. The ransom amount seemed off: $6.5 million is such a precise number, almost too exact. Most kidnappers ask for $10 million or some other nice, round figure. $6.5 million obviously stood for something. It had to.

The one person who could find out was Chapo. He practically ran Mexico, and nothing went down without him knowing. If Peter and Junior were going to get to the bottom of it, they had to fly to see him.

My husband and brother-in-law each packed a small bag and decided to head out the next morning for Culiacán. They weren't going to be gone long; they were just as worried about me and Olivia as they were about their dad.

Before Peter walked out the door, he looked at me and said, "Mia, I think you should go somewhere. If this ends badly, I don't want you to be here."

"I'm not going anywhere. I'm waiting for you."

"Then I'll call the second I get there. Please know I'm so sorry. This is not what I want for you. This is not the honeymoon you deserve."

"Peter, it's okay," I said, lying to him. "I love you." But it wasn't okay. *I* wasn't okay. I was sitting in a dirty hotel realizing that loving Peter, that being married to him, wasn't just about accepting his lifestyle. It was about living through all its terrible moments, over and over and over.

He kissed me hard on the lips and walked out the door. I knew he'd be fine, but for the first time since our wedding my ideal world shattered, and I thought, *Why are we living like this?*

Olivia

They weren't gone long, but the meeting was productive. El Chapo told them a lot more than they expected.

He revealed that back in May Uncle Pablo had dodged a meeting he was supposed to have with him. When the boss sends for you, you don't ignore it, so Chapo declared Pablo his enemy and decided to tap his phone and keep him under surveillance.

Mia

Months later, Pablo's $6.5 million debt to Chapo went unpaid. Then Peter and Junior's dad got kidnapped, under incredibly suspicious circumstances and with a $6.5 million ransom demand. While Chapo couldn't confirm that Pablo was the kidnapper, he strongly suspected he was, and he ordered Peter and Junior not to pay the kidnappers one penny until he investigated.

Olivia

The kidnapper had to be Uncle Pablo. Goddamn Pablo who'd taken Peter not even seven fucking months before had snatched his dad and his baby to pay back a $6.5 million debt he owed the Sinaloa Cartel. That man would stop at nothing.

Mia

Chapo hadn't just ordered Junior and Peter not to pay a ransom; he'd also told us we should go back home, and that he'd send someone to check on us.

That person was his main *sicario*, or hitman, whose name was Rambo.

Olivia

When you're the most powerful man in Mexico, you're going to have some pretty ruthless people working for you. The most dangerous of all of them was Rambo.

Rambo looked like he was in his late forties or early fifties. He was stocky and light-skinned, with super short hair and a mustache. He was always on edge, very serious, especially about his "operations." As I got to know him, I could tell he didn't really trust anyone because when a new person came around, he started to actually *look* like a hitman. Like deadly serious. Yet around Peter and Junior, he'd crack jokes. Anyone felt comfortable around them.

Mia

A few days after Peter and Junior got home, Rambo showed up with a group of men. Peter led them to the back of our house, and Junior sent Olivia and me to pick up dinner for everyone.

When we got back with the food, we walked into the kitchen, which was full of about twenty *sicarios*, dressed head to toe in military gear. Laid out neatly on the table were the kinds of weapons I'd only seen in movies: high-capacity automatic weapons, rounds of ammo, cartridges stacked up ten high, and grenades scattered on the island. The men looked like they were ready for battle, and it made me sick to my stomach.

This is not who Peter and Junior are, I thought to myself. *It's one thing for us to have security; they're there for protection. But it's another to see an army of assassins.*

I realized, right then, that the cartels were about *way* more than making money. They were about death and domination, at all costs.

Olivia

But was that something you'd take personally? Apparently, never. While Mia and I were putting down the food, worried sick and slowly dying inside, Rambo turned to Peter.

"You know, one of my men kidnapped you in April. He's right over there, my gift to you." Rambo pointed to one of the *sicarios* and motioned for him to come over.

The kidnapper started walking fast toward Peter, and, I swear, he couldn't have been more than twenty. *That well-dressed kid kidnapped my brother-in-law?* I thought.

Suddenly, Peter grabbed one of the guns off the table and pointed it at him. As the *sicario* froze, Mia let out a loud scream. Peter put his weapon down and began laughing.

"I'm just kidding," he said to his kidnapper. "I know you were just doing your job."

Then he took his hand and shook it. The kid gratefully hugged him while the entire room burst into laughter.

I was shocked, but I stomached it. I don't know why someone would ever want to hug their kidnapper, but I realized it was in keeping with who Peter was. He could be upset one minute and totally forgiving the next.

I looked over at Mia, though, and she wasn't half as sympathetic. She had fire in her eyes. I thought to myself, *Seeing those twenty* sicarios *and their guns is horrifying to her. Worse than that, watching her husband hug his kidnapper is dredging up memories of the worst time in her life.*

I decided to do my best to console her.

"These guys are professional hitmen, Mia," I said as I pulled her into a hug. "What he did to Peter wasn't personal."

"I know, I know," she said. "But we can't be living like this."

I paused and hugged her tighter. "I think about that every day."

Mia

Soon after Olivia and I walked out of the house and pulled ourselves together, we learned from our husbands what was happening.

Apparently, Chapo had discovered from his surveillance that Pablo was back in his hometown near San Juan. Around Christmastime, there were these big carnivals called *ferias* that went on for weeks. Entire families, whole towns, would go out to them and drink and listen to music all night. Chapo was positive that Pablo would be there. The *ferias* were all about pride and showing how much money you were worth. If you were Uncle Pablo, it wasn't the kind of event you'd even dream of missing.

Olivia

Still angry about Pablo skipping out on a meeting with him and eager to collect his debt, Chapo planned to send some *sicarios* to kidnap Pablo and his two sons right in front of everyone, right there at the *ferias*. Pablo was his enemy, and Chapo wanted to send him a clear message: don't mess with the boss. The operation would be headed up by none other than Rambo.

When Junior and Peter found out, they felt hurt and upset. Regardless of what Pablo had put them through, they never wished harm on anyone.

"His sons have nothing to do with it," they said.

Rambo responded, "I'm just following orders from Señor."

Less than three days later, the operation was complete. Chapo's men snatched Pablo and his sons at the *ferias*, holding them hostage and doing God knows what to them.

Mia

We didn't hear anything for more than ten days after that. The phone went silent, and we thought for sure that our father-in-law and his baby were both dead.

Then the kidnapper, El Comandante, called. When Peter answered the phone, it was clear that the Old Man wasn't giving him orders anymore. The kidnapper was practically a pussycat.

"I've heard so many great things about you, Mr. Flores," he said. "And I'm sorry this all happened. Because of that, we only want $2 million now. Give that to me, and I'll let your father and his son go."

Peter was furious. "Don't fuck with me. I'm not playing with you, so don't play with me. Bring my father and his son back *now*." He slammed down his phone so hard I thought he'd broken it.

The kidnapper called right back.

"I'll take a million," he said.

Peter looked at Junior, and together, they agreed. Even though Chapo gave them a direct order not to pay one penny, they had to do what was best for their family. After all, Chapo hadn't been thinking of them. He had his own agenda.

"Please drop the money in the black Ford Explorer at the McDonald's on 54th and Pulaski."

Peter paused with his mouth wide open. "In Chicago?"

"Yes."

"Then you are working for Pablo," he said. "No one else would ask for a drop off in our city."

"Yes," he said, ratting out Pablo without even a thought. Then, things got weird when he continued. "But I'm actually a Mexican federal agent, and this is my side job. I'd much rather work for you and your brother."

Peter hung up. He didn't even give him the dignity of an answer. In his mind, kidnappers are the lowest of the low, the toilet scrubbers and garbage men for the cartels. They're just thieves, and thieves would never work for them.

People in this world will do anything for position, I thought. *It's more than about money. It's about selfish power.*

Olivia

The day after Peter and Junior had the ransom dropped in Chicago, their dad and his little boy came home. It had been a brutally long three weeks, and every horrible minute showed on my father-in-law's face. When Junior first saw him, he didn't look much different than Peter had after his kidnapping; his hair was long and unwashed, and he was covered in bruises.

"They never let me or the baby go hungry," he told us. "And they never laid a finger on him."

But that wasn't much relief. The little boy couldn't stop crying, and he'd been having nightmares. He would for a long, long time.

Mia

Peter and Junior never saw Pablo again. After Rambo kidnapped him and his sons, Pablo settled his debt to Chapo by signing over $10 million in properties. Rambo then released his sons, but under Chapo's order, he executed Pablo.

The lesson was that no one disrespects the boss. Ever.

CHAPTER 14

The Peak of Their Careers

Olivia

Junior and Peter's peak year was 2006. By early that winter, their business had started growing faster than they ever imagined, and they were Sinaloa's and the BLO's golden boys.

One of the main reasons it happened was because they took advantage of opportunities and connections that no one else had. Chapo and El Mayo were sending Junior and Pete four hundred kilos, minimum, every five days, which was unheard of. Most months they averaged selling two to three thousand kilos, but one time they broke the record and sold two tons in ten days. In Chicago, they'd sold one to two thousand kilos a month.

As for prices, they typically paid $15,000 a kilo. On each load, the cartels allowed them to buy 10 percent at cost as an incentive, which was $10,000 per kilo. This was just insane; the cartels could mark up anything they wanted to, but for Peter and Junior, they actually gave them a steep discount. Chapo and El Mayo also wanted to start sending them twenty tons of weed, but my husband and brother-in-law didn't want to sell it because the weed was too bulky and smelled too much. Unfortunately, when Chapo's the boss you just can't say no, so they had to do it.

After everything was paid off, they started making $5–7 million a month on average. In Chicago, they'd been making half that, like $2–3 million after expenses. They could have made more money, but they were giving their wholesalers the cheapest prices because they wanted to help them grow. The wholesalers were not only a big asset; they were their friends and not just guys they did business with, so Junior and Peter knew that if they made them happy, it was good business all around. Plus, wholesalers lost a lot through raids, seizures, and theft, so not having hefty price tags meant they could afford to take losses and still be able to make payments.

El Mayo told Junior that one of his guys once complained about their prices. The man had said, "The *Cuates* [twins] are selling the kilos too cheap in Chicago! Please tell them to stop giving them away because they're messing up my money."

Junior got nervous. He thought El Mayo was going to start regulating his prices. Instead, El Mayo laughed and brushed the guy off. "Whatever the Flores brothers want to make is their business," he said.

Junior joked, "You tell him that the next time he wants to move work in our city, he needs to ask us for permission."

People might as well have because, believe me, the way Junior and Peter tackled different parts of their enterprise, business wasn't just good, it was great.

Mia

Peter excelled at running the US-based details. The numbers, the logistics, and the ins and outs of who needed what and when made his brain light up. I've never seen anyone roll calls like he did. One cell phone would ring, and he'd bark some orders about moving a shipment of cocaine from here to there, then another would ring, and he'd hang up and work out some numbers on another call. There were no days off.

He'd become more serious and withdrawn emotionally after his kidnapping, so focusing on straight business, nose to the grindstone, actually seemed to provide some relief for him. He felt like he'd been handed so much responsibility when they hooked up with the cartels that there was no room for error, and he became 100 percent pure perfectionist. He and Junior had taken too many losses and dealt with too much heartache and stress, so all they wanted to do was be great at what they did and never fuck anything up. They aimed to be the best traffickers ever, and, in 2006, they were on the way to achieving that goal.

Olivia

While Peter was more on the logistics side, Junior excelled at the personal side. Peter used to call Junior a kissass because of the way he handled their suppliers, customers, and associates. He'd take them out, entertain them, and make them feel really special, and sure, it seemed a little excessive sometimes, but they loved it. Junior's a real people person. He enjoyed talking about stuff outside of business, which made everybody warm up to him fast.

He spent so much time beefing up their relationships and connections, but it wasn't to the exclusion of everything else. He also set up the infrastructure in Culiacán, Mexico City, Juárez, Guadalajara, Mexicali, Toluca, and LA, which meant we were traveling nonstop. He had to get stash houses, warehouses, workers, and put together businesses that could serve as fronts. When these things were in place, he had to negotiate a contract with El Chapo, El Mayo, or Arturo Beltrán for a specific amount of coke, usually three or four tons set at a fixed price. If the street value went up or down, there was no renegotiating.

Even though they were still receiving shipments for the bosses, they also worked for themselves. In Chicago, their wholesale price for a kilo was $18,000, but they were getting it at $15,000. That's a $3,000 profit on each one. But in LA, their cost was $12,000. Realizing they could double their profits if they relocated their shipments to LA, they decided to start their own route. Junior set up an infrastructure there, with stash houses, stash cars, warehouses, and workers, while Peter set up the routes, trailers, and drivers.

Mia

When the supply costs were settled with the cartels, Peter would negotiate prices with his wholesalers. Then, it was time for things to move. Junior would fly wherever the cartel's shipments had landed to make sure the cocaine was quality grade. Once everything checked out okay, Peter would coordinate with Junior and make sure all his drivers were in place, with a deposit payment in hand.

Junior would then pay the *fleteros* (independent contractors who move shipments of drugs to various locations) to pack up the commercial buses that held the stashes. Junior would call his contact person to clear all the military checkpoints so the buses could make it safely to the border. They paid $50,000 each month for this luxury.

Before they actually drove into California, Junior would have their workers unload the buses in Mexicali. Then, he'd pay *cruceros*, who are independent smugglers, to jump the work across the border using underground tunnels, cars with fast passes that allowed them to drive into Mexico without being checked, or however else they saw fit. Later, when they got access to La Puerca's tunnels, they eliminated the *cruceros* and began using their own people.

When the shipments made it to LA and a deposit was paid, Junior's workers would load the drugs into SUVs with stash compartments and take them to various stash houses. There, different workers would clean the bricks of kilos, repackage them, and vacuum seal them.

Then Junior's workers would take the kilos to a warehouse and wait for the drivers that Peter would send. Workers would load up tractor-trailers with the kilos and then drive to Cincinnati, Columbus, DC, Philly, New York, Detroit, and their main hub, Chicago. Peter was meticulous about keeping daily tabs on the drivers; the shipments had to get where they were intended to go. There could be anywhere from two to four semis on the road at a time, either with drugs or money, but they never carried more than three hundred kilos each.

Olivia

Once the shipments arrived at their destination, the same cycle started again. Peter had his workers unload the bricks, take them to the stash houses, count them, and keep inventory on them. They would never keep more than two to three hundred kilos or $5–7 million at a time in a single house, and they nicknamed every stash, warehouse, courier, and wholesaler so that if the feds were listening they'd have no idea what and who they were talking about. For example, if there was a 7 Eleven nearby, they'd call a stash house "the 7 Eleven."

Then, he'd serve his wholesalers, most of the time on the same day, and they'd dole out the bricks to their dealers.

Mia

The last part of the trafficking equation concerned money. Peter got the couriers in each city to collect cash from the wholesalers, and his tractor-trailer drivers would take it to their main hub in Chicago. Then, his couriers would carry it to their stash houses. Peter would have them sort through the bills using money counters, bundle it up in certain denominations, package it, vacuum seal it, and transport it to the tractor-trailer drivers. His workers would be up all night counting while his couriers were delivering drugs to his wholesalers, and he wouldn't sleep till they all got home. It wasn't just that he wanted to make sure everything was in order; he needed to be sure his guys were safe. They were counting millions of dollars, so it wouldn't take an hour. They'd be working till four a.m., so he and I wouldn't go to bed till five or six.

He was tired every day, but it was worth it because nothing ever came before his employees. They needed to know they were more valuable than any amount of money or drugs.

Olivia

With the money all loaded up, the semis would get back on the road and drive to LA, where Junior's workers would hand the cash to the same person they picked up the work from. The cash would make its way across the border on a commercial bus to Mexico City or Culiacán, and once it was there, Junior would have his employees take inventory of the money and make sure it was accounted for. Junior would deposit it immediately because there was no such thing as consignment in Mexico, ever. All work at cost had to be paid upfront.

But if Junior negotiated a contract in LA or Chicago, they would have their workers unload the shipments at their warehouses, and then deposit the money in either city. The money always had to be paid in the city where they received the shipment.

Moving money was actually worse than moving drugs, and taking care of it was a job in and of itself. Junior and Peter served the wholesalers, who served the drug dealers, all the way down the line until someone reached the little guys on the street corners who were collecting ones and fives from dope fiends. People imagine the cash involved in drug trafficking is like a scene in the movies, when one person hands another a suitcase full of clean $100 bills, all tied up and positioned in neat rows. It's not like that. You have a hell of a lot of small bills on your hands, and you've got to figure out what to do with them.

Sometimes, these bills aren't just a headache, they're a real problem.

Once, Junior went to see El Chapo, and Olivares became furious with him about the small bills they'd given him.

"You turned in $1.6 million in ones and fives!" he yelled. "That money filled up a whole fucking shipping container. You better come pick them up right now because I'm not accepting your bullshit money as payment. If you don't get it fast, I'll burn it all."

Junior was stunned, but he didn't want to show it. Instead, he looked at Olivares and Chapo and leveled with them. "We have to pick up $6–7 million just to get $1 million in hundreds. We didn't have the time to change the rest into larger bills. My brother's depositing faster than the workers can run through the money and package it. Since you needed to transport the money quickly to Mexico, we had to do it this way."

Chapo thought for a minute, then nodded his head. He understood that Junior was doing his best. "Let it go, Olivares," he said. "Let it go."

Olivares was beyond upset, but Chapo was the boss, and his order was going to stand.

Mia

While Peter took control of the ledgers, keeping track of all the inventory and the accounting in meticulous detail, he and Junior took equal responsibility for hiring and training employees. As far as their people were concerned, they were one voice, and, together, they always stressed one thing: their workers should act, not think. "Leave the thinking up to us," they'd say, knowing there was no room for error.

Their employees were their eyes and their ears, and they maintained close relationships with every one of them. Peter always made sure they knew that they were *not* replaceable, and he and Junior would never choose money over them. Because of the respect Junior and Pete showed them, their workers would do anything for them—or us—at any given moment.

Olivia

I remember one time when Junior's associate and close friend Payo picked us up from the airport in Culiacán. Even though we had new identities, airports were always nerve-wracking, especially that day. As soon as we stepped off the plane and walked past the gate, I could see the federal police. They were walking quickly toward us, looking right at Junior. My heart dropped.

Oh, God, I thought. *This is it. He's going to jail. They're going to drag him away.*

Instead, the police were there with Payo to escort us out of the airport safely.

That day, I began to realize how powerful Junior and Peter were. They didn't just have everyone—including the federal police—on their payroll, but these guys were prepared to do anything to protect them and us.

Mia

When we'd travel, Peter and Junior would take meetings during the day, and Olivia and I would go shopping or out to lunch, then meet them for dinner. Junior would entertain their clients, while Peter would sit back, a little serious. Still, it was always clear they were on the same page about anything and everything.

When we were out on the town, though, their associates just couldn't understand why Olivia and I were always there. They'd just stare at us like, "Do you always have to be with your husbands?" In Mexico, women don't go out with their spouses if there's business involved; they're home taking care of the kids or cooking.

Olivia

Junior and I went to Culiacán all the time, and it was always another world to me. The whole city was plugged, just completely cartel-infested. We'd sit outside and eat at the taco stands, and hundreds of pickups would pass by with armed men hanging out of the truck beds, in broad daylight. As I tried not to look too hard, one of them would jump out and walk right past me to order, a radio strapped to his waist and a machine gun lying across his back. Entire families, with little babies, would be eating tacos, and it wouldn't even faze them. They'd become numb.

Then, you'd hear shots in the distance, and someone's radio would go off. A muffled voice would bark orders, and the men standing in line would turn around, march back to their pickups, load up, and burn rubber toward whoever was shooting.

Mia

Olivia and I never went into the mountains to see Chapo, though. That was strictly off-limits to women, unless you were a stripper or a prostitute. But according to Junior and Peter, there were plenty of them there because El Chapo loved to pay for girls and always had them around. If they were young, all the better, and sometimes, he'd specifically ask for virgins.

Every inch of Chapo's compound was spotlessly clean, and he had this thing about always taking showers and practicing good hygiene. Why? Because he always had a girl on standby, and he wanted to look and smell nice for her.

Olivia

Peter and Junior weren't into that, though. After watching how their father acted, and all the heartache their mother went through, they wanted to be different with us. They were devoted to me and Mia and didn't even think of cheating on us.

They made that clear when they were in the mountains, too. Chapo had twenty satellite phones, and every time Junior would land at Chapo's compound, he'd call me on one to say he'd made it there safely. Then before I went to bed, he'd call me again to say he loved me. Chapo and El Mayo would laugh at him every time he grabbed one of the phones.

"Your wife is *muy carbona*," one of them would say, meaning, "She must be the boss."

Once, when Vicente was there with his dad, he laughed, adding, "You must be scared of her!"

Junior would just shake his head, smile, and joke, "I'm more scared of her than Chapo." Then everyone would burst out laughing.

All that power, and he still chose to think I was in charge.

Mia

Chapo was the boss, but he was a real person, too. Peter said he had this unique, super sharp sense of humor and was always kidding around. But not in a goofy way. He'd just say little things, and you couldn't really tell if he was messing with you or not. He was really engaged, really perceptive, and was always making a very deliberate effort to stay on his toes and keep you on your toes. He was taking B12 shots and flying in special vitamins from Europe every week. "I like to keep my mind strong and my body healthy," he'd say.

Olivia

That's probably one of the reasons he liked Junior and Peter so much. They kept him feeling young.

Junior and Pete were just kids, in their midtwenties. Chapo and El Mayo were thirty years older than them, and it was fun for them to have these young guys in their inner circle. Plus, as Americans, they were different, exotic almost, and Chapo just soaked that up. Chapo adored American food, and he once shut down a Burger King just so he could eat there. He loved talking about their business across the border because he knew how hard it was to work in the states. The challenge was exciting to him. It was a whole other world.

Mia

Junior and Pete being American wasn't just good for stories or thrills, though. They knew how to deal with their American workers in a way the Mexicans never would.

Most of their wholesalers in Chicago were black, and people from Mexico didn't trust them. They'd never dream of giving them work because they don't have family in Mexico, and south of the border, the only thing that matters is where your roots are. Family is the cartel's insurance. If you don't pay up, they'll kill your wife and your kids.

This psychological barrier existed on the other side, too. The black wholesalers and dealers didn't respect the *paisas*, or their Mexican connections. They'd say, "Those *paisas* in sombreros don't speak a lick of English!" There was no one to bridge that divide till Junior and Peter showed up. They built these new networks, business boomed, and suddenly everyone was happy.

Olivia

Their meetings with the cartels became natural and easygoing because of it. The more they got to know Chapo and El Mayo and the richer they made them, the more relaxed things became. They started to be like family to them. When they'd get to the *palapa*, El Mayo would stand up from his chair, motion for them to sit down, and say, "No, Pedro, Junior, take my seat." He'd always state both of their names, one right after the other, because he couldn't tell them apart.

El Mayo started taking care of Junior and Peter because he loved how humble and appreciative they were. In Mexico, giving gifts to say thank you is expected, but Peter and Junior were the best at it. They'd gifted Mayo's sons with $150,000 Rolex Masterpieces and $150,000 choppers, and even though El Mayo never let his kids ride motorcycles because Vicente's four-year-old son had died on one, he still expressed his gratitude.

Chapo adored Junior and Peter and looked at them like sons. He even pushed them to be good influences on his youngest kid, who was sort of immature. Today, Alfredillo's kind of famous for posting Instagram photos of stacks of cash, his Lamborghini, hot girls in bikinis on yachts, and his pet cheetah. Back in 2005, though, there was no Instagram, and Alfredillo was known to be just a rich narco junior. He lived in Guadalajara near us, and sometimes we'd see him driving his white Lamborghini way too fast past our house. Chapo got on him for this, and made a point of telling him to stop and hang out with Junior and Peter.

"You're good for my son," he said to my husband and brother-in-law.

Sure enough, Alfredillo started coming by our house after that.

Mia

Chapo and El Mayo used to make jokes about how big Junior and P were. Chapo would laugh and say, "You can feed all the pigs in the world with the scraps you leave behind." Basically, that means that you're making so much money that you can afford to drop some for the pigs that are sniffing around under you. To them, Junior and Pete were these wonder twins, capable of almost anything.

Olivia

Things were so relaxed that sometimes the jokes were aimed at Chapo.

It was hot in the mountains during the day, so a lot of the time Peter and Junior wore shorts when they flew there. For Americans, this was normal. When it's hot, you're sure as hell not wearing jeans. But in Mexico, shorts are for women, and if a man wears them, people think he's feminine. Even though Chapo understood American culture, it wouldn't stop him from poking fun at them when they'd visit.

"I know you have the money to buy the other half of your pants," he'd say.

Junior and Pete loved kidding around, so one day before flying out they found out Chapo's size, bought a pair of shorts for him, wrapped them up nicely with a box of Viagra, and presented them to him as a gift. It became the biggest joke out there in the mountains.

Mia

At home, we never joked about business or Chapo, much less talked about it. In fact, we hardly discussed all the money that was coming in.

By 2006, cash was something that was just *there*, free for the taking and spending. In fact, I felt jaded, almost unfazed, like a banker who walks into the vault a few times a week and sees millions of dollars in front of him. I never stopped and said in shock, "Oh, my gosh! We have so much money!" I just knew we had millions and could spend as much of it as we wanted. In fact, a few steps away from our bedroom was a room where Junior and Pete stored their cash. Probably $2 or $3 million was piled up, all tied in little bundles, and if I needed some, I'd just walk in and grab a few stacks.

I got new pieces of jewelry all the time. We bought a new car every couple of weeks, and Peter would give away the old car to one of his low-level workers or one of our cleaning ladies. Or anyone, really. These people's families probably couldn't afford the gas, but here they were, with a brand new car in their garage.

Olivia

A $10 million loss from a raid, theft, or seizure used to be a huge deal, but that year, big losses were just part of the game. Sometimes, they wouldn't even tell us about them, and they never made Junior have a bad day. You hear of husbands coming home from work, stressed out after terrible days and taking it out on their wives or ignoring their kids, but not Junior. He was always so positive.

Once, all of us were out at this really nice Italian restaurant, and Junior's phone rang. In the middle of the conversation I heard him say, "$10 million gone? Okay. We'll just have to make it up this week."

I flipped out. "Make it up this week? You lost ten million dollars?"

"Don't stress, Liv," he said. "It's just a part of business."

Mia

Peter wasn't the type of guy to get really *happy* about making money, though. He never said, "Hey, baby, I made a million dollars today, let's go out to eat!" Both of us came from nothing, and millions of dollars hadn't made our lives better. Sure, it made things easy and nice, but better? Not really. If anything, things were just more complicated.

Olivia

Honestly, I always felt that money was the root of all evil. I'd see people with wads of cash they'd made all of sudden, and it had turned them into monsters. Junior would always say to me, "No, you don't understand. They didn't become assholes overnight. They were always like that; they just didn't have the means to show it."

I couldn't wrap my brains around how that could happen. When I was a teenager, I thought being in the scene and making money would make me truly happy, really complete me, but pretty fast I figured out there's more to life than that. Life's about family and love and putting good into the world, I learned. Since then, there have been times I've had millions of dollars and times I couldn't pay my bills, and my heart's been the same through all of it.

Same with Junior; money never changed him. He was different from all the rest. He would have been the same, good person if he'd worked from nine to five every day.

Throughout 2006, it would be something I'd have to remember—because while life couldn't have been better at home, the Mexican drug trade was about to reach a boiling point, with all of us caught in the crosshairs.

CHAPTER 15

"This Is Going a Little Too Far"

Olivia

Not only was 2006 the best year, business-wise, for Junior and Peter, it was also one of my happiest years at home. I was so caught up with Brandon, trying to be a good wife and mother, that I stopped being a busybody and stayed out of Junior and Peter's business. I was obsessively in love with my family, encased in this bubble, in complete denial of what was really happening around me. But I didn't care. I felt safe and secure, and most of all, happy.

I even let go of my music career. For two years, I'd been flying from Mexico to Miami to New York, then back to LA, to record, and it had started exhausting me. Junior and I had spent so much time bringing famous producers, songwriters, and engineers down from the States to Mexico City, and we'd huddled in our recording studio, working with them. We had strong ties and close relationships to music executives and top artists, and if there was a connection, it was ours. I was even presented with the opportunity to sign Drake before he was with Cash Money Records.

But the music was too consuming, and the business was too demanding. My family needed me. I let my career slide, and Junior supported my decision; he just wanted me to be happy.

With more time on our hands, Cancún became our favorite spot. We'd take the whole family down on long vacations with us, sometimes months at a time, and once we realized we were in Cancún constantly, we decided to buy a condo there. All of Junior and Peter's wholesalers and employees came to visit, and when we weren't there, they used it as a vacation house.

Sometimes Mia and Peter would watch Brandon while Junior and I would go to dinner. The next night, they'd head out to the same restaurant, and the waiters would give the guys dirty looks because they thought they were living double lives.

During the day, we did family things like going out to the pyramids, or we'd take Brandon in the pool. He'd swim around with his floaties, then beg Junior to throw him up in the air and catch him as he came up from the water like a little fish. When he'd get tired, the three of us would lie in the cabana as he fell asleep on his daddy's chest. As we watched the sunset, Junior and I would hold hands.

It was heaven. And I know I was just fooling myself, but at the time I thought, *Why try to fix something that isn't broken?*

Mia

It really was heaven. Peter and I moved into a five-thousand-square-foot penthouse that had been owned by the famous singer Alejandro Fernández, the son of legendary singer Vincente Fernández. It had white Italian marble everywhere, twenty-foot ceilings, and windows wrapped around from one end to another. The master walk-in closet was the size of a studio apartment, and the elevator opened up right at the front entrance.

The only things I had to worry about were how I looked and whether Peter was stressed about his day. I never had to cook or clean, and I always tried, but Peter wouldn't let me.

"Mia, what are you doing?" he'd yell at me. "You better not be cooking!" Then he'd come up behind me and kiss me.

We never wanted to leave that house, and there we shared our deepest feelings and secrets with each other. There was hardly a minute when we weren't laughing about something. We'd sit on our balcony, listening to music, looking over the city every single night. We decided we were tequila connoisseurs, and we tried every top-shelf tequila known to man.

Plus, their business was still growing by leaps and bounds. El Chapo had called every day during Peter and Junior's dad's kidnapping, just to check on our family and ensure that nothing bad had happened to us. Life was just getting easier, and money was rolling in. Peter and Junior had branched out to Atlanta and New York and into Canada, and because of that, my husband's brain was just lighting up with ideas. Every day it was something new, made possible with the help of all the new people he and Junior had met.

Olivia

After their dad's kidnapping, Junior's friend Sobrino, who he'd met at Tony Roma's, set up a meeting with his uncle, La Puerca, or El Animal. His real name was Manuel Fernández Valencia, and he was both Chapo's close associate and Mochomo's *compadre* in the BLO.

La Puerca lived in Mérida in the Yucatán in a beautiful, twenty-thousand-square-foot hacienda with horse stables on his grounds. As Peter and Junior sat in one of his grand rooms, their voices echoing as they discussed business, La Puerca told them he had his own tunnels from Mexicali to Calexico and his own routes to the border. They partnered with him, which allowed them to grab less work in the States and more in Mexico. Apparently, greater risks came with huge profits.

Mia

Through El Chapo, they'd connected with one of his lifelong friends, Alfredo Vásquez-Hernández and his wife, Maria. Chapo and Alfredo were so close that Chapo had named his son Alfredillo after him. Alfredo was Chapo's logistics operator, making sure the cartel's drugs were loaded onto their trains, semis, or 747s. In Mexico, there was no credit, so Peter and Junior had to pay for their loads upfront.

Maria owned a currency exchange, and she started changing our money from pesos to dollars or vice versa, getting it from point A to point B. She would charge 5 percent from Chicago to Mexico and 3 percent from LA. This sounds like a lot—when they moved $20 million, she could net up to a million—but it was additional security because the money was guaranteed. Suddenly, they'd solved one of the difficult parts of getting money across the border.

The cash was coming in faster than Peter and Junior could move it, so they invested in a private plane with Maria, paying a million each for it. Maria would go shopping and use her bags to take the attention away from the suitcases of $5 or $10 million she'd picked up from Junior and Peter's workers at a small airport by the naval base in Kenosha, Wisconsin, near Gurnee Mills mall in Illinois, Torrance, California, and Long Beach, California. After she handed over the cash to them, Peter and Junior would reinvest it that day.

Olivia

Their infrastructure in LA was one of their biggest challenges. They had to build a machine from the ground up in a city that wasn't familiar to them, and it took research, time, and learning from other people's mistakes to bring together a great team. But it paid off. At their peak, the route through LA was so successful that they had two to four drivers on the road constantly.

Junior and Peter always had a plan B, though. They invested about $600,000 in a furniture company that used trains to ship goods. They'd hide drugs in the walls of the rail cars. It was slow, but it was guaranteed with hardly any risk.

The furniture company was their only legitimate business, but they also spent money on dozens and dozens of semis with hydraulic stashes that concealed their drug shipments. These semis and trains would bring the drugs into a city, but to get the drugs from place to place within that town, they commissioned custom-fitted cars.

These vehicles were crazy. To get to the hidden drugs, you'd have to get in the car, fasten your seatbelt, put the car into drive, then press a certain button like the defrost or back window to trigger it. You'd hear this *whoosh* sound, and the whole back or floor would open using hydraulics. In these secret compartments, you could fit about one hundred kilos, or maybe $1 or $2 million. Bigger vehicles like pickup trucks could hold 150 kilos. The people who drove these cars wore ties and dress shirts, like white-collar guys, not drug runners. They didn't want to attract the cops' attention, so they were clean cut, and they didn't run red lights or speed. This was ground-level drug transport, but Peter and Junior had elevated it to an art form, with a fleet equipped with the latest technology.

Mia

With more direct control of transport, things became increasingly intense. Peter became such a micromanager, making up all kinds of rules for his workers. "Don't even say where the stash house is over the phone." Or "Walk through the house exactly the same way every day. Don't leave any mail in the mailbox." He'd make his people confirm accounts every time they went into the house, and if they took any kilos away from the stash, he would have them put them to the side, then recount the kilos that were there. He even made them wear gloves so they would never leave fingerprints on the kilos. He knew that cleaning up the mess from a problem was harder than just getting it right the first time.

Olivia

Their employee relationships got more sophisticated, too. They had this idea to build a team, so they'd have not only the best prices but also consistency. There are a lot of traffickers who don't have a steady drug flow, which means no cash flow. You need stable, happy employees who are on your team, pushing the drugs out and bringing the money in.

This was a dangerous business, so the more comfortable you were with the people you worked with, the better. Junior and Peter spent a lot of time building trust and good relationships. They wanted serious commitments, not a bunch of "one-night stands" with suppliers or customers. That can cause a lot of trouble; you could end up with the wrong person and get burned.

Mia

With so much more to manage—and so many more people—Peter and Junior went from having twenty lines each to thirty or forty each. It was insane. They never put two people on one phone. Their cash counter at one stash house in Chicago got one, the guy who delivers money got another, and the head of their furniture company had another. We would put little stickers on each phone with someone's initials. These phones would last a few weeks, then they'd destroy them and get another burner phone with a new number. We even had one phone designated for pizza orders because, in this business, you never had a home phone.

Olivia

Before Chapo met Junior and Peter, he'd never answer his phone. He had people do it for him. But seeing Junior and P with all those burner phones must have inspired him because he started doing it himself. He labeled them just like my husband and his brother did, too. Those phones were the first thing Sean Penn wrote about in his *Rolling Stone* story about his meeting with Chapo, and when I read it, I just laughed and thought to myself, *I bet Sean Penn thinks Chapo's so original. Little does he know.*

Mia

Our husbands were so busy, but it didn't take them away from us emotionally. If anything, they wanted us closer to them. Having a wife and family took a lot of the pressure off, or at least some of it. Peter wanted his life to be as routine as possible outside of work, which is why he went everywhere with me. I remember, once, I was about to leave to get a manicure.

"Where are you going?" he said.

"To get my nails done."

"I'm going with you," and he followed me right out the door. I sat under the UV light waiting for my polish to dry, and there he was with his bag of phones, just hanging out with me. It's not that he didn't trust me, and he wasn't worried I'd be hurt. After his kidnapping, we had security to make sure nothing ever happened to one of us. He just wanted to be with me, like a regular husband who was so bored he'd decided to join his wife at the nail parlor. I suppose it made him forget all his problems. I imagine it gave him a sense of peace, like it could make the violence and weirdness go away.

Olivia

The Mexican government had started to squeeze the cartels in 2006 and 2007, and everyone from El Chapo down was feeling it. They were reacting to it with full-on terror.

On December 1, 2006, Felipe Calderón was elected president of Mexico, and ten days later, he sent 6,500 army troops to the state of Michoacán, just southeast of Guadalajara, to fight the cartels. They fought back, and over the next six years, almost 85,000 people would die because of cartel violence.

Mia

Terrible things were happening near the border. In 2007, Chapo and El Mayo went to war with the Juárez Cartel in an attempt to take over the highly active, lucrative drug smuggling route from Ciudad Juárez to El Paso. A city of over 1.5 million that's just over the Rio Grande, Ciudad Juárez had always been different than its smaller sister city, but when the turf war began, the gap between the two grew even bigger. In 2007, Ciudad Juárez recorded 300 homicides. By 2008, that number hit 1,500. In 2010, there were over 3,000. Over all that time, El Paso's murder rate hovered around three to five per year.

Olivia

All during 2007, Junior and I took business trips to Ciudad Juárez, and we witnessed the mayhem. I remember seeing the streets filled with police agents, thinking how obvious it was that the Mexican government had sent up the army to fight the cartels. I would sit there and worry my head off, thinking, *I've never felt more uncomfortable in my life.* Then I'd cross the border and go shopping in El Paso just to get away, and it was like night and day.

The violence had gotten worse in Culiacán, too. When Junior and I would go there a few times a month, the newspapers would be full of pictures of dismembered people, their body parts scattered everywhere. Or photos that showed dozens of bodies hanging from bridges, with banners on them sending messages to their enemies. Newspapers in Mexico are not like in the United States, where they blur out blood or gunshot wounds. There, they show *everything*.

Those images were one of the things that pulled me out of the bubble I'd created after I had Brandon. When I saw them, I realized, *That could be Junior*. I started thinking about these people's poor wives and kids who would have to grow up without a father. I'd been the wife whose husband got murdered, so I knew what it felt like firsthand.

It was eating away at Junior, too. With so many people dying because of the cartel wars, it was beginning to be too much—for Junior and Peter, and for us.

Mia

Then, all this talk about submarines started.

Olivia

Chapo's transportation system had always been out of hand. To get drugs from Colombia to Mexico, he'd taken control of thousands of container ships and had a fleet of 747s, more than even Aeromexico had. In each plane, he took out the seats, then filled them with clothes or supplies, supposedly for humanitarian missions. He'd unload those goods in Colombia, then reload them with twelve thousand kilos of coke. That's fourteen tons. All that coke would make its way back to Mexico, where corrupt federal officials would help unload it, then it would find its way via train, tractor-trailer, bus, or secret tunnel to the vehicles with secret compartments that my husband had built.

These systems weren't foolproof, though, and Chapo was always looking to improve his transport. So he decided to invest in submarines. He bought one sub from the Russians, then started manufacturing them in Colombia for $1 million each. The plan was to have ten submarines in the water at a time, holding eight to ten tons of cocaine each. That would be over a billion dollars in the water, and Junior and Peter were invited to be in on the load.

The subs were managed by different men Chapo and El Mayo trusted. Alfredo Vásquez-Hernández was in charge of one of the subs, and he stopped by our house one day to talk to Junior and Peter.

"How much do you want to put in?" he asked.

"Let's do twelve hundred," Junior said.

The way it worked out, though, is that when Alfredo put the load together, Chapo and El Mayo would end up getting 20 percent, or two tons, for free. You know how much two tons is? It's like $20 million for free every time each submarine goes. It sure paid to be the boss.

Junior and Peter were responsible for turning in their 1,200 kilos to the Colombians to load onto the sub. To do this, they started working with a close friend named Andy, who was their contact out of Colombia, and a part of our extended family. He would purchase, mark, and deposit the work with the people in charge of loading the subs, and even when the bosses were short on kilos, he'd go to Colombia or Panama and put in the difference.

Once the subs got to Mexico and were unloaded, though, guess what the cartels did with them? They'd sink them, because they didn't want to risk sending them all the way back. They'd use them once, then sink them every time.

Holy shit, I remember thinking. *This is going a little too far.* Sure, I knew about the 747s and the tunnels across the border, but submarines were on a whole different level. Only the navy had submarines. Regular people didn't have them.

But at that point, we were *far* from being regular people. Yet we didn't try to change that till we almost lost our lives.

CHAPTER 16

The Strip Club Incident

Mia

I hadn't felt comfortable in Puerto Vallarta since our wedding. I lived for the beach, but that immigration officer who'd tried to extort us was there, and being anywhere close to him was terrifying. Plus, the last time we'd been out in Puerto Vallarta, a few weeks before we got married, we'd run into a Chicago police officer at a club downtown. He'd looked Peter and Junior right in the eyes and said, "I know who you are." Then he pulled out his cell phone and snapped a photo of them.

At the end of January 2008, though, Peter and Junior had business associates in from China, and they wanted to go to the beach. If you were looking to impress someone and take them out, Punta Mita, which was right outside of Puerto Vallarta and where Olivia had gotten married, was the place to go, so Peter and Junior planned a short trip.

"I don't want to go," I said to Peter. "That immigration officer might find out we're there."

"There's no way. We're going to be so far away from their office downtown. We won't even be on their radar."

I relented, and the next morning, we packed up our things.

Olivia

The two guys who'd flown in from China owned an import/export business, and they were there to talk about these things called buckets.

Junior and Peter had gotten into the meth business recently, and the buckets were the key to the whole operation. They were five-gallon tubs, sort of like a paint barrel you might pick up at Home Depot, and they were full of pseudoephedrine powder, which everyone just calls "pseudo" and which is one of the main ingredients in meth. They had a contact in Canada who was getting them from New Delhi, India, but the Chinese guys promised to sell them cheaper. Each bucket cost $150,000, and there were forty buckets in a ton. If Junior and Peter bought four tons, that would cost $24 million. The pseudo was worth way more in California than Mexico, and they could sell it to a manufacturer over the border for $80 million, a profit of $56 million. It was hard to buy pseudo in bulk in the United States since the government had cracked down with all kinds of new laws, so Junior and Peter were in a great position to make a lot of money.

The day before the men from China were set to show up, Junior explained to me how he'd transport the buckets once they'd made the deal.

"The guys from China ship the buckets over," he explained. "I'll pay off the *piso* to clear customs agents at the port in Manzanillo, and then I'll have the *fleteros* send them up to Mexicali. Then La Puerca helps get them over."

Junior and Pete had just moved their infrastructure to Mexicali, so they were seeing La Puerca, who controlled the tunnels from Mexicali to Calexico, a lot more regularly. I liked La Puerca; he was handsome and very charismatic, older than all of us, but I always thought he was fun to have around. He'd become one of Peter's best friends, in fact.

Junior added, "These Chinese guys approached me years ago about buying buckets, but I didn't think much of it till Chapo and El Mayo were talking to me about wanting pseudo because they have a chemist in California. I looked at them and said, 'I know who to talk to.' Then I thought to myself, *You have no idea how long these guys have been bothering me about these buckets.*"

Mia

A few hours later, buckets were the last thing anyone was talking about when we sat down to dinner with the Chinese businessmen and their associate.

"We'd like to see some girls," they said.

"Then we know exactly where to go," answered Peter.

When associates came into town, they always wanted to go to strip clubs. It was just what you did. And because Olivia and I went everywhere with Junior and Peter, they asked us to join them. I was reluctant, though.

"Can't we just have some girls come over to our house? I'm worried about being out."

Peter looked at me and burst into laughter. "Brandon will be home. These are strippers, not babysitters."

He had a point. Brandon had just turned two, and he'd be staying home with Adrian and Daniela. I finally relented, and it was just after dark when we piled into a few SUVs and drove about twenty minutes away.

Olivia

It was a Saturday night, and the club was packed. The music was pumping, we were popping bottles, having a good time. We were seated in the VIP section, in a roped-off area the owner had specially reserved for us. He'd called a bunch of girls over, and they'd started dancing for the Chinese guys, who looked like they were having the time of their lives.

In Mexico, women *do not* go to strip clubs, so I could see some guys nearby staring at us. I shrugged it off; it had happened a lot, and wasn't a big deal. As I scanned the room about five minutes later, though, I noticed one guy who looked strange. The expression on his face just didn't seem normal. It was like he knew us, or like he wanted something from us. I turned to my husband.

"That guy is staring at us, Junior. Something's wrong."

"No, babe, it's fine. He's just not used to somebody's wife being in a strip club. He probably thinks you should be home cooking and cleaning." He laughed a little bit, and I did, too, nervously.

A few minutes passed, and he kept looking. I pulled on Junior's arm. "This isn't good. I don't like that guy."

Junior grabbed my hand, "It's okay. We're fine."

But it wasn't. I just *felt* it.

I went back to drinking my champagne, watching a parade of girls make their way over to our table. This wasn't a high-class, VIP strip club like some we'd gone to in Guadalajara, but the customers were well dressed. They were spending good money. But the guy who'd been looking at me and Mia was different than all of them. He had something on his mind, and it wasn't a lap dance. Another minute passed, and the man stood up, walked past us, his eyes glued to the side of my head, and moved out the door.

As I turned to tell Mia, I saw the front doors swing open. A group of men dressed in black poured in, their faces covered and AK-47s drawn. They began shouting in Spanish, "Get down! Get down!"

The music cut off. It sounded like something from the movies, when a DJ's record stops spinning, the needle scratches the vinyl, and the speaker blasts, *errrr*... I saw half-naked girls running back and forth on the stage, screaming at the top of their lungs. Then, I watched a crowd of masked men sprinting toward us. Mia had been right next to me, but there was no sign of her. Junior and Peter were still across from me, and in what seemed like less than a second, the men reached us and shoved the points of their AK-47s into the backs of our heads, forcing us to the floor.

I'm going to die right here in this fucking strip club, I thought. *God help us.*

Just then one of the men who'd been hightailing across the floor picked me up like a rag doll. I started fighting, kicking, and punching like a wild woman, and he dragged me toward the door with my shoes scraping across the floor as I flopped around. When he got me outside, I saw about five Suburbans lined up, their windows blacked out. In front of each car was a line of men, all armed with semiautomatic weapons. The man who'd pulled me out of the club pushed me forward, then picked me up and threw me into the passenger seat of one of the Suburbans.

Peter and Junior were in the backseat with two armed men sitting behind them with guns to their heads, and someone outside slammed the door shut.

Mia

When the music stopped, I was already on the floor, next to Olivia. Men and naked girls were running toward the door, screaming. It was a madhouse. As people were scrambling past me in every direction, the girls who'd been dancing for the Chinese guys grabbed me by the arm and dragged me. I glanced back, terrified, and saw Peter. He was looking right at me, his eyes big as saucers. Then someone ran up to him and put a gun to his head.

The girls hid me in a room in the back. It had been their dressing room, but right then it looked like a refugee camp.

I was on the floor, hysterical, and I could hear men screaming, "Get down! Get down on the floor!" Then, a stripper put her arms around me and said, "Stop crying. Be quiet. If they hear you, they'll come for you."

We sat in that room for five minutes. I think I was the only one with a top on. There was makeup scattered on the floor, bras and panties in piles in the corner, and sniffling, half-naked women everywhere. But we were all as quiet as we could be, with just a few whimpers every now and then. Right then I heard footsteps coming toward the back, and a voice called, "Where is she? Where is she?"

My God, I thought, *They're coming for me.*

A man broke through the door, pointed right at me, and then picked me up from my stomach. My legs dangled off the floor, and I kicked and screamed with all my might, trying to get away from him while he yelled, "Shut the fuck up! I'll kill everyone in here if you're not quiet!" Then he dragged me toward the door, marched through the club, opened the exit to the outside, and threw me into the front seat of a waiting SUV. In the back were the two Chinese guys and one of their associates.

I saw my chance. The window was cracked, and the car was running. I'm small, and I knew if I could get that window down just enough I could escape out of it. I pushed the button, bounded up, and threw my body toward the window. But the man grabbed my neck and pulled me to his lap.

"Stop fucking moving," he said.

Someone in the back added, "Stop fucking moving or he's going to hurt you."

Olivia

Junior, Peter, and I could see Mia being dragged into the truck's front seat. I watched her squirm around, then face the window. I saw a hand reach up to her neck, and then I saw her pull back and freeze up. That's when Peter spoke up.

"If I had a gun, I'd shoot her myself."

In Mexico, you never want a woman with you when shit's going down. The things kidnappers do to women are inhumane: they torture, rape, and sodomize them. Knowing this, I realized, *He doesn't want to see her suffer.*

Then it hit me: *What the fuck was going to happen to us?*

I had to do something.

I'd left my purse in the club, but I still had my phone with me, in my back pocket. It was a Nextel flip phone with a walkie-talkie, and I slowly reached toward it, pressed the button that started up the two-way feature, and prayed that it would connect me to someone. I moved it below me so no one could see it, and then I began yelling at the kidnapper next to me, who was wearing a mask.

"What do you want? How much do you fucking want? You want $10 million?"

"I don't want your fucking money!" the man in the passenger seat said. He was speaking English.

I kept going. "Junior, tell them you got money. Tell them who you are."

"I said I don't want your fucking money," the kidnapper said, banging on the dashboard. "They fucked me. They should have paid me when they had the fucking chance." He was wearing a mask, motioning toward Junior and Peter at this point. "The US is coming for you, and you're spending the rest of your lives in prison."

I had my finger still pressed to the side of my phone. If I took it off, I knew it would beep, so I held my finger there like my life depended on it. I was thinking the whole time, *Please. Please someone be listening to this.*

I had my hands hidden behind my back, clutching my phone, but my eyes were glued on the guy with the mask. I watched him move his hands toward his face, then pull off the mask. He faced us.

Holy shit, I thought. *It's that customs agent from Mia's wedding, the one who extorted us. Chapo and El Mayo told Junior and Peter not to pay him, so he's back for revenge.*

Mia

I don't even know how long we drove. Maybe twenty minutes? All I remember is thinking, *I'm going to die. I'm going to die,* as the car I was in pulled up to this little building on the outskirts of town.

The kidnappers took me, the two Chinese guys, and their associate out of the car. They pushed us inside, slamming a steel door behind us. I noticed a poster on the wall with the AFI (Agencia Federal de Investigación, which is the equivalent of the FBI in Mexico) emblem on it. There were two ratty sofas shoved up against the wall, with Peter, Olivia, and Junior smooshed up altogether on one. They were handcuffed. This building didn't seem like a place where government officials worked; it looked like a spot where you tortured someone.

Someone threw me onto the sofa with Peter, Junior, and Olivia, and the three other men piled onto the other. A man with an AFI uniform on slapped handcuffs on me, then moved away and started talking to someone else, who was wearing a different type of uniform.

Holy shit, I realized. *It's that customs agent from my wedding. The one who extorted us.*

Peter turned to me and started whispering. "I'm sorry. I'm so sorry."

"It's okay," I said. "We're together. I just don't want to be without you."

"It's not okay. You don't deserve this, Mia."

I told him again to stop, that he hadn't done anything, but I couldn't shut my brain off. *I never got a chance to be a mother. I never got to say goodbye to my parents.* I'd started crying so hard I could hardly breathe, but I still choked out, "Peter, be honest with me. Are we going to die?"

My husband turned and looked me straight in the eyes. "No, we are not going to die."

Even with handcuffs on, in a room full of armed men who looked like they wanted to kill us, I believed him.

Olivia

I'd spent the entire car ride trying to negotiate to get us out of there, but when we'd been dragged inside and pushed onto those nasty couches, I decided to shut my mouth. These men were not playing, and I was out of my league. Mia and I were the only women in that room, and that was a position that no girl should ever be in.

Finally, Junior started talking to the customs officer. "I'll give you $1 million for each girl. They have nothing to do with this."

"I told you. I don't want your fuckin' money. I just want you."

I looked over at Junior. Tears were coming down his face, and right then, I knew we weren't getting out of this one. Junior had always been my rock. He'd always kept me strong and made me feel protected, but he looked broken. *I'm helpless,* I thought. *If he thinks we're fucked, we are.*

"I'm sorry, Liv, you're going to have to raise Brandon alone," he said.

"Stop, Junior. Don't say that."

He looked down to the floor and grabbed his head in his hands. "My poor baby. My poor girls. Please take care of them."

"Junior, you're scaring me."

"I'm sorry for not listening to you about changing my life. All those years. I'm sorry for not giving you a normal life. I'm sorry I couldn't give you another baby."

"Junior, you're getting out of this. I love you. Be strong."

"*You're* getting out of this. You and Mia. But I don't know how the rest is going to play out."

Right then, I knew he was right. Despite all our near misses and all our last-chance saves, the danger we'd always faced was bound to catch up with us sooner or later. The moment of reckoning had come, and I thought to myself, *Our beautiful family is about to fall apart, and there's nothing I can do.*

Then suddenly, everything stopped.

Mia

The immigration officer's phone had started ringing. He looked down at the caller ID screen and answered it. After some back and forth, lots of "Sí, señor. Sí, sí," with him pacing around nervously, looking like he'd seen a ghost, he put the phone down and turned into an animal.

"Who the fuck did you call? Who the fuck did you contact?" He was screaming, and veins were popping out of his neck. He started waving his gun around near Peter and Junior. Some spit shot out of his mouth, and his hands were shaking. I'd seen really irrational people act like this before, and it's never good. *This guy is scared out of his mind,* I thought. *And that's worse than if he was just angry. The way he's acting, he's going to shoot one of us in the head.*

Olivia

Peter and Junior hadn't called anyone. But I had, back in the SUV. I'd reached Adrian, and he must have heard me trying to negotiate a ransom. I'm sure he hung up and dialed up someone important, and whoever that was had just called the officer's phone.

Then I suddenly realized I still had my Nextel phone in my back pocket, and I squirmed a little further back on the couch, manipulating it and wedging it in the crack of my ass. I knew if the agent saw it, he would pop me right between the eyes.

Mia

Olivia and I had been handcuffed together the whole time. We were terrified, holding each other's hands. It felt like hours, but during that whole, awful time, our relationship shifted. It was our turning point. We had always been sisters-in-law and family no matter what, but right then, we became sisters.

I squeezed Olivia's hand harder as the immigration officer paced furiously and waved his gun around. Then the AFI official in charge called Junior over to the phone.

"It's *el jefe*, Arturo Beltrán," he said. "He wants to talk with you."

Someone removed Junior's handcuffs. Junior took the phone into another room, talked for about ten minutes, and returned, all business.

"Take the shackles off the girls right now," Junior said. "They're free to go."

Olivia

I had been red-faced and crying the whole time Junior was in the other room. Peter was apologizing to Mia, begging her to be brave. But the second Junior walked back into the room, and we heard that we were free to go, Peter snapped out of husband mode and into business mode. He looked at me.

"Pay attention to every word I'm about to say, okay?"

"Of course," I said. "What is it?

"When you get out of here, go to LA. But don't let anyone find out. If they know we're locked up, they're not going to pay us. There's $40 million out there, owed to us. Here are the wholesalers who are set to pay." He started going through a list of names, asking me to repeat each one.

"Slow down!" I said. "I got this, but slow down."

"Make sure you get that money. Your life depends on it."

I knew he was right. If we didn't take care of this, it didn't matter where Junior and Peter were. The cartels were going to want their fucking money, and if we didn't get it to them, they'd decapitate our whole family for it.

Then the officers took off our handcuffs and led us to the door. I turned around and looked at Junior. "Go. Just be careful," he said. "I'll see you soon."

I started crying hysterically again. "*No!* You're lying to me. I'm never going to see you again. You cut a deal. You're just trying to save us. I'm not leaving you!"

Peter peeled me away from his brother, stared at me, serious, and said, "Go now before they change their minds."

Mia and I looked back in disbelief, like it was our last goodbye, and shuffled out the door, followed by the two Chinese guys and their associate. One of the officers handed me a set of keys, pushed us into the SUV that we'd driven to the club, and walked away.

Then I started up the truck and began driving the five of us away from the scene of our own kidnapping.

Mia

The Chinese guys were so relieved. The whole time they'd been inside, they'd thought Junior and Peter had set them up. Unfortunately, though, their problems weren't over because we had no clue how to get home.

In 2008, nobody had GPS in Mexico, so Olivia had no idea where she was going. We were out of our minds, hysterical, and I wasn't sure Olivia could see well enough to drive. She was swerving, saying things like, "I have to get back to Brandon. Brandon needs me."

I was so out of sorts that I didn't know what to do or where to go, and I started yelling, "I don't want to leave them! Go back!"

"Hell, no," she responded, finally in control of herself. "We're going home."

Soon, though, we began seeing signs that we were leaving Puerto Vallarta, a place I'd been so terrified to go the day before. Yet here I was now, and what had happened was just as bad as I feared.

"Get out a pen and paper," Olivia said. "I need you to write down these names."

As she reeled off the list of wholesalers, I took notes. There were so many names I couldn't figure out how she remembered, but she had. Minutes later, we drove into our beach house driveway in Los Ranchos. As soon as we got through security, the three guys jumped out of the car like their pants were on fire and ran into the house, and we followed behind them.

We quickly realized we had a problem, though. The house was way too quiet. Adrian and Daniela were nowhere to be found, and wherever they'd gone, they'd taken Brandon with them.

Olivia

The beach house was huge, with rooms on the left side and an equal number of rooms on the right. The back was all windows and doors that opened out to the sea, and there was an upstairs, too. I ran through each of those rooms screaming my head off, "Brandon! Adrian! Where's my baby?" But there was no one there.

Adrian hadn't been answering his phone as I'd been driving back home, and I was terrified. I walked into Brandon's room, and his little bed was unmade. His stuffed animals were scattered around, and the blankie he always carried around was sitting on the bed, all balled up. In the corner of the room, there was his car seat.

Shit, I thought. *Not only did someone take him, but they took him without his car seat.*

Then, way down the hall, I heard one of our maids, who lived way back in another part of the house. She was just waking up as she stumbled toward me.

"They're gone," she said, and my heart stopped. "They left in the middle of the night."

Mia

I'd been pacing around the kitchen, looking for Peter and Junior's papers and phones, when Olivia ran into the kitchen. She was totally out of breath when she said, "Adrian and Daniela left with Brandon."

"That's great! They're safe. Where did they go?"

"I don't know. But they forgot to take his fucking car seat! He's not safe without his car seat!"

Of all the things to focus on right then, that car seat had apparently become the most important thing in the world to her. I tried to get her attention off of it. "What do we do? Do we go back to Guadalajara?" I was pretty much screaming at her because somebody had to make a decision, and it wasn't going to be me. I hadn't slept, I'd just been kidnapped, my husband was probably on a flight back to the United States, and I'd cried so much I could hardly see. But Olivia didn't answer.

"Let's wait," I finally said.

Olivia calmed down just enough to respond, "You're crazy. We have to get the fuck out of here."

But I'd made up my mind. "No," I said. "I'm waiting for Peter."

Olivia

There was no way I was staying in that house. No fucking way. We had to make sure the deposits in LA were safe, we had to get the hell out of Puerto Vallarta, and most of all I had to find my son.

We ran upstairs and started packing. We hadn't planned to stay in Puerto Vallarta long, so we didn't have much. I threw everything into one bag and could hear Mia doing the same. She'd started crying again, and every few seconds there would be a little whimper or sniff. After about five minutes, they were getting less and less frequent, and there was more silence than tears.

Then, suddenly, I heard what sounded like the Mexican army coming down our driveway. I became terrified all over again, and I thought, *Someone's coming to take our asses off to jail.*

Mia

Oh my God, it was insane. I ran to the window in my room and saw pickup trucks with armed men in the back, Suburbans, Jeeps, and pickups rolling down toward our house all in a line. There was car after car after car, windows all blacked out. I thought about heading downstairs, but I couldn't move a muscle and couldn't have run if I'd wanted to. Then it hit me. *What the hell is going on? Whoever's in those cars is going to kill us. You have to do something.*

I saw the door of the first pickup truck open up, and it was Peter. I sprinted down the stairs and out the door faster than I'd ever run in my life.

Olivia

In my mind it was Junior that jumped out of the car first, but they look so much alike and I was so out of my mind that, honestly, it could have been Peter. I was so happy to see both of them that it didn't make a difference anyway.

After we'd finished hugging and kissing, Junior motioned for us to go inside. When I say, "us," I mean the horde of guys who'd just stepped out of the five hundred cars that had driven toward our house. There were dudes everywhere.

Our dining room had a table that seated about twenty people, and everyone filed in toward it. I immediately knew who was in charge; his name was Nemesio Oseguera Cervantes, who everyone just called El Mencho. El Mencho's now the head of the Jalisco New Generation Cartel, which is pretty much the most violent cartel in Mexico right now. He uses shoulder-held rocket launchers to shoot down military helicopters, and he actually once set part of Guadalajara on fire. But at the time, El Mencho ran the plaza in Vallarta. He was a semi-regular drug lord in 2008, even though everyone—from the police all the way up to federal agents—feared him because he was a total maniac.

We all sat down at the dining room table and listened to Junior and Pete relate what had happened.

Mia

When Olivia had called Adrian on her Nextel from the back of the blacked-out Suburban, she had no idea whether or not he'd answered. Luckily, it was Adrian, and he had answered, and he'd heard every demand, scream, and threat. He understood his marching orders, and he quickly sprang into action making phone calls.

One person called another, moving the SOS up the ladder, until someone finally got the ear of Chapo, El Mayo, and Arturo Beltrán.

At this point, Adrian, Daniela, and Brandon had decided to get the hell out of Puerto Vallarta because it wasn't safe, and Adrian realized that although he couldn't protect his little brothers, he could save his nephew. They loaded up their car so fast they forgot Brandon's car seat, then started driving toward Guadalajara—a long, five-hour trip, where cell service was spotty.

Olivia

In the meantime, while Adrian's car was winding into the mountains and we were tied up in that torture chamber, Arturo Beltrán Leyva called and demanded to talk to Junior about the ransom he and Peter were prepared to pay to set us free.

"What did you get yourself into, and why are you offering so much money?" he said firmly.

"Because I have to," said Junior. "I have no other choice. I'm not going back to the States."

"Look, we're going to get you and your brother out," the BLO boss said. "But it's not going to be easy. What is the most important thing to you both?"

Junior didn't have to think twice. "Getting our wives out of this mess."

"It's done," Arturo said. Then he paused and added, "Keep this phone on you from now on. And remember: *tú mandas cabrón!*" (meaning "You tell them what the fuck to do.")

Mia

That's when the AFI officer started freaking out. He agreed to let Olivia and me go, knowing that if we got hurt, they'd be in deep shit. Then he released the Chinese guys and their associate because they weren't worth anything to them.

Olivia

Chapo, El Mayo, and Vicente then got on a call together to figure out what to do. They realized they had $5 million sitting in a plane on a runway in Juárez, and if they rerouted that plane, they could get the money to Puerto Vallarta in two and a half hours.

Vicente called the AFI office to negotiate.

"Keep the Flores brothers safe," he demanded, "and we'll pay you in exchange for their freedom. But it's going to take about two and a half hours."

"We don't have that kind of time," the official said.

Unfortunately, two and a half hours wasn't going to work. The AFI and immigration officer had been serious about wanting to send Peter and Junior back to the United States, and they'd called the US feds.

"The US Marshals will be here in half an hour," the AFI agent said. "They're taking Peter and Junior. We can't make a deal."

The drug lords huddled together on the phone again and quickly came up with a plan B. They tapped Vicente to call the AFI officer right back.

"We could do this the easy way or the hard way," he said, "but regardless, you're not sending the brothers back to the US. And since you're apparently insisting on keeping them, we're going to do things the hard way."

Mia

As a matter of fact, the cartels were prepared to go to war to save Junior and Pete from being sent back to the United States; El Chapo, El Mayo, and Vicente had begun amassing an army to come get them.

Olivia

The AFI agent knew he and his men were going to be outnumbered by whoever the cartels were sending, so they suited up in full war gear and shuttled Peter and Junior out of the station as fast as they could. They didn't give them bulletproof vests, but they did push them into a bulletproof Suburban, with two armed agents stationed on either side of them. The US Marshals were supposed to arrive by one p.m., and they had to meet them the minute they showed up.

The AFI agent got behind the wheel and began driving around the streets of Vallarta, frantic. After a few minutes, his phone rang. It was Músico, Arturo's right-hand man. Músico made all phone calls for Arturo and was one of Junior's closest friends, and right then, he was demanding to speak with Junior.

The AFI officer handed the phone back to Junior and Pete. Then, Músico started talking.

"We have hundreds of men ready to fight for your lives. Every road that leads to the Puerto Vallarta airport is blocked off. Every street is barricaded. There's no way you're getting on that plane. There's no way you're going back to the US."

As he listened in, Peter paused for a minute and realized just what was happening. But before he could say anything, Músico started to talk again, his voice cracking. "I don't know if there will be a shootout. This might not end well. But whatever happens, Junior, please know it's been an honor knowing you. Knowing the both of you."

Mia

When Músico said that, Peter thought about a million things, but three really stuck out. First, he remembered what his dad always said to him: "Don't ever let them take you to jail." Next, he thought about me. Finally, he said to himself, *Junior and I came into this life together, and I guess we are going to leave this world together.* Then he grabbed his brother's hand, closed his eyes, and felt hot tears start to run down his face.

Olivia

Junior choked up as he was talking to Músico. "We're ready. But… our family."

Músico replied, "Don't worry about your family. You have my word that I will guard them with my life and get them out of Mexico safely. I promise I won't let anything happen to them."

That was the signal for the AFI officer to make his move. He rolled down his window, put on his turn signal, and as he inched toward the side of the road, he motioned for his caravan to pull over, too. Then he jumped out of the car and made a call.

As he held the phone to his ear, he began pacing back and forth, clearly distraught. The US Marshals were about to roll into town, guns blazing, ready to capture the Flores brothers, and they were going to run right smack into the cartel's army. Something devastating was about to happen, and the AFI officer knew he'd put his men in the middle of it.

Then, he got back in the car and drove slowly toward the plaza in downtown Vallarta. As he rounded a corner, he saw almost a hundred men holding AK-47s, their guns drawn. Probably half of them surrounded the AFI officer's caravan, and El Mencho walked up to where Junior and Pete were sitting.

"*Cuate?* Time to go."

The AFI officer looked at Peter and Junior, put his gun on the floor, and exited the car with his hands up. As he opened their door, El Mencho said, "*Vamos,*" signaling for them to get out.

Junior and Peter slid off the seats just as two of El Mencho's men took their places in the back. They were decoys, intended to throw off the Marshals, who were getting closer.

Then Junior and Peter walked quickly toward a waiting car. Before they reached it, though, Junior turned around, approached the AFI agent, shook his hand, and told him, "You did the right thing. Don't worry, I'm not going to let anyone harm you. My brother and I are going to look out for you."

Mia

That's when they started driving back toward Ranchos, where our beach house was. They were in a massive procession of bulletproof cars. Every guy on the passenger side had his window rolled down, his gun peeking out, ready to fire. There were also men piled in the back of pick-ups, weapons drawn, in broad daylight.

They got to the first army checkpoint and switched cars, joining El Mencho. When they entered the second checkpoint, El Mencho rolled down his window and the Mexican army waved them through, their guns also drawn.

Not long after, they rolled up to our house, and Olivia and I ran out the door screaming.

Olivia

Before we headed back to Guadalajara later that day, Junior had one more phone call to make. He needed to reach Adrian to tell him we were on our way back.

"Adrian!" he yelled. "We're safe. We're driving back to Guadalajara. We'll be there tonight."

I ran to my husband and grabbed the phone right out of his hands, mid-conversation. I needed to know if my baby was okay *that second*.

"Brandon's fine," Adrian said. "He misses you but knows you're coming."

I was too upset to even hear what he said. "You took my baby without his car seat," I yelled. "You forgot the fucking car seat."

I hung up the phone and heard a room full of guys—including my husband—burst out in laughter.

CHAPTER 17

Do-or-Die Time

Olivia

Right after Junior and Peter came back to our beach house, some Mexican federal agents drove all of us back to Guadalajara in two armored trucks. It was me and Junior in one and Peter and Mia in another. The whole ride back, I remember thinking, *If I ever really wondered whether or not the federal government was assisting drug lords, this sure as hell settles it.*

In fact, agents were so in the cartels' pockets that Peter and Junior decided to pay the AFI officer who helped them escape the US Marshals $2.25 million, just as a thank you.

Chapo, El Mayo, and Arturo Beltrán had saved our husbands' lives once again—and ours for the first time—which cemented Junior and Peter's position in the cartels even further. Just like any big company that has executives, they were now at the top, and that afforded them benefits. Chapo gave them special passwords to let paid-off government officials know which cartel they belonged to, and to make them feel even safer, he specifically told them they'd never have to worry about extradition. After all, he was always notified when the United States was planning to pay a visit.

Mia

Even with that kind of protection, Peter and Junior were feeling less and less safe every day. They added extra security at the perimeters of our houses and invested in new cameras, so they could have a record in case anything bad happened. We'd always had cameras everywhere, and there wasn't a single blind spot between the two of our homes, but having even more scared me to death. I remember thinking, *It's like I'm living in a police state or war zone.*

Olivia

But Junior and Peter weren't ready to get out entirely.

"Pete and I have been talking about scaling back, baby," he said to me, "I think maybe we could just slow down, not grab any more work from Chapo, El Mayo, or the BLO, and just get start sending up our own work."

I was skeptical. "What does Peter say?" I asked.

"He's mostly concerned about our workers. We're everything to them. We're responsible for eighty families, and we can't just back off. They need to make money. But he also thinks that we can never really get away. We make all the money for the cartels, and every time we throw in loads with them and send work to the United States, we're in debt to them. If something gets seized, we'll owe millions." Junior paused. "My brother may be right; I'm not sure we can ever leave them without getting killed."

"There's no halfway, is there?" I knew it even before I asked.

"I don't know, so that's what we need to discuss."

Mia

The bad taste of our kidnapping was still with us, and we knew it would never leave. Even though the cartels had promised to protect us, there was nothing *truly* stopping anyone from trying to kidnap us again. There was nothing keeping the Mexican government from arresting and extraditing Peter and Junior, either. Sure, the cartels had told my husband and brother-in-law they were untouchable, but if there's anything we'd learned in the last four years, it was that life could change at a moment's notice.

By March 2008, that realization—and the question of what we

should do about it—felt even more urgent because Olivia and I had just discovered we were both pregnant.

Olivia

I always said I wanted my kids a grade apart. I loved being a mom, and I adored being pregnant, and before I'd had Brandon, I felt so close to Junior knowing his baby was growing inside me. I loved how attentive he'd been and how much he catered to me; he would kiss my belly and rub my feet every night, saying, "You've never been more beautiful to me."

Still, I knew Junior was hesitant about having another child. His worst fear was something bad happening, and me having to raise our babies alone. But understanding how much I wanted another child, and how much he loved our family, he went with it. He and I started trying to get pregnant again pretty much immediately after Brandon was born.

We tried and tried and tried every month, but nothing happened. After a year, I was like, "What the heck is taking so long?"

Then I got kidnapped.

I guess I should have known I was pregnant that night. I mean, I suspected—I'd been pretty up and down emotionally—but I hadn't confirmed it. But then, bam, we got dragged out of that club, and I was a thousand times more crazy and hormonal than I usually am. I'd never cried so much or so loudly. As soon as we got back to Guadalajara, I took a test, and sure enough, there were those two little blue lines on a stick.

I was *so* happy when I found out. I wanted nothing more than to be a devoted wife and mother. Having Brandon with Junior had been the greatest thing that had ever happened to us; we developed such an intimate bond, a closeness that was almost unexplainable.

Junior was just the best dad, too. He and Brandon were glued at the hip. They took naps together. Junior sterilized his bottles and watched every Disney movie with him. We had three housekeepers—one per floor—to make sure the house was spotless, but Junior would not let the señoras touch Brandon's bottles. His associates started calling him Mama, and when you'd see Junior, he'd be carrying his messenger bag full of phones and our boy's diaper bag, one per shoulder and crisscrossed in the back. When I'd walk in front of Brandon, he'd turn his little head on me because he just wanted to be with his dad.

It was going to be another new beginning for us, or so I told myself. But deep down, I knew: *We can't really start again unless we give up everything. It's do-or-die time.*

Mia

Even though Peter and I were married over two years before we decided to have a baby, I'd always known I'd wanted to be a mom. I'm a nurturer—I like to take care of people, really listen to them, and let them know they're loved—and I knew Peter would be a wonderful dad. But we'd put it off, mainly because we wanted to enjoy each other's company. One morning in 2007, though, Peter woke me up. He was kneeling by the bed, and he took my hand.

"I have to ask you an important question," he said.

"Is it something bad?"

"No, it's not bad. Just listen to me. I want to know if you want to have my baby."

I was a little confused, but I went along with it anyway. "Yes. I'd love to have your baby! We've already talked about this."

"No, serious. I want to make sure this is forever."

I was getting more confused by the second. "We're *married*. Of course this is forever. What are you saying?"

"I don't want you to say anything today. I want you to think about it. I want to offer you $5 million, and you can go if you know that you can't be with me for the rest of your life. If you know in your heart that you can, then we should have a child. But if you know that this is not what you want and *I* am not what you want, and this life is not what you want, then I'd rather see you happy somewhere else."

I was floored. I started thinking, *Why is he doing this to me? Is this a trick?* But I realized he couldn't bear to have me live through another kidnapping. This was not an easy life, and the future—the next day, even—felt so uncertain. Having a child was momentous and final in a way that just being married wasn't. Because if he'd died or disappeared before having a child with me, it would just be my loss. If the same thing happened with a baby, it was a loss for an entire lifetime. Peter knew that having a child was the biggest decision we'd ever make, and right then, I realized it, too.

The next day, though, I said yes. Peter was my life. Our future family was my life. And one morning in March 2008, just two months after our kidnapping, I got the news I'd been dreaming of.

I love pizza. I could eat it three meals a day and still go back for more. Yet one night, Peter and I ordered pizza, and I couldn't stand to look at it, let alone eat it.

"Get that away from me," I said to Peter.

I went to bed early, still hungry, and the next morning, I woke up and walked to the bathroom. Sitting on the vanity was a cup holding one beautiful flower and an unopened pregnancy test. I removed the test from the cup and walked back into the bedroom to talk to Peter.

"What's with this?" I asked, smiling.

"Go back in the bathroom and take that test," he said. "I have a feeling it's going to be good news."

Less than five minutes later, I saw those two little blue lines on a stick.

Olivia

For all of us—me, Mia, Junior, and Peter—the Puerto Vallarta kidnapping became our second chance. When Mia and I were tied up, thinking we'd die right there before having more babies, our husbands were thinking the same thing. They were asking themselves, *Is this the life we want for our wives and children? We can't do this to them anymore. If this happens again, it's going to end in tragedy, and everyone, including our kids, will be dead.*

I also realized how lucky we'd been. If the Marshals had taken Junior and Peter back to the United States, they would have been facing life behind bars. I would have been left alone, pregnant, with two babies to raise by myself.

That's why Junior and I started talking almost nightly about getting out.

"I won't ever forget what you looked like at K's funeral," he said to me. "You were pregnant, lying on the ground in agony. I felt it then and I feel it now: *That can't happen again.*"

I was on the same page. I just *couldn't* go through that again.

We knew it wouldn't be easy, though. The Sinaloa Cartel and the BLO had just gone to war with each other, and Junior and Peter saw that things were headed in a bad direction, like worse than ever. They were on the fringes of the kind of personal retaliation they'd never seen before.

Mia

On January 21, 2008, Mochomo was arrested in Culiacán with $900,000 in cash and an arsenal of rifles, automatic, weapons, bullet-proof vests, and grenades. The Beltrán Leyva brothers believed that it was El Chapo and the Sinaloa Cartel who had tipped off the authorities to Alfredo's hiding place in a Culiacán safe house, and they were enraged, vowing revenge. This incident sparked the beginning of the feud that quickly turned BLO against the Sinaloa Cartel.

Olivia

The arrest of Mochomo infuriated his brothers. With Alfredo behind bars, Arturo took the helm of the Beltrán Leyva Organization, vowing he'd get back at El Chapo. Violence in Culiacán shot through the roof, and the months of February and March—and beyond—saw all-out warfare on the streets of Culiacán. El Chapo's men were cut up into pieces, which were then thrown into the trunks of their cars. BLO workers were shot at random in the mom-and-pop bars they frequented at the end of every work day. It wasn't uncommon for safe houses to be firebombed, with the workers inside so badly burned that their bodies couldn't be identified.

Mia

Right away, Peter and Junior had found themselves in the middle of the two warring factions. Both the BLO and the Sinaloa Cartel needed them desperately, though, so while they felt somewhat protected, the heat was on. To each side, the obvious way to get more power over the other was pull Peter and Junior closer into the fold, so each brought up the idea of a *plaza*. The BLO wanted them to control Tijuana, while Chapo and El Mayo hoped to turn over Mexicali.

Olivia

A *plaza* is a piece of real estate specific to trafficking. There was *plaza* in Vallarta, another in Culiacán, and more in pretty much every major drug center in Mexico. The head of a *plaza* controlled that area, coordinating which drugs were coming in and which were going out. He negotiated police protection, and anyone who sold drugs in that area would have to get his permission. It was a powerful position to be in, and to a lot of the cartel members in Mexico, it was the highest you could go without actually being the boss.

The idea was to have Junior and Peter control a plaza together—after all, they'd always run a dual business—and there was no way one would go to one cartel and the other go to another. They were a team, and two heads weren't just better than one, they *were* one.

But they respectfully declined. "We don't want that kind of power," they said. I'm sure El Chapo and the Beltrán Leyvas just shook their heads and looked at them like they were crazy, but Peter and Junior just weren't chasing that kind of massive ego drug lord life. This was just a business to them, and they were always going to choose family over everything.

Mia

They knew that if they got a *plaza*, they would have had to send us back to the United States to live. Just like Chapo or all of the other cartel bosses, they'd have to go into hiding, and we'd only see them once they sent for us. Chapo didn't care about being in the mountains; he'd just have girls come to him. But Peter and Junior wouldn't think about giving us up. It was totally out of the question.

Olivia

They could turn down a *plaza*, but they couldn't escape their associates who'd started putting pressure on them.

One day, after Mochomo got arrested and the Beltrán Leyva brothers soured on Chapo and El Mayo, Músico called Junior. He wanted my husband to come see him, but Junior said that he couldn't.

"I can't come see you because Rambo's here," he said. "He's been in town on an operation and said it's not a good time for me to come out."

If Músico had a problem with Junior hanging out with Rambo, he didn't say it on that call. Sure enough, though, the next day Junior found out that Rambo had picked up Arturo Beltrán's right-hand man, a guy they called El Comandante, taken him back to his ranch, and killed him in front of his whole family. The "operation" Junior had mentioned was a deliberate act against the BLO, and Músico was pissed.

He called Junior and said as much. "Rambo killed El Comandante! You better tell me where the fuck Chapo is, because I'm going to kill him myself!"

Junior just sat there, so worried. He had no idea the operation was a direct blow to the BLO.

"Músico," he said. "You know my brother and I have nothing to do with this war. We're not fighting. You know us. You know we don't get involved. Don't be mad at us, we're just working."

But Músico kept screaming. "You better pick a side! Pick a fucking side!"

Mia

You could see the stress on Peter's face. I'd been with him through three kidnappings, but I'd never seen this kind of pressure bubbling up inside him. He and Junior were two warring cartels' biggest and best pipelines for sending drugs into the United States, and bodies were piling up to their right and their left.

He came to me just a few weeks after I found out I was pregnant.

"I think Junior and I need to stop doing this."

Without taking a moment to think about it, I pulled him to me, looked him straight in the face, and said, "Yes."

"Let's go talk to Junior and Olivia then."

Olivia

Mia didn't know that Junior and Peter had actually been talking for days. Maybe it was because Peter had tried to protect her, like he always did, or maybe she was just so happy about being pregnant that Peter didn't want to spoil that moment for her. But I was always in Junior's ear, and I'd been begging for this more than anyone.

Junior was scared of walking away and giving up the only life he'd ever known. But he'd seen how I'd grown into a different woman since we'd met; I didn't care about snitching or what people thought. I loved my family so much I was willing to accept what had been unthinkable. *If Junior's willing to change his life for me and our children, then that's the ultimate gift,* I thought. *I respect and love him for making such a courageous decision.*

Mia

We initially started talking, all together, every few weeks after dinner. Some conversations were vague, and some were specific, with names and details and dates. We were scared. After all, we were considering changing everything in our lives.

Olivia

One night that April, we were sitting around the kitchen table at Mia and Peter's place. I don't know who started talking first, but I think it was Junior.

"P, things are changing, and we have to put our family first. I just don't think we can slow down and scale back," Junior said. "And if we move overseas, the cartels are just going to hunt us down. There's no walking away from them, and we'll have no protection. We risk the feds grabbing us and extraditing us."

I don't think Junior had to convince him. He already had his mind made up.

Peter got really serious and said what we were all thinking. "We should call our lawyer and see if we can cut a deal." He looked over at Junior and continued, "We can't keep doing this to our family."

Mia

Peter and Junior had put their blood, sweat, and tears into their organization, so leaving it all behind wasn't going to be easy. But there were three things weighing on us.

First, we had unborn children. Bringing them into the drug world wasn't just unsafe, it perpetuated a cycle that had started the day Junior and Peter were born. They didn't want our kids to be raised the way they had been, and Brandon had already been exposed to too much. There was security around the perimeter outside where he played, a room packed with millions of dollars in cash next to his nursery, and two parents who didn't come home one night because they were handcuffed in a torture chamber.

Second, this life wasn't guaranteed. Sure, Peter and Junior had worked day and night to build their business, but all of it could change at a moment's notice. The people they'd helped make rich could betray them anytime, then kill them and our whole families and not lose a second of sleep over it. People were dying left and right, families murdering families. They wanted no part of that, and neither did we.

Finally, what they were doing just wasn't right. Peter and Junior had morals, but their job didn't. People in Chicago, a city we all loved, were strung out on drugs they'd shipped. Mothers had lost their teenaged sons in cartel crossfire. Olivia's second husband had been murdered by a gang that was fueled by drug dealing.

Peter and Junior turned to us. With one look of doubt from either me or Olivia, they would have had a change of heart.

"What do you think?" Peter said.

Olivia and I nodded our heads in unison. *Get out.*

It was decided. Pedro and Margarito Flores were going to become federal informants, bring down the cartels, and dismantle everything they'd helped create.

PART FOUR

INFORMANTS

CHAPTER 18

No Promises

Olivia

By 2008, Junior and Peter's organization was pumping almost $50 million worth of cocaine onto US streets every month, and they had over one hundred employees in ten cities.

Yet they hadn't stepped foot on American soil in almost five years. They were fugitives, and if they'd taken that risk, they would have been arrested on the spot.

Mia

They had to take precautions, so they steered clear of the United States no matter what—even to talk to their lawyer about how to become the biggest drug informants in US history.

Someone had to fly to Chicago to lay the groundwork, though. It wasn't going to be them, and it didn't make sense for it to be me, either. Junior and Peter's lawyer was just a voice on the phone to me, and I didn't have the background or the experience to effectively relay all that he needed to know.

"Who's going to do it?" asked Peter one night.

"Olivia," Junior said. "No question."

We all turned and looked at her, knowing she'd be perfect.

Olivia

It had to be me. After all, I'd had a relationship with Junior and Peter's lawyer, Joe Bonelli, long before I got together with Junior. When

I was married to K, and the government asked me to wear a wire to gain intelligence against him, I'd decided I needed to talk to a lawyer, so I'd called Joe. He'd defended people in the drug trade, and on the street he was considered to be the best in the business.

He'd also represented Peter and Junior's employees, wholesalers, and any big drug conspiracy case in Chicago. He'd defended Adrian before he was sent to prison in the 1990s, and he'd stayed in touch with Junior and Peter over the years. He seemed to care about them, in fact. He never failed to ask about our family, and when I called and told him I needed to meet with him in Chicago, he seemed genuinely pleased.

Joe had always been sharp. He was tall and handsome and wore nice, tailor-made suits, so he looked the part, but he acted it, too. He was a great speaker, really commanding. I'd never seen him stumble; if anything, he was so confident he almost seemed cocky. But in March 2008, when I walked into his fancy office in the Loop, all business, and started talking, he became a different person.

"Junior and Peter want to tell everything they know about Joaquín 'El Chapo' Guzmán, Arturo Beltrán, and Ismael 'El Mayo' Zambada." I said their first and last names and nicknames just to be totally clear and avoid any confusion. El Chapo wasn't all over the news like he is now, and most Americans, aside from the government, hadn't heard of him. "Junior and Peter have been working with the cartels for four years, and they know where the bosses are hiding. They're willing to do anything to bring them down."

Joe sat behind his big wooden desk with his mouth wide open. He was holding a pen in his hand, but I think he'd forgotten that he wanted to take notes because he suddenly stared at the papers at his desk and hunched over, then started writing really fast. I realized he didn't know what to ask, so I kept on talking.

"I can tell you exactly how many tons Junior and Peter are bringing in every month, how many workers they have, and where the tunnels are that they use to get loads across the border. Chapo's been investing in submarines, and he's asking them to purchase rocket launchers from the military, and Junior and Peter own a fleet of tractor-trailers they use to transport loads…"

"Slow down. Stop. Did you say 'rocket launchers'?"

"Yes. They'll tell you every single detail of their business and how they're working with the cartels. They want to cooperate. Fully." I put extra emphasis on that last word.

Joe finally looked up and paused. He was thinking. Then he started talking slowly.

"So, if I call this DEA agent I've worked with, maybe he can tell me exactly what you need to do." He went a little white. "Wait, you don't have a wire on you, do you?"

"What?"

"A wire. Is anyone listening?"

"Why the hell would I be recording you? Are you okay?"

"Yes, yes, I'm fine, sorry."

I'd known this guy for years, and he was usually cool as a cucumber. He never got paranoid. Then I realized I was putting him in a sticky situation. He was a kick-ass defense attorney who represented guys on the street, like regular drug dealers, and he probably didn't want to be known as the person who represented snitches. No one likes a rat, and they like their lawyers even less. To top it off, even though Joe had ten times more experience with the drug trade than any other lawyer in Chicago, one of his clients cooperating with the government—on the international stage—was on a whole different level. Cooperation wasn't just a thing. He wasn't just nervous; he might even be in over his head.

"Look, relax," I said. "I brought a secure phone. Let's call my husband and Peter."

Mia

Olivia had given us a heads-up that she'd probably call us from Joe's office, but Peter, Junior, and I were still so nervous, sitting there in our penthouse with Brandon. We had no idea if Joe would even want to take the case, and we were really depending on Liv to tell him everything.

Plus, I couldn't stop feeling strange; we had this secret that no one else knew, and it occupied my mind constantly. I trusted Peter completely, and I knew his decision was 100 percent in my best interest, but still, I was seeing him—and everything—in a new light.

When the phone rang, Peter grabbed it and proceeded to tell Joe absolutely everything he and Junior wanted to do. Then he put it on speaker so we all could hear.

"Peter, Junior, Mia, hello," Joe said, deliberately. "Are you sure this is what you want to do?"

Junior spoke up. "Absolutely. We're sure."

"Because there's no turning back."

"Yes. Definitely," said Peter, then he stopped. "But do *you* want to do this?"

Joe paused. "Do I have a choice? I don't want you guys to talk to the wrong people and then have something happen to you and your families. Just let me make some calls. I need to reach the right people."

Peter leaned in toward the phone and lowered his voice. "Joe, listen to me. Be careful who you contact, because half of the people we know in Chicago and half the people you represent have ties to the cartels. Chapo and El Mayo have lawyers and officials on both sides of the border who weed out rats and snitches. They report to them weekly. If anybody finds out what we're doing, they will kill my whole fucking family. You got that?"

"I got it."

"So what's going to happen next?" Peter asked.

"I'll call you after I speak to the feds. After that, the ball's in their court."

"But you've got our backs, right?" Junior asked.

"I do." Joe went quiet for a second. "Look, I can't promise you what kind of deal you'll get, and I can't even promise the amount of prison time you'll get, but I'll give you my word that I'll defend you no matter what. I'm on your side from here on out. That's probably the only promise you'll get this whole time."

"We trust you," Junior said.

"I'll call you in a few days. I hope. No promises." Then Joe hung up.

The next thing we knew, Olivia was on a flight home.

Olivia

"No promises" became the theme of those first few months Junior and Peter were cooperating. Like, *Sure, we'll tell you we're assigning a bunch of agents to your case, and they'll probably call you at some point, but we can't promise when.* Or, *Give us all the intelligence you can, but we can't promise you how it might affect your case.* We knew nothing—like absolutely zero—in the beginning.

The only thing we could do was try to take care of our situation at home, which meant deciding who'd meet with the feds, whenever the hell they did call. It didn't take Peter long to make a decision.

"I don't trust the feds," he said. "When we meet with them, they could arrest us and extradite us right then and there. We can't go together."

"Then what are you thinking?" Junior asked.

"I'll go alone. I can't separate you from Brandon; if he loses you right now, I couldn't live with myself."

Junior looked at Peter and slowly nodded his head. There wasn't even a need to say thank you; they were in this together, like they'd always been. Junior had put his life on the line during Peter's kidnapping, flying into the mountains to meet with Chapo and hammering out an arrangement to free him. Making sacrifices for each other was just what they did.

We planned, and we waited. Joe was our only lifeline.

Mia

We called Joe all the time, and he was patient and reassuring most of the time, but sometimes, he was as concerned as we were. "It's going to take a while," he'd say. "And, seriously, I wonder if you boys are making the right decision."

Joe had come to realize what we had: that Junior and Peter were making an unheard of decision, by far the most difficult one they'd ever made. They were doing what few people in their right minds would even consider: risking their lives by walking away from the drug trade at the height of their careers.

We finally heard from a DEA agent named Sam in April, who wanted to set up an initial meeting between Peter and the feds in Cancún soon. To Junior and Peter, it was one of the most gut-wrenching conversations of their lives. The second they picked up the phone and said "hello," they officially became rats.

Olivia

I think that call made the whole situation hit home. After that, they were beyond sick. They completely went against everything that had been instilled in them since childhood because growing up, the feds were the bad guys, the enemies. They were the people who'd sent their dad away before they were born. They were the guys who'd helped put away Adrian. In their minds, they'd always been doing what they needed to do to support their families. Sure, they were making excuses to justify their wrongdoings, but coming from where they did and being bred into the world they were, that was the way it had always been.

To make things right, they knew they had to sacrifice themselves, walk away from their loved ones, and go to prison for a very long time. They were heading down an unknown path, and their lives were going to turn upside down and become a living hell because of it. But they had to break this cycle and do what was right. It was the only thing—and the most selfless thing—they could do for our families and the well-being of our children.

Junior and Peter had always said, "It's easier to do wrong and so hard to do right." In the weeks leading up to their first meeting with the feds, for the first real time in their lives, they began doing the latter.

CHAPTER 19

The Feds

Mia

The feds scrapped the Cancún meeting. A few weeks later, they set up another one in Cabo San Lucas, but when Peter and I arrived there, we found out that it had been canceled, too. The feds hadn't been able to get clearance from the Justice Department.

Traveling back home to Guadalajara, we were in a panic. At the airport, the garbage man taking out the bathroom trash looked like a cartel member. Then we saw two American men eating at a fast food restaurant, and I froze up.

"Peter," I said. "They look like undercover agents."

"Just keep walking and look ahead," he answered. But I realized, *He didn't disagree with me. He knows as well as I do that dozens of people know about his meeting. We could be ambushed at any moment from both sides: the cartel* and *the feds.*

Olivia

Thank God, Mia and Peter came home safely. When they did, we continued to discuss our plans almost every day. We'd huddle in the bathroom in my house, running all the spa jets, the rain showers, and the six-person Jacuzzi and whispering together in case one of Chapo's employees was driving by, picking up conversations from the air.

During one of our bathroom conferences, we came up with a plan B. If Junior or Peter was captured or killed, Mia and I would get on a private plane and fly to a safe house in Mexicali. There, we'd wait for further instructions.

Then, finally, in May 2008, the feds called again. They wanted Peter to hop on a flight to Monterrey, Mexico, and be prepared to talk—for hours. The feds were ready to hear what he and Junior planned to disclose and who they wanted to betray, and they were prepared to give them instructions on how to become federal informants.

Apparently, though, they weren't at all ready for a case this big.

Mia

Peter and I hated the idea of going to Monterrey, not just because it was so close to the border but because we'd be entering enemy territory. Monterrey was controlled by Los Zetas, one of Mexico's most dangerous and violent cartels, and they were at war with Sinaloa. The second we got there, Peter was looking over his shoulder.

But that didn't stop us from taking a walk the night before his meeting, something we did every night we were together.

"If this doesn't work out, you know where I'm going. I want you to know that I love you, and I did this for us. We'll be fine. *You'll* be fine," Peter said to me that night.

For the first time since I'd been in Mexico, I began to believe that maybe he was right. Even though the possibility of him going to jail the next day felt very real to us, I thought to myself, *If I was strong enough to agree that Peter should change his life, I'm strong enough to live on my own.* Joe hadn't given him any promises about what would happen when he sat down with the feds, so we knew an arrest right then and there was possible. Still, I felt a small pocket of strength stirring somewhere deep inside me.

I needed that confidence the next morning, though. When we woke up and sat together on the edge of the bed, holding hands, our hearts pounding, part of me was convinced it was all going to go south. I couldn't stop thinking, *Oh my God, this is it. It doesn't matter what he says or does, I'm going to have to raise our baby by myself.*

"I love you," Peter said as he pulled me toward him. "But I may have to let you go for a little while so I can hold on to you forever."

I was sobbing. "This is the hardest thing we've ever had to do. What if they don't let you come back to me?"

"If they don't," Peter answered, "please take care of yourself and my baby." Then he turned and looked me straight in the eyes. "I'll see you soon. Keep the door locked, and if you see anyone suspicious, leave right away." He stood up and leaned down to kiss me, then my belly. Then he walked out the door.

I didn't know when he'd be back, so I stayed in that room, pacing back and forth nervously all day. I kept thinking, *What did I let him do?* I didn't open up the curtains. I took a few bites of food I'd pulled out of the minibar, but nothing tasted good. I tried to turn on the television, but I was terrified I'd see a news report with Peter's mugshot plastered on the screen, saying he'd been taken away. I'd slept so badly the night before, but I couldn't nap. All I could do was wait, and wait.

I couldn't stop thinking about what might be happening. I knew how corrupt the cops in Mexico were, especially near the border, and the barbarism of Los Zetas made me sick to my stomach. Peter had demanded that there be no officials from Mexico in the room, but there were going to be American agents in the meeting who were stationed in Mexico. How could we be sure the cartels didn't know what was going on? For all I knew, Peter had walked into that hotel and been shot in the elevator.

The only thing that really reassured me was that our lawyer, Joe, would be there, along with two DEA agents who knew their case better than anyone. The agent from Chicago's name was Eric Durante, and he was young, smart, and eager. A case this big was a new world for him, and he needed to learn from Peter and Junior to advance in his career, so he was taking it on with an open mind. He wasn't cocky, like all the other agents they'd run into in the past, and he didn't treat them like criminals. He actually seemed astounded by their courage in putting themselves in such a dangerous predicament. He realized this was a big decision for them, and he knew they wanted to make a difference in their lives.

His colleague from Milwaukee was named Matthew McCarthy, and he'd actually been the guy who'd raided Peter and Junior's houses, along with their sister's house, back in February 2004. Peter and Junior knew he'd just been doing his job, though.

Still, Eric, Matt, and Joe were the only guys Peter felt comfortable with in that room. Everyone else was an unknown, and that was a risk.

I sat there in the dark for six long hours before Peter walked in.

"Baby! You're back!" I screamed and ran to him.

He looked almost as bad as he'd been when he came home from being kidnapped. He was pale, and his face was sunken. He seemed bone tired. He slumped toward the bed, sat down, pulled me close, and started bawling. He looked absolutely defeated. Finally, he began talking.

"We went to a hotel and entered through the basement. I took the elevator up with Joe. I thought I was going to throw up, but he was so relaxed, like totally nonchalant. He knocked on the door, and when someone answered, he walked right past him and started talking with everyone else in the room."

"How many people were there?"

"About eight, other than me, and Joe knew all of them." he said. "The federal prosecutor, whose name is Tom Shakeshaft, some US Marshals, a few FBI officials, Eric and his colleague, this agent named Matthew McCarthy, and Joe. Someone frisked me for weapons, sat me down, and started asking questions."

At this point he'd settled down a little bit. I was trying my best to be calm, but I was terrified.

"How did it start?"

"I began when I was a kid. I talked about Junior, Adrian, and our dad. I went through everything—getting kidnapped in Chicago, leaving the country, building up our business from here, and how it all works. I went from A to Z."

"How did they react?"

"Everyone except Joe sat there with their mouths open. Some female agent from Milwaukee was running the show." He paused. "Joe sat there with his feet kicked up on the end table half the time."

I couldn't fucking believe it. My husband was about to rat out the cartels, and not only was a small town agent running things, but our lawyer was acting like he was thinking about hitting the beach. Then again, he was a distinguished lawyer in the biggest, most dangerous case of his career. Maybe he actually *did* need a long vacation to deal with all of this.

"They kept asking about numbers, like they couldn't get how big we are. They couldn't comprehend the level we're on." He paused to hold me tighter, and then started getting worked up again. "They were asking about street dealers, for God's sake. And customers. They wanted to know about Chicago, not Mexico. I was sitting there saying, 'I'll give you Chapo and El Mayo,' and they were like, 'Tell us more about where your stash houses are.' I was talking submarines and cartel members, and they were asking about all these little people."

Peter was usually so calm, but he could go from zero to ten, with ten being totally furious, in seconds. He was at about an eight right then.

"They're clueless. They have no idea what they're fucking doing. Can they handle this information? I'm about to give them Chapo, the most violent, dangerous, and powerful criminal in the world, plus everyone who's helped build his empire. This is bigger than Chicago; it's a global issue. It's fucking narcoterrorism. Yet they asked me to draw a diagram of who's on top in the cartels and where Junior and I fit in." He pulled a piece of paper out of his pocket. It was from one of those notepads you find next to a hotel bed, with a ballpoint pen on top. Written in Peter's handwriting was this:

```
Chapo  —  El Mayo
    /         \
 Peter  ← →  Junior
```

I was floored. "Fuck."

"Yeah, right? All this time I thought they knew everything about us, that they were building this huge case against me and Junior and could grab us at any minute, and they knew jack shit. They're in over their heads. I finally couldn't take it anymore and said, 'You're going to do this my way. If you want information out of me, this is the way we have to do it.'"

"Did they agree?"

"Yes, they had to. They *have* to. Everyone in that room understood how important informants are, and that a huge case like this doesn't just fall into their laps. I worry that they aren't grasping the complexity and how huge this case is going to be. I don't think they realize that we can dismantle everything. Like the entire North American drug trade. We can bring in El Chapo if we do this right."

Olivia

Junior and Peter knew they could be the most important informants the feds had ever encountered. The work they were going to do wasn't just a matter of law and order; it was about changing their lives and the world around them.

Yet right from the beginning, they knew they were taking a leap of faith, praying that everything would work out for the best. There were no promises, no sense of security, and absolutely no guidance.

And, unfortunately, when they started to record, things didn't get much better.

CHAPTER 20

Recordings, Raids, and Seizures

Olivia

Junior and Peter's agreement with the feds was basically unheard of in the history of US drug trafficking investigations. They'd tape all their conversations and phone calls, gather information and intelligence, facilitate massive seizures of drugs and money, and secure indictments and extraditions of the United States' and Mexico's highest-ranking cartel members. If their workers unloaded a shipment of drugs in Chicago and Peter was on the line to supervise it, it went on tape. If Peter arranged distribution to the wholesalers, it was recorded. If Junior negotiated prices for their loads, the DEA and US Attorneys were going to hear it.

Mia

Who everyone really hoped to get, though, were the leaders of the Sinaloa Cartel and the BLO. In 2008, there was no direct criminal evidence against El Chapo, El Mayo, Alfredo Beltrán, or any other member of the two cartels. Sure, there was a trail of clues that may or may not have led back to them, and a pile of bodies building up on either side of the cartel wars, but no one had the leaders on tape. In fact, there weren't any recent photos of El Chapo, and even his appearance remained a mystery to US authorities. In order to get an indictment against him, they needed solid evidence that would prove that the heads of the Sinaloa Cartel were actually involved in drug conspiracy in the United States—and especially in Chicago.

That's what they were counting on Peter and Junior for.

Olivia

In exchange for all the information Junior and Peter gathered and turned in, they'd receive leniency when it came to their crimes. But as with everything involved in their cooperation, there were no promises. They might get five years or they might get thirty. In fact, the specifics weren't even discussed during their conversations with the lawyers or the agents; they couldn't be because the ultimate sentencing decision—which might not happen for years—was up to a federal judge.

Mia

The guidance they received about recording was just as unclear. If you think the feds came into our houses and put secret cameras in our walls or microphones in our ink pens, like in a James Bond movie, you're dead wrong. Peter and Junior had the opportunity to unravel the entire North American drug trade, but they didn't even have the necessary equipment. They had to buy their own recorders at places like Radio Shack. They'd fill up a few recorders a week, upload the conversations onto USB drives, then hand them over to the agents.

Worse than that, the government couldn't be responsible for their lives, so they wouldn't advise them on what they were supposed to say when they recorded. Everything they did or said was at their own risk.

Olivia

Junior and Peter worked with the DEA's and US Attorney's offices in Chicago. All information came from Chicago, and all reporting went back to them. There were government officials, such as the DEA, FBI, US Marshals, and Homeland Security stationed in Guadalajara, but those agents had no jurisdiction in Mexico, so they were powerless. The cartels could run right over them if they'd wanted to.

In fact, it seemed like anyone might be able to. In our part of Guadalajara, we used to see them around, just out and about like sitting ducks. They weren't hard to miss; they looked like American tourists and drove around in cars with diplomat plates. One used to work out at Junior's gym, and when Junior would walk in, he'd just smile and nod at him.

There was no reason to be scared; Junior was protected by the cartels, and there was nothing some random fed could do about it.

On a few occasions after they started cooperating, Junior and Peter were debriefed and questioned at random hotels or hidden side streets, but the agents just fed information up the pipeline to Chicago. They'd tell Peter and Junior what was happening in Mexico, though. One time, they revealed to my husband and brother-in-law that an informant had just been killed. Believe me, that scared the shit out of all of us.

Mia

Another big problem was that the Chicago office was making things up as they went along. Or at least that's how *we* felt. There had been cartel bosses that had cooperated in the past, but only once they were captured and sent to prison. There hadn't been any on-the-streets and in-the-mountains federal informants on Pete and Junior's scale in anyone's lifetime, and especially not ratting out the heads of the cartels. Our husbands had reached the peak of the drug trade, and because of that, the DEA's office had no idea what kind of information they'd be getting from them. It wasn't like they could prepare Junior and Peter for what to ask.

Olivia

Even as anxious and unsatisfied as they were, though, Junior and Peter felt a huge sense of responsibility when it came to the agents they were working with. Undercover agents stationed in Guadalajara were putting their lives in Junior's and Peter's hands, and if the cartels found out who they were, they'd be executed on the spot. Because of that, Junior and Peter were amazed at the degree of bravery and integrity these guys possessed. They were doing the right things for the right reasons. And by ensuring their safety, Junior and Peter were finding hidden depths in their own integrity.

Mia

Peter got hundreds and hundreds of phone calls on his burner phones every day, and he recorded each one. He figured it would just be easier to stay home, where he always had his recording devices set up and could use his two-way earbud in private. Outside it was much more dangerous. What if he was out on the street, got a call, and had to put his ear bud in and turn the recorder on? Somebody would see that, and he'd be dead.

At home, he kept his earpiece in when he was on calls, or if people were around, he'd take it out and hide it. He stashed it in drawers, next to the TV, or anywhere else that no one could see. Even though the government told him explicitly not to record in person, he had to sometimes. I remember him hiding the cord in the back of a book, with the bud sticking out from the pages. When he met with people in his office, he'd try to position himself as close as possible to the bookshelf, with them sitting nearby, so he could be sure every word they said got on tape.

The whole thing made me a nervous wreck, and I did everything I could to make his days better, less stressful. Then, anytime anyone came over, I'd spend half an hour running around making sure the recorders were hidden. After they'd arrive, I'd try to figure out what to do with myself.

I'd tell Peter, "I don't know what to do when people are here and you're recording. What if they can read my face and body language and know I'm hiding something?"

"Relax," Peter would say. "Just try not to be around."

So I'd go in the other room and pretend to be busy, all the time worrying that the battery on the recorder would run down and start beeping.

I just didn't want us to die. It was as simple as that. I didn't want to be tortured or have my baby gutted out of me, and I knew that was a real possibility if we got caught.

Olivia

Many of the calls Peter and Junior made were to their associates in Chicago, making sure that the shipments were arriving where they needed to be, on time. They had to keep their business moving along, yet no one could know they were undercover. So they were constantly hitting the feds with information like "There's a load in LA," or "There's a stash house in this neighborhood in Chicago." Then the feds would swoop in and bust those locations, seizing the drugs and arresting everyone. Little by little, everyone they were working with in the United States was going to get hauled in.

Mia

The first seizure was one of the most stressful things they'd ever been through.

On August 9, 2008, Junior and Peter were expecting a load from a line they'd been working in Mexicali. This shipment in particular was 250 kilos, which was about the norm. The load had made its way through a network of tunnels, crossed the border, was placed on tractor-trailers, and was en route to Chicago, with a precise pick up time of six a.m. Saturday.

As always, Junior and Peter had done a dry run before the shipment hit the road, so everything was running like clockwork. They had the fastest routes picked out and knew the best ways to avoid taking too many streets. They'd planned to stick to highways and busy roads so that the trucks would just blend in.

Olivia

Peter had given the feds the exact address of the warehouse in Melrose Park, a western suburb of Chicago, walking them through the location using Google Earth so they knew exactly where to park without anyone noticing them. The night before, Eric Durante and Matt McCarthy went there and staked the place out.

Then, they set up an undercover DEA agent to receive the load, called a controlled delivery, explaining to their workers that there was "this new guy" there for pick up. Peter called the worker who was in charge of driving the shipment to Chicago and started speaking in code.

"Is Pancho there?" he asked in Spanish.

"On behalf of whom?" asked the driver.

"On behalf of Donald Trump."

He'd cracked the combination. Things were ready to move.

Mia

After he hung up, Peter was a wreck. We had this little white Maltese named Gigi who was his baby. That dog followed him everywhere, and I swear, if he had to choose between me or the dog, he would have chosen her for sure. The entire night before the raid, Peter kept walking back and forth to his computer, checking Google Earth to see which streets the agents could park on. Gigi hung right at his heels, her tiny pink painted toenails clacking on the floor. As I struggled to fall asleep that night, thinking about the choices he and Junior had made, and how exhausted Peter was by this life, all I could hear were those toenails, back and forth on the hardwood.

Olivia

The next morning, the workers were in place, ready to receive the load; the feds were on the ground; and Peter, Junior, Mia, and I were up bright and early, stationed near the phone. Eric finally called.

"The truck just pulled in. We're ready to go."

Hours later, when Eric rang and said that they'd taken down the truck and confiscated the kilos, Peter called Olivares, Chapo and El Mayo's lieutenant, to let him know that the load had been caught.

"Well, whatever," Olivares said. "Too bad. It happens."

To Olivares, it was just another raid, just another shipment lost. But to Peter and Junior, it was the beginning of the end.

Olivia

It went on and on like that for months. A raid here, a raid there, kilos and kilos of drugs being seized. They were losing millions of dollars in potential revenue because they were responsible for their loads, and when they got seized, they also lost the 10 percent that they paid up front. Junior and Peter personally paid back $5 million on their first seizure alone.

And at the same time their workers and associates in Chicago, LA, and every other city where they did business were getting arrested. These were people they'd known all their lives, men and women they loved. They felt guilty; we all did.

There was danger on every corner, too. Not just to them and to us, but to everyone they were even remotely connected to. After they repaid Olivares for a seized 250 kilo shipment, the lieutenant confronted Junior and Peter because too many loads were falling, one after another.

"I think it was the trucker who ratted you out. It was his first run. We don't know him, and it's suspicious that the feds let him go."

Peter said, "No, no. I checked him out. He's not a snitch."

Peter and Junior kept arguing and eventually saved the driver's life, but it planted a particular kind of terror in their minds: Even with just the *smallest* bit of suspicion from the cartels, with just the *tiniest* shred of doubt about their honesty, the cartels wouldn't hesitate to have them killed.

CHAPTER 21

The Countdown to the End

Olivia

During the summer and fall of 2008, nothing in our lives was certain. I was super pregnant and taking care of Brandon, Junior and Peter were recording as much as they could, and with every call, they were positive their world was about to come crashing down.

They knew their cooperation couldn't go on forever, yet there was no end date, no exit strategy, no direction, and, in their minds, no plan in place. They were just hanging by a thread trying to stay alive, and sooner or later, after dozens of raids and millions of dollars of lost revenue, their money was going to run out. If they couldn't repay the cartels, their days were numbered.

That's why, early that fall, they did what they felt they had to do to continue to make payments: they shipped a load of 276 kilos into Chicago without reporting it to the feds. Honestly, they were worried that the US government wasn't going to ensure that the cartels didn't come after them or us, so while they knew not disclosing the sale was wrong, they felt they had no choice. They were responsible for keeping their family alive.

Mia

It wasn't just their phone conversations that left them exposed. That summer and fall, they were frequently called into the mountains by El

Chapo. There, they had to look him in the eyes, knowing they were betraying him.

One early August mountaintop meeting was especially rough. As Peter and Junior sat at El Chapo's table with his top lieutenants, discussing business as usual, Chapo spoke up.

"Everyone, leave. All of you but the Flores brothers."

There was an army of men in the *palapa*, and one by one, each of them stood up and filed out the door. Knowing that Chapo was all too aware that their loads kept getting seized by the feds, Peter and Junior were terrified. There had always been a silent language between them, a way they could communicate just by looking at each other, but they couldn't do that here; Chapo was watching them, dead serious. They thought the worst; the boss had found out they were snitches, and they were about to die.

"I know everything you do," Chapo said. Junior and Peter looked around and saw guns on the table and ammo hanging on the walls. "I know who you work with and how you make every dollar."

Junior breathed in, slowly. He had no idea where Chapo was going, but not talking would look suspicious. "Yes," he responded. "And we hope it's benefiting you. Right, Señor?"

Chapo paused, and you could have heard a pin drop in the room. Finally, he smiled. "Yes, yes! I have your backs one thousand percent." Then, he got serious. "I know you're businessmen, but I need to say this. From now on you are only to work with us. Not my enemies. Let this be your first and final warning."

Peter was so relieved that someone hadn't come in the room and shot him in the back of his head, but he put his game face on. "I understand, but we need to make money."

Chapo interrupted. "And I'm happy you make money! You're good at it, too. If you were triplets, you'd be the richest people on earth. But understand me; I need you on my side."

So this wasn't about Peter and Junior being informants; it was about them being caught between the cartels. It wasn't the last breath they'd take after all. El Chapo had simply put them on notice.

Olivia

That September was such an emotional time for me and Junior. We were so excited about having our second baby, and yet every time their customers and Chapo's associates called, Junior wired up, ready to record, and we instantly became terrified.

Still, I knew what Junior and Peter were doing was for the best, and that gave me some peace. We weren't chasing the cartel life anymore; we were chasing what my parents had. Despite the fact that my husband was going to go to prison at some point soon, I thought, *At the end of the day, this is going to give our children the simplicity I always wanted.* We were on our way to creating a new story for our children, and I felt deep down it was one that would someday have a happy ending.

Early one morning that month, Junior and I left Brandon with Mia and Peter at our house and drove to the hospital before the sun came up. After I checked myself in and got into a room, Junior and I held hands and couldn't stop looking at each other. I don't know what it is, but knowing you're bringing a baby into this world is the warmest, most loving feeling you can ever have. I felt like I was living a dream. The moment that the doctors laid our beautiful son, Benjamin, on my chest, it literally took my breath away. As he wiggled on my body, I felt safe and protected, like I always had with Junior. A warmth washed over me that was so calm and peaceful, and I wanted to hold on to that moment forever.

Mia

It was back to business almost immediately. Peter and Junior kept recording, they kept seeing their loads get seized, and through it all, we feared that every day could be our last in Mexico. When Chapo summoned Peter and Junior up to the mountains in October, saying he had an incredibly important meeting, they really believed it was do-or-die time. If the feds couldn't catch Chapo at that meeting, was their cooperation even worth it?

Olivia

When El Chapo called a group of his people together, it was always a big deal. But this one promised to be bigger: El Mayo, Olivares, Vincente, and 150 of his top lieutenants would be there, together in one room for the first time ever.

"I think you should stay behind," Junior said to Peter. "If someone there finds out we're informants, they'll kill both of us."

Mia

The truth was that most of the time, Junior went to the mountains alone because Peter needed to stay with the phones. Meetings with Chapo lasted all day and were drawn out, so someone needed to be at home running the day-in, day-out operations.

This time, however, they prayed Chapo wouldn't call attention to Peter's absence. It was such a big meeting, and Chapo had asked them both to come, but they hoped to hell no one would think things were off.

"I'll stay, Junior," agreed Peter. "But, just please, be safe."

Olivia

Junior called Eric and the DEA's office beforehand.

"Eric, everyone's flying in. One hundred fifty cartel members are expected to be there. I can tell you the exact coordinates of where the meeting is. All of these people have never been in the same room together, and this is your chance to get them all. This only happens once in a lifetime, and I'll even take an agent with me."

But Eric refused. "It doesn't work like that, Junior. I can't risk any of my agents."

"Then give me a wire or a camera."

"I can't take that risk, even with you."

Junior was getting frustrated. "Peter and I will gift Chapo a plane. We just need you to install a GPS tracker on it. Chapo trusts us so much, there's no way in hell he'll have it searched."

"I'm sorry, Junior," Eric answered. "Just go in there and get what you can."

Mia

Peter got so upset when he heard what Eric had said. "What's the point of recording if we're giving them Chapo's exact location?" he yelled. "I don't understand why they just don't go get him."

But that was the nature of the game. Record, wait, conduct business as usual, put on a brave face, and record more.

Olivia

Like he'd done more times than he could count, Junior hopped on a tiny plane in Culiacán, and less than an hour later, landed uphill in the mountains, the plane kicking up dust all around him. He followed the same path with the same people, probably rode in the same Jeep. But when he got there, Chapo looked disappointed.

"Where's your brother?" he said.

Junior laughed it off. "We can't both be here. Who's going to take care of business and get you paid if we're both stuck in the mountains?"

Chapo started laughing, too, but Junior wondered if it was genuine.

Mia

All the while, their loads kept getting seized. They'd always pay the cartels back, but after a while, it started to look suspicious.

Olivia

Felipe Cabrera Sarabia was one of Chapo's top lieutenants. During one particularly big seizure early one morning that fall, Felipe called Peter, unprompted.

"Someone's tailing my driver," he said. "What's going on? Are you rats?"

"You've got to be kidding," Peter said, then talked him down and brushed it off more. He put Felipe at ease, but not himself. He was so freaked out he ran into our house at probably six a.m. and woke Junior up. When I saw the look on his face, I knew it was serious.

"Junior, Junior," Peter said. "Something's wrong. Felipe Sarabia's on to us. The feds are all over his driver. He accused us of being rats."

"Let me call Eric," Junior said.

Junior called the DEA agent and woke him up. He started yelling so loudly that Benjamin began crying. As I held my baby in my arms and gave him a bottle, I could hear my husband screaming.

"You're going to get us killed! How can you leave us out in the open like this? Tell your agents to back off because you could have blown everything! I'm here in Guadalajara like a sitting duck. I have my family and a newborn baby, for God's sake, and Peter's wife is pregnant. Don't you know the cartels could come kill our whole fucking family?"

Eric couldn't really say a thing. After all, he knew Junior was right. He and Peter had everything to lose, and the DEA had everything to gain.

Mia

Unfortunately, though, Peter and Junior still didn't have Chapo on tape. Through all their meetings with him that summer and early fall, they'd never recorded him saying anything that was incriminating.

On November 15, 2008, when I was so pregnant I couldn't see my toes, all that changed.

Olivia

Two weeks before their baby was due, Mia and Peter walked over to our house. Just like he always did, Peter had his recorder in his pocket.

Mia

Everything seemed normal. Junior had some friends and associates over, and we were all planning to sit down outside and have dinner. A few people commented about my big belly, but in a cute way. Peter kept looking over at me and smiling. "My beautiful, pregnant wife," he'd say, and I'd squeeze his hand under the table.

After dinner, Peter spoke up. "I have to call Chapo," he said, then pushed back his chair and headed inside and up the stairs.

He returned not two minutes later.

Olivia

I saw Peter motion to Junior, who was right next to me. Then he came up to us and whispered, "I just missed Chapo."

"Let's go upstairs," said Junior. They turned, walked away from everyone, and escaped up to the bedroom.

Mia

Olivia and I knew what was about to happen. Junior and Peter had told us that night was the night they were going to get Chapo on tape, so when they went upstairs, we moved inside, too, and situated ourselves on the couch.

We couldn't talk much; there were too many people around. But we were both thinking the same thing: *If Junior and Peter get this recording, they won't have to spend a lot of time in jail. The government's going to be so grateful they may actually pardon them. After what we've been through, it's the least they can do for us.*

Of course, it was all wishful thinking. And when Peter and Junior came back downstairs, the looks on their faces made any happy thoughts go away.

Olivia

Peter was holding the recorder in his hands like his life depended on it. He looked like something was horribly wrong, like he'd just seen a ghost.

"What's wrong?" I asked.

"We got it," Peter said.

Junior added, "I think we've nailed Chapo."

In the home I'd built with the love of my life, and, only six weeks before, carried our newborn baby into, I suddenly knew there was no turning back. My family was about to be torn apart.

Mia

Peter had called Chapo back, and he'd answered.

"Hola, amigo!" Chapo said happily. "How is your brother?"

Over the course of only a few minutes, Peter negotiated the price of a twenty-kilo shipment of heroin down from $55,000 per kilo to $50,000. It was business as usual, and in fact, it was warm and friendly.

Olivia

But with that one call, the countdown to the end was over. Chapo had incriminated himself, and the United States had officially netted the biggest drug dealer in history.

It was time to bring Junior and Peter home.

CHAPTER 22

Surrendering

Mia

About two weeks before my due date and days before Peter got Chapo on tape, I started to have a bad feeling in my gut. Something was telling me that Peter and Junior's cooperation was going to end soon, and that they'd be taken away. At a time that I had so little control over anything in my life, and when the stress was becoming almost too much, I needed some peace. I wanted Peter to spend as much time with the baby as he could, so I told him we should schedule a C-section as soon as possible.

"Pay the doctors more if you have to," I said. "I just need to have the baby early."

Thankfully, the doctors were fine with it. When we checked into the hospital, I was a bundle of emotions: so scared of childbirth but so excited about being a mom. I'd never wanted anything so badly in my life.

After we ate dinner together, Peter helped me take a shower, and we made love. Then I got in my hospital bed, and he set up his bed on the couch. We started to talk and joke about all the memories we'd made together over the last decade, remembering everything from the first time we laid eyes on each other as teenagers to the day he fell to his knees on the beach and asked me to marry him. We talked about how excited we were to bring our baby girl in the world, and I said how proud I was of him for sacrificing his freedom for our family. Peter told me that I'd grown into a beautiful woman, one he was privileged to be married to and one he was so grateful was about to be a mother for the very first time.

"I never could have done anything good in my life without you by my side," he said.

Every now and then, Peter's phone would ring. He'd put in his earbud, press record, and answer the call. When he hung up, we'd start talking and laughing again. Finally, I dozed off. Then I woke up in the middle of the night to the sound of the phone ringing.

"Please, baby," I said. "Don't answer it. We need rest."

"Okay," he said, and he willingly let the phone go to voicemail for the first time in his life.

"Get off that couch and come to bed with me," I added with a smile.

He crawled into my hospital bed and didn't answer a single call till the next day, after our daughter, Bella, was born.

When they wheeled me into the recovery room, I looked around and couldn't find Peter. Junior and Olivia were there, though.

"Where's Peter?" I asked.

"He's in the nursery, just staring at the baby," Olivia said.

For the next eleven days, I don't think he left her side once.

Olivia

For almost two weeks, we did our best to keep on living just like we always had. Even though Tom Shakeshaft and the feds were in a panic about the possibility that their star witnesses might be murdered by the cartels—something we didn't know at the time—and despite the fact that Junior and Peter owed at least $15 million to La Puerca, we tried to stay calm.

On Thanksgiving, I cooked a massive, picture-perfect dinner.

Thanksgiving isn't celebrated in Mexico, but in my house, it was. Our friends and associates were always so amazed by how we did things, and that Thanksgiving, I made sure everything was bigger and better than ever. We had four huge birds and every side you can imagine. I set the table with white linens and put flowers and candles everywhere. Our babies were so tiny, but they still filled the house with warmth. Brandon was loving every single second, too, because everyone spoiled him with attention. I remember Junior looking at me in the middle of all of it, and I knew what he was thinking. The same thing was going through my mind: *This may be our last holiday together. I just wish to hell we could freeze this moment forever.*

Of course, we couldn't.

Mia

Junior and Peter didn't just owe La Puerca money; they were also running a huge debt to Sinaloa, somewhere over $40 million. The DEA was about to search and seize a few of their warehouses in LA, and the feds were concerned that Chapo would be on to them any minute. If that happened, our heads were going to get separated from our bodies.

All that's why, three days after Thanksgiving, on Sunday, November 30, our world changed.

Olivia

Sunday had always been our day to relax and watch TV, just sitting around our house. We always had people cooking and cleaning for us, but on Sundays we didn't want anybody around because it was family day. I'd get up and cook breakfast, then later Junior would make lunch. At night Junior and I would cook dinner together, and Mia and Peter would come over. Now that we had these little angels, we'd put them next to each other in their bassinets while we ate.

In the morning, all Junior wanted to do was be with Benjamin. He'd rock him, give him his bottle, and just sit there, looking at him. That Sunday, he was holding him like he always did when his phone rang.

He answered, listened for a little, and finally said, "I see, yes. Okay. I understand." Then he closed the phone, jumped, and brought the baby to me. He was dead serious. "We have to turn ourselves in."

I fucking flipped out. "What do you mean? What are you talking about?"

"We have to report to Guadalajara International Airport in two hours. You're going to have to pack up the babies and get out of the country now."

"With you?"

"No, with Mia. They're taking me and my brother back to the United

States. If anyone comes here and finds out we're gone, they're going to kill you. Liv, I need you to take our babies and leave. There's so much money at stake. We owe so much." Junior turned away from me and started packing up. "I have to call P."

I was in disbelief, but not just because I was about to lose my husband. I realized right then, *I may also lose my life.*

But if there was anything I'd learned in my years—from battling my way out of an abusive marriage to keeping my head on straight in jail to escaping from a kidnapping by the skin of my teeth—it's that I could never, ever stop fighting for myself and my family.

"We're US citizens!" I screamed. "How could they just leave us here to die?"

Junior grabbed me. "Listen to me. I need you to be strong, Liv. You have to keep our family safe. You know how to get to the border. I need you to grab only what you need and go. If they find you, Liv, they're going to kill you, Mia, and our babies."

I knew, right then, my babies needed me. My family needed me. I had to get us out of Mexico.

Mia

Bella was so tiny, just a totally innocent little thing, when Junior called that Sunday morning and told Peter they had two hours to get to the Guadalajara airport. I was busy throwing a few outfits and a toothbrush into a bag for Peter, and tossing bottles into my diaper bag. Then, I stopped and looked around. There was my husband on the edge of the bed, cradling the baby. He was holding her tight in his arms, staring at her and talking to her softly. She was looking back at him, her eyes barely open. It was like she believed as much as he did that they had to hold on to this one moment for as long as possible.

The phone ringing broke the silence in the room. It was Junior on the other end of the line.

"We'll be right over," Peter said, putting the baby on the bed. "Mia's just packing up. You should call Adrian, too. He'll need to drive us to the airport."

I walked over to him and sat down. "I don't think I can do this. You can't go."

"Baby, I have to." Peter pulled me to him, and for another moment we just sat there, the three of us.

We'd finally moved into our dream home. It was our sanctuary, where we could escape all the madness, and Peter's favorite room was the nursery. When we finally stood up and started walking, Peter stopped outside the nursery and just stared into it. He loved that nursery; he'd spent days and days making it perfect for Bella.

He's saying goodbye, I thought. *And I'm going to have to accept that I am, too. I just hope that one day Bella knows that she's the reason her father wanted to change his life.*

Then we both turned and headed toward Olivia and Junior's house next door.

Olivia

Mia and Peter came in with the baby, looking like they'd just come back from a funeral. They were moving in slow motion, holding hands, and generally looking awful, which is how we all felt. I watched Mia sit down slowly on the couch and take the baby from Peter, then just sit there staring off into space.

How the hell is she so calm? I thought. After the feds had called, I'd sprung into nonstop action.

I'd been running around the house like a freaking tornado, checking for papers or anything that had our information on it. I'd been yelling orders, "We have to get everything out of here! There can't be any sign of us! Get rid of everything!" I had a stack of magazines with our names and Chicago address on them in one hand and a pile of papers in the other. I ran to the garbage and ripped them up, then grabbed a garbage bag and headed over to the walls to get the framed wedding and family photos that were hanging on them. I threw the garbage bag at Junior and screamed at him, "Take that out to the car!"

We had video cameras scattered around our house for security. I ran through every single damn room and pulled down each and every one, then headed outside and got up on a ladder to pull down the cameras that were hanging near the roof. I hardly thought about those cameras most of the time—we'd lived with them for so long that I forgot they even existed—but at that moment, they were the most important thing in my world. I had to get rid of them.

When all that was done, I started looking for my kids' birth certificates. There was no way we were getting across the border if I couldn't prove that they were my babies. Benjamin was so little he didn't have documentation of his dual citizenship, so getting his paperwork together was pretty much a life-or-death situation. I went through every drawer in our house, and finally I found the papers.

Why weren't we prepared for this? I kept telling myself. I suppose we thought we'd have a few more months, maybe years. Or maybe we were in denial, thinking we could all be together forever. The truth was we'd known nothing. No clue how much more they'd need to record, no idea of whether or not what they'd gathered was useful, and no idea if fucking Rambo was at our back door ready to kidnap us. We'd had no protection, no feedback, no nothing.

And now, we had no instructions about how to get the hell out of our house and make it to the border without being killed.

Mia

I remember just sitting there on Olivia and Junior's sofa, holding Bella in one arm and her diaper bag in the other. Olivia was running around from room to room, looking like a crazy woman, pulling photos off the wall and throwing pieces of paper into garbage bags. I wanted to help her—to do *something*—but I was just too lost. My in-laws—who Peter and Junior had told about their plans a few months back—had just come over. While my father-in-law looked disgusted, my mother-in-law was crying her eyes out. I didn't even think she noticed me, but days later she told me, "When I saw you on that sofa holding Bella, I don't think I've ever seen you look so small."

I'm tiny, one hundred pounds most of the time, but that morning, I felt like I'd shrunk. My head wasn't on straight, and I couldn't even move. *How am I going to go through life without Peter?* I kept thinking. *I can hardly sleep without him beside me.*

Peter approached me, took Bella from my arms, and removed her changing pad and a diaper from my bag. "I've got her," he said. Then he placed her gently on the sofa, cradling her little head and neck, and changed her diaper. "Here you go," he said as he passed her back to me.

I watched as he walked to the kitchen to make her one last bottle. When he came back, he handed the bottle to me, leaned down and kissed me.

"What is it?" I asked. He looked so serious.

"Mia, it's time," he answered.

Then I watched the man I love do the absolute hardest thing he'd ever done in his life: turn and start to walk away from his family. Even though my heart was breaking, I remember thinking, *I've never been more proud of him.*

Olivia

I'd been racing through the house for the last hour, but I'd made a point of putting Brandon in his room with some toys. He didn't need to see his mom breaking down. I was frantically crying and couldn't believe that Junior had to leave us. Junior was my rock, my everything, and I was terrified of being alone. As strong as I'd always been, at that point I was at my weakest. The only thing that kept me going was the deep sense that I had to protect my babies, and if I couldn't keep it together for myself, I had to do it for them.

I have to keep going, I told myself. *Just keep moving.*

But as I walked downstairs into our living room, the enormity of everything hit me again. We had our Christmas tree up already. I'd already put out all my little Santa Clauses and decorated the entire house. Brandon's birthday was a few weeks away, and Christmas right after that. *Junior's going to miss them both,* I thought. *Thanksgiving was our last holiday as a family.*

Daniela saw me and came out of a side room, leading Brandon by his hand. Junior was standing by the door, holding his bag. Brandon had always been Junior's little best friend. If Junior had to leave the house, our son would literally cling to his dad's leg while he started walking. Junior would pry him off, then walk him back across our hardwood floor. There were even a few times that Junior canceled plans because he didn't want to leave Brandon behind.

When Brandon saw his dad by the door, he ran toward him.

"No, don't leave!" he said, diving toward Junior's legs. "Don't go!"

Junior looked broken. "Brandon, it's okay, baby. Daddy's going to come back." Junior pulled him up close. "I love you, and I promise I'll be back. You have to take care of Mommy, and never forget how much I love you. You're my little best friend."

I carried Benjamin over to the two of them, and we stood together in the foyer, holding on to each other for dear life, trembling. I wanted to fall to my knees and beg him not to leave me. As selfish as it was, I thought to myself, *I should have never pressured him to change his life. I'm not sure breaking up my family is worth it.*

Then Junior let us go, and he and Peter moved together toward the door. When they walked out, I heard the click of the lock.

Mia

When Peter and Junior closed the door and started heading toward Adrian's car, I heard a loud cry. It was sort of like a high-pitched siren. I looked over and saw that it was coming from Brandon, who was hanging from the doorknob with both hands, screaming, "No, Daddy, no!"

Seeing a child in that kind of pain is agonizing, and when I looked over at Olivia, shaking as she rocked Brandon back and forth, I wondered why we'd ever decided to put ourselves through this.

Olivia and Junior had installed a deadbolt way high up on their front door, not for security, but because Brandon had learned how to unlock the bottom lock and let himself out. Before they put the deadbolt on, Peter and I would sometimes see him toddling out the door toward our house, wearing his little onesie and carrying his blankie. Peter would always go scoop him up, give him a big kiss, then call Junior or Olivia and say, "Your son just came over to play with my dog."

I realized that if the door hadn't had a deadbolt, Brandon would have sprinted right out, dragging his blankie behind him, and run after that car all the way to the Guadalajara airport.

It was the most painful thought I'd ever had in my life.

Olivia

If I could have taken away Brandon's pain, I would have. But I had to stay strong and come up with a plan to get us the hell out of there. My family's life depended on it.

It was Sunday morning, so the only staff around were our body-guards, who stood outside our house and did surveillance of the neighborhood. But I knew people would be coming around soon, and there was no way our security could protect us from them. Everyone had tabs on Junior and Peter, and cartel members were always doing business with them on the weekends. If they drove up and couldn't find them, they'd know something was up. Not only that, but they'd act on it.

I had to come up with a decoy.

Just then, one of their associates walked over and knocked on the door.

"Where are Junior and Peter?" he said when I opened it.

"They'll be back," I answered. "They went to talk to someone."

He left, and five minutes later, Junior's friend Payo came by. As I saw him walking toward the house I thought, *Oh my God. Time to act.*

I grabbed my bag in one arm and the baby in the other. I marched out the door to the car and put Benjamin in his car seat, bundling him up. I left the car door open, then ran back toward the house, screaming loud enough that Payo could hear me.

"Mia, let's go! My motherfucking husband, how could he do this to me? I'm leaving him! Junior cheated on me, and I'm leaving him and this fucking country!"

I could see Mia standing up slowly, staring at me like I'd lost my mind. She gave me a look like, *What the hell?*, then realized what I was doing and grabbed her diaper bag.

I kept on going. "That fucking bastard! I'm out of here!"

"What?" Payo said when he saw me racing back toward the car, trying to get the hell out of Dodge. "Oh, hell no, that's not true."

He thought I was just acting crazy. There was no way in hell Junior would have cheated on me, but as far as Payo knew, I'd made up my mind that he had.

"Where are you going?" he said.

"None of your business. And if you see him, tell him I don't want anything to do with him. Come on, Mia!"

I went back to the house and picked up Brandon. Mia had started putting Bella in her car, and she'd already loaded up a handful of stuff in her backseat. I pretty much threw Brandon in his car seat and slammed my car door, started it up, and pulled away as fast as I could. As I drove down the driveway, I could see Payo and my neighbor in the rearview mirror, their hands up in the air.

Mia was right behind me in her car, and we met Daniela, Adrian, their kids, and my in-laws outside the gates of our subdivision. Then we started driving, a line of luxury SUVs so conspicuous they might as well have had flashing neon lights on them, toward the Mexican border.

CHAPTER 23

Crossing the Border

Olivia

Nuevo Laredo was the closest border crossing to Guadalajara, and it was a twelve-hour drive away.

I knew Nuevo Laredo all too well; it's where I was arrested when I was a teenager. Unfortunately, it wasn't just the center of *my* drug smuggling. In 2008, it was ground zero for cartel violence.

The Gulf Cartel had always ruled Nuevo Laredo, and their armed wing, Los Zetas, did their bidding when they needed to fight the police, the government, rival cartels, or members of their organization who'd wronged them. Los Zetas were ruthless; gunfights and kidnappings were common, but in one attack, the militia cut out six victims' hearts, carved *Z*s into their chests, and left their bodies in caves. In 2004, thinking that the Gulf Cartel was losing their hold on Nuevo Laredo, the Sinaloa Cartel moved in, looking to expand, and a turf war broke out. By 2008, Sinaloa had a firm grasp on the city, and everyone at the border was Chapo's eyes and ears.

Mia

In Nuevo Laredo, one call from one person who'd noticed that Junior and Peter weren't home and smelled a rat would guarantee an automatic hit on our whole family. It was even possible that Los Zetas would spot us, figure out who we were, and kill us just to rub it in El Chapo's face.

Yet here we were, driving blind toward one of the most dangerous cities in Mexico, with no help, no protection, and no exit strategy.

Olivia

I had Benjamin and Brandon in the backseat in the car seats, and it was the first time I'd driven alone with them. Junior had always been in the car with me, and I'd always sat in the back with my boys. Luckily, Benjamin was so tiny that more than half the time he'd be asleep, and Brandon was so used to driving long distances in Mexico—like back and forth from Puerto Vallarta to Guadalajara—that I knew we wouldn't have to stop much. Probably only for meals and potty breaks.

Mia was alone in her car with my poor niece, who wasn't even two weeks old. Adrian was driving with Daniela and their new baby; Daniela's kids were driving another car; and my in-laws were in a fifth car.

We probably could have piled into fewer cars, but we all thought, probably stupidly, "We have warehouses full of vehicles, so why not take as many as we can?" Still, we had to leave a dozen behind.

Mia

We abandoned everything that didn't have sentimental value or that we wouldn't need on the road. We scrapped our Ferraris, ATVs, and even our plane. There just wasn't time to grab any of our valuables. We knew it would all get stolen in a matter of time, and we later found out that within a few weeks, Junior and Peter's associates had taken everything: designer clothes, handbags, man bags, Viking appliances, ATVs, Jet Skis, motorcycles, and all of our cars. They even took the chandeliers and light switches off the walls. It was a free-for-all for everyone, even their closest friends.

Olivia

We couldn't care less about our stuff, and it was the last thing on our minds as we started driving. We just wanted to make it to the border, to our safety zone. Without stops, Nuevo Laredo is a good twelve-hour drive from Guadalajara, and we didn't get there till three in the morning.

We were terrified at the idea of using our phones on the way. I kept thinking, *What if someone's listening in?* so I didn't call my family to tell them we were heading home to Chicago. I wasn't prepared to tell them the truth. I couldn't tell anyone because it sounded like a suicide mission.

We were so paranoid, but with good reason. A line of Range Rovers, BMWs, and Mercedes trucks, driving like bats out of hell, is pretty much like standing out in the middle of the street with a sign that says, "Hey! We're a bunch of drug dealers escaping for our lives. Come kill us!"

When we finally got to Nuevo Laredo, we stopped at the Hilton to change the babies and get them ready for the long ride. I pulled my sleeping children out of the car, looking over my shoulder every five seconds.

"We're not staying," I said to Adrian. "We have to keep going."

He'd made up his mind. "Crossing in the middle of the night is a huge red flag. Let's just wait till morning."

"No, we have to leave now," I said. "We have to get out of Mexico."

After we stumbled back into our cars, we lined them up, with my truck leading the way since I'd crossed so many times before. As I exited the parking lot, I was so nervous and scared that I swerved out too far and hit something in the road, hard. I couldn't be sure, but I think it was a divider. I heard a muffled "flap...grind...flap..." and as my wheel rim started to scrape against the road, I knew what had happened. I had a flat tire, right there in the middle of cartel-infested Nuevo Laredo.

It was a bad one, too. Whatever I hit ripped my tire right off the rim. I jumped out of the car, my babies still in the back, grabbed my head in the middle of the street, and started freaking the fuck out.

"Let's just leave it. I don't care! Let's forget the car!"

Bear in mind that this was a $150,000 Range Rover. In Mexico, you can't use credit or get a loan for a car purchase, so we'd paid all cash for it. I loved that stupid car, but I loved my life a hell of a lot more.

My nephews hopped out of their car and started to jack my Range Rover up.

"Stop!" I screamed. "Let's just leave it!" I walked over to them to try to push them back in their cars. I swear to God, I thought that, at any minute, someone was going to drive by and shoot all of us.

The truth was they might have because Adrian's phone had just started ringing.

Mia

Adrian and Daniela were in the car behind me. I kept looking in the rearview mirror and seeing Adrian lift his phone to his ear, then start barking something or other into it. I knew none of it was good. It wasn't even dawn on a Monday morning, and in drug dealer time, the workday had just begun. People had started calling Junior or Pete, heard their calls go straight to voicemail, and figured something was up. Junior and Peter *always* answered their phones. No one had my number or Olivia's number, but they all knew Adrian's.

"They keep calling! What the hell am I supposed to tell them?" Adrian shouted at Olivia, who was still railing against Daniela's boys to just give up and let her ditch the Range Rover.

"How the fuck do I know?" she said. "Just tell them they're still sleeping!"

With new babies and jobs like theirs? No way. There was no possible way their workers wouldn't realize that things were really off. We couldn't get around it.

I couldn't believe the situation we were in. My C-section stitches hadn't even healed, and I was still in pain. Any time Bella had cried during the drive, I'd had to pull over, hop in the backseat, and nurse her. *We're so close,* I thought as I looked straight ahead out my windshield. *I can see the border.* There were agents with huge guns pacing back and forth, questioning cars and letting people through. *God damn it, we're so close,* I thought, and then, suddenly, I just lost control. It had all become too much. I grabbed the steering wheel and exploded.

"We're never going to get out of here! We're going to die here!" I loosened my grip, raised my fists, and started pounding as hard as I could on the steering wheel. I paused, felt even more helpless, and started pounding harder, screaming at the top of my lungs. I didn't care if I woke Bella up; she was a baby, and she wouldn't remember. But if I didn't let out my rage, I thought I actually might get out of the car and try to run for the border.

Then I saw Olivia's car start moving.

Olivia

Daniela's son fixed my tire faster than anyone at Midas ever had, and I got the hell off that street as quickly as I could. Seeing the border crossing in front of me, I gunned it. The other cars fell into line right behind me, and I zipped right along toward an open booth. It was so early that most of the lanes were actually open.

"Hello," I said as I rolled down my window, handed the agent my passport and my kids' birth certificates, and waited to move right through.

The officer looked at my stack of papers a little too closely, for a little too long. "No, you can't go," he said. "You have to turn around."

My heart stopped. "What the fuck? What do you mean?" Now, I know that's not how you're supposed to speak to an armed government official, but I was in no mood to be polite.

"You have Mexican plates and your children were born in Mexico. You have to have a proper visa for them to cross." He stepped back and moved his arms, like he wanted me to pull over.

I was desperate but was trying not to sound like it. "But, I'm their mother, and my baby is two months old. I'm an American! How are we going to get in?"

"Go back and get proper documentation for the minors, and we'll let you through." The guard motioned once again for me to turn my car around.

I just sat there in park and stared at him. Being nice wasn't going to work, so maybe being bat shit crazy would. I started yelling. "They're going to kill us! We're all going to be fucking killed!"

The guard backed up, acting like he was either going to bring out reinforcements to arrest me, or run because he thought I was a suicide bomber. I kept going. "Let us through now, or we're all going to die!"

I looked around me, and I could see everyone else getting out of their cars. My father-in-law was arguing with someone, and Adrian had just thrown his hands in the air. Mia was white as a ghost. The border patrol officer had lifted up his walkie-talkie to call for backup. I didn't know what else to do, so I jumped out of the car and started screaming. "They're going to fucking kill us if you don't let us through!"

Mia

Before we'd left, I'd been careful to gather together all the paperwork I'd stashed away next to my bed. I had my birth certificate, as well as Peter's. I had my passport and Bella's birth certificate. I even had a notarized letter, written by Peter, stating that our daughter could cross the border. But it was no use. They wouldn't let me through because Bella had been born in Mexico, and I didn't have a visa for her.

I was so in shock that I hardly remember walking into the border agent's office. All I can recall was how cold it was when I stepped out of my car. It was that kind of predawn wetness you often feel in Chicago but rarely in Mexico—the type of chill that you just can't shake off unless you bundle up right away. As I wrapped a blanket around Bella and zipped up the only coat I'd brought along, I just remember thinking, *It never gets cold like this in Mexico.*

But all bets were off at that point. It could have started snowing, and honestly, I wouldn't have been fazed.

Olivia

When I walked into the border agents' office and saw Mia sitting there shivering, I jumped into mama bear mode. "You cannot just let her sit there like that," I said. "She's freezing!" I would have done anything to protect my family at that point. I was so desperate to get us across the border.

Finally, though, I had an idea. I pulled out my phone and dialed a saved number. On the third ring, a person on the other end picked up.

"Good morning, this is Matt," said a friendly voice on the other end of the line. *Thank God he's up,* I thought. I knew that a lot of DEA agents started the day before dawn, so I wasn't all that surprised that he'd answered. I was totally wired, but I explained the situation to him as calmly as I possibly could.

"Let me talk with the border guards," he said after listening, and I handed my phone over to one of them.

They talked for what felt like forever. But when the agent closed up the phone and motioned for me and Mia to come over, I realized we might be okay.

Matt must have told them to search the hell out of us because, when they took us outside again, they scanned our cars from top to bottom. We stood there for probably three or four hours while they X-rayed the insides and outsides, then brought out the dogs to sniff every inch. The whole time, I was like, *Do they honestly think I'd be trying to bring drugs over the border when I'm running for my fucking life?* Then it hit me: We were always going to be treated like criminals. Because that's what our husbands were.

Everything checked out, so the agents led us toward our cars. We put the babies in the car seats, got in ourselves, turned the keys, and put them in gear.

As I glanced in my rearview mirror, I was afraid of what was behind us, but I was more terrified of what was to become of us. Still, there was nothing I could do. Just as during every other bad thing that had happened in my life, I had to make a decision, take action, and hopefully learn something and be a better person because of it.

Here goes nothing, I thought, and I began driving across the US border toward the rest of my very uncertain life.

Mia

Adrian, my father-in-law, and one of our nephews were stuck at the border. Adrian had been deported the day he'd been released from federal prison years before, my father-in-law had a huge criminal history, and our nephew didn't have his birth certificate with him, so they weren't going to get clearance to cross till they got their papers straight with US immigration. Daniela, her children, and my mother-in-law stayed back with them, but that didn't make us feel any better.

Olivia

They hugged us goodbye and said, "Don't worry, we'll switch hotels every day. We'll be fine," but we didn't know if we'd ever see them again. Matt had promised to work on their paperwork, but he hadn't offered to protect them. Adrian's phone was still ringing off the hook, and it was a matter of days before someone was going to put two and two together and start to search around Nuevo Laredo for him. I'd always been close to Adrian and Daniela, and I felt like I was saying goodbye to them forever. I honestly thought we would never see our family again.

After we crossed and got back into our cars, I said to Mia. "Let's just keep going. All the way."

"Are you sure?" she asked. "We're exhausted."

"Yes, definitely." My adrenaline was pumping, and I felt like I could drive all the way to Canada if I had to. It was going to be a twenty-some hour drive, and I'd be damned if I was going to stop for the night.

Mia

When you have 1,400 miles ahead of you and what feels like a lifetime in your rearview mirror, you have a lot of time to think. I spent half the drive worrying about Bella in the backseat and the other half wondering what was happening to Peter, but when I actually stopped and took stock, I realized, *This is the first time in almost five years I've been alone.* Peter had done absolutely everything for me. I'd never had to step up to the plate and take care of myself. Now I had to do that *and* protect my daughter.

Olivia and I had bought new phones after we crossed, and I'd called my mom right away. Now she was calling every five minutes to find out where I was. I'd told her everything, finally: that Peter and Junior were traffickers, that they'd become informants, that they'd surrendered at the airport, and that we'd escaped with our lives. Every detail had made Mom frantic.

"Are you okay? Where are you? Why don't you stop?" she kept saying.

I'd respond, "Mom, I love you, but I'm trying to drive. I can't have you calling me all the time. I have to keep my full attention on the road."

Four-plus years of time and distance, and I was still her baby. I guess some things never change.

My plan was to go to their house while Olivia checked into a hotel. This would be the first time my family had met Bella, and I kept hoping that she'd take some of the pressure off. I needed it, desperately. With our lawyer's assistance, Peter had finally gotten clearance to call me midway through our drive, and while I was so happy to hear from him, it had left me a complete wreck.

"I can't believe it took you so long to get over the border, baby," he said. "I was worried sick about you the whole time. I've been so scared thinking something happened to you."

I didn't want to dwell on it, so I changed the subject. "Are you okay? Where are you?"

"They have us hiding in some random hotel in Mexico City. To get us here the feds covered our faces, locked the hotel down, and snuck us in."

"Mexico City?" *Why the hell were they there?* I thought. Mexico City was one of their main hubs.

"We're a block away from one of our stash houses. We can actually see it from our hotel window. They've still got us recording all the bosses and lieutenants. But we've also met with every single bureau you can think of: Homeland Security, immigration, the DEA, the FBI. We've been answering questions and getting debriefed, but no one's been willing to tell me anything about you. All I've done is ask about my family, and no one's told me a fucking thing."

So not only were they in as much danger as we'd been, but they were totally in the dark, flying blind just like we were.

Olivia

It was twenty-four hours from the border to Chicago, and we made it there the next day. Twenty-four freaking hours on the road, and we only stopped when we had to feed the kids, change a diaper, or use the bathroom. When we got to Chicago, I said goodbye to Mia, then checked in to a hotel near the airport.

Mia

I thought about going to the hotel with Olivia, but I couldn't stand the thought of not being with my family. I needed them just to feel safe.

When I arrived at the house I grew up in, my parents, brother, and sister were standing in the doorway, already crying their eyes out. I parked the car, then carried Bella in her car seat up the steps. Mom looked at me for a split second, grabbed the car seat from me, and carried it in. Then she placed it on the kitchen table and unstrapped my daughter, her second granddaughter. As my dad held me around the waist with one arm and my sister grabbed my hand, I watched my mom—who'd been practically a baby herself when she'd had me—lift Bella up to her shoulder and hold her, rubbing her back.

"It's all okay. You're home. You're safe," she whispered to her.

I knew she was, but I wish I'd felt the same. As I watched each member of my family pass my daughter back and forth, kissing her sweetly, I thought to myself, *This is not my home anymore. It's my parents'. My home is with Peter, and I may not ever have that again.*

Olivia

I called my parents as soon as I got Brandon and Benjamin situated in the hotel room I'd checked in to. I still hadn't told Mom and Dad the full truth. I'd never wanted to hurt them, especially after I'd put them through so much already. But I kept them in the dark so they could sleep better at night.

When they came over, I broke down and told them everything. I couldn't lie anymore. Still, the look on my dad's face was pure disgust. I'd wanted so badly to protect him and Mom, and instead, I'd broken their hearts.

When they left, I tried to collect myself. I felt so empty and alone, and as I stared at the ceiling, I wondered if Junior was doing the same.

Then, I called Joe.

"Olivia, you shouldn't be in the city," he said. "Your lives are in danger. Check into a hotel far out of the city."

"Where are Peter and Junior?"

"They're going through the process. They'll go to the correctional center downtown soon. They'll be well guarded, and they'll be together. But if anyone figures out you're in town, you might not be. Go somewhere outside the city limits."

"I'll go to my house, then." I'd kept a house in the suburbs for years, so I gave him that address.

"Someone will meet you there tomorrow to talk about next steps for you and Mia."

Next steps could have meant anything, so it wasn't worth asking. Instead, I packed up what little I had and left with my sons. While I was on the road driving the few miles out to my house, I called Mia and told her that she should meet me there the next morning.

Mia

When Olivia called and said we weren't safe in the city and had to leave, I was devastated. I didn't want to endanger my family, but I hated the idea of being without them. I'd had Bella less than three weeks before, and I was still in pain from my C-section. I barely had anything but the clothes on my back, and I didn't just need help, I needed love. I wanted my family, and I ached for Peter. *I'm really on my own,* I kept thinking. *And this is what it's going to feel like for years and years.*

My dad was crushed when I left with Bella. "Baby, just stay," he said. "I can protect you."

I know he felt like he could; but let's be honest, no one was really able to. Olivia and I were on our own, and that's why we had to get away.

Olivia

My house was about forty-five minutes out of the city. I'd decorated it exactly like my home in Guadalajara: Decorative pillows covering big, plush couches, and huge rugs spanning wall to wall. But there were none of the little Mexican knickknacks and touches that I'd put everywhere in Guadalajara. It felt empty, not warm or full of love like my home with Junior. It was an American home, far, far away from Mexico. Hugging my babies, I just sat on the steps and bawled my eyes out, thinking, *I don't even have the strength or will to keep going.*

Mia

Looking around it, I suddenly felt sad all over again. *I'd never been happier in my life than in Mexico,* I thought. *I know it was a dangerous life to live, but we were all together. We were a family there.*

Olivia

Joe had hired twenty-four-hour security for us, so when Mia arrived, there were these armed guards waiting to greet her. A few hours later, they let in a woman named Carol Williams from the Witness Protection Program.

Carol was friendly, with a warm, pleasant smile. She seemed nice enough, but honestly, I don't think she knew what she was walking into. Peter and Junior were prepared to be the biggest drug informants in US history, and we had targets on our heads just because we were married to them.

"Good morning," she said when I offered her a seat. Then she dove right into the subject that had brought her to my house. "So, as you know, your lives are in danger, and we'd like that not to be the case..."

I wasn't going to pull any punches with her, so I cut her off. "We've been telling you that for the last three days, but no one from the government has helped us. Not one fucking bit, except for Matt McCarthy, and I made that happen. It took us hours to get across the border, and our in-laws just got out yesterday. The US Attorneys had to work to get them clearance; that took a few days, and they had to jump around the border from hotel to hotel. They could have been killed on your watch. *We* could have been killed. We're not going to be your sitting ducks."

Carol just sat there, straight-faced. But she didn't apologize.

"What we can offer you now are two spots in the Witness Protection Program. We'll give you new names and relocate you and your children."

Mia and I had talked about this beforehand, but we still had real questions.

"When would we see our husbands?" I asked, knowing what the answer would be.

"You'll be far away from their prisons, but even if you travel to see them we can't allow unscheduled visits. You'll see them once a year, maybe, and it's entirely scheduled and supervised. We can't permit calls unless we set them up weeks in advance." Then she paused. "Your lives will be very different—and very separate—from your husbands'."

"Would we be near each other?" Mia asked.

"No. You'd be in different parts of the country."

I didn't even look at Mia when I started talking for both of us. We were on the same page about this, no questions asked. I couldn't lose the only person in the world who understood me, and she couldn't give up the only person in the world who reminded her of home. We were sisters, and no one was going to separate us.

"Never," I said. "We gave up everything. Our husbands sacrificed themselves for the love of our family and to give our children better lives, and the last thing we want to do now is break our family up. Our husbands need us, and we need them, and there's no way our babies are going to grow up not knowing their dads. Mia and I only have each other, and we cannot get through this alone. So our answer is absolutely, no."

Carol looked at both of us in shock. "You're making a huge mistake. This is a terrible risk."

"It's a risk we want to take," Mia said.

Carol nodded slowly. "Then it was wonderful to meet you, and I wish you all the best."

Together, we walked her to the door and showed her out, thanking her for her time. Then we went back to the couch, sat down, and without saying a thing, reached for each other's hands.

We're in this together for the long haul, I thought. *It might be twenty years till we're back with our husbands, and we'll sure as hell never be living on the beach in Mexico again, but we'll always have each other. And we're not giving up.*

PART FIVE

PURGATORY

CHAPTER 24

Chicago

Olivia

Christmas 2008 was our first without Junior and Peter, and it was the most depressing of my whole life. My parents were still disappointed and hurt, but they loved me no matter what, so they'd invited me over. Holidays and being together meant everything to them. Mia and I were too worried about being in the city, though, so we decided to spend the day alone in my big, quiet house in the suburbs. The most I did to decorate was go to Walmart and buy a plastic tree that I put up on a side table, with a few glass balls that I'd found right at the checkout aisle.

We didn't hear from Junior or Peter, and we had no clue when we'd get to see them.

Brandon's birthday had been a few days before Christmas, and he'd kept asking, "Where's Daddy? Why isn't he here for my birthday?" He spent most days hiding under Benjamin's bassinet, holding his blankie and sobbing for Junior. I tried to be strong for him, but sometimes I couldn't hold it together. As tears rolled down my face, I'd just turn off the lights so he wouldn't see me.

If you thought I was bad, though, Mia was worse. Bella was colicky, and she would cry all day, every day. Mia finally gave up trying to be strong around her, so she'd just sit and sob right along with her.

Mia

I'd hold Bella all day and night trying to soothe her, but it didn't help. I bought a sound machine, but still, nothing. I remember thinking, *I'm just glad Bella's too young to remember this. She and Benjamin will never know how bad this is.*

Olivia

I'm totally OCD when it comes to cleaning, but that December I didn't give a shit about anything. I'd roll Benjamin's dirty diaper in a ball and just throw it on the floor. Then I'd walk outside in the middle of the night in the freezing cold just to get away. Mia and I felt guilty for the little we did have, and after hearing through our lawyers that Junior and Peter were in jail, starving and freezing cold, we started taking cold showers as some sort of punishment.

Mia

I talked to my mom every day, and she'd always beg to come over. Finally, I let her, and she was shocked when she arrived. The house was a mess, and we were worse.

"What are you thinking?" she said. "Snap out of it! Your babies need you!"

But I felt stuck. Olivia and I were too depressed to do anything but just exist.

Olivia

We didn't hear from Junior and Peter till after New Year's, when we were allowed our first visit. We were about as excited as we'd been on our wedding days, but getting to the federal building where they'd been transported was a total scene. We had to drive downtown, practically to the center of the Loop, and we packed everything: diaper bags full of wipes, bottles, and formula, a change of clothes for the kids, and bags of snacks. It was like we were going on a freakin' field trip. Armed guards picked us up and drove us downtown into an underground parking deck, and when we stepped out of the cars we were met by US Attorney

Thomas Shakeshaft, the assistant US Attorney Michael Ferrara, and Eric Durante from the DEA.

As Mia and I lifted the kids out of the cars and loaded them and all our stuff into our huge Orbit strollers, we must have looked like we were ready for a week-long trip because the agents all stared at us like, *What the hell?*

I didn't care. I was about to see my husband.

Mia

We got into a back service elevator, since the main elevator was used to transport prisoners to court, and we couldn't risk being seen. When we got off, we walked into a room that had two long windows on each side of the door. It looked like a conference room in a regular old office building. We stood inside waiting for them, with Brandon holding Olivia's hand, so excited that he was jumping up and down. I'd taken a million pictures of Bella and had written to him almost every day. I never wanted him to feel like he was missing out, so I hoped that when he saw her, he'd as much as know her.

Suddenly, we saw Peter and Junior through the skinny windows, walking toward the room, shackled at their hands and feet.

Olivia

"Daddy! Daddy!" screamed Brandon, and he ran toward his dad and grabbed him around the knees.

Junior's face lit up, and I couldn't stop staring at him. I loved and missed him so much that I ached deep down, and all I wanted to do was hold him and never let him go. Still, underneath his huge smile, he was clearly a different person than I'd known before he went away. He looked like he was suffering from malnutrition and smelled like he hadn't showered since he'd left Mexico. He kept staring down at Brandon, like he was ashamed to hold his head up. After a moment or so, I lifted up his chin and looked him in the eyes.

"You're the handsomest thing I've ever seen," I said. "And the bravest, most courageous man in the world."

Mia

When I saw Peter, I couldn't believe how skinny he was. His hair was long and ratty, and his beard had grown out. The prison officials hadn't allowed him to take a shower in four weeks.

He didn't even want to hug me. "I'm so sorry you have to see me like this," he said. "I'm so sorry. Please forgive me."

"I've missed you," I said, pulling him toward me. "I'm just happy to be here with you."

I didn't want him to apologize. Just for that one afternoon, I didn't want to think about how our lives were upside down. And, luckily, it wasn't hard with Bella in the room.

Peter couldn't keep his eyes off of her. She'd grown so much over the last month that she looked like a different baby. The agents took his handcuffs off and let him hold her, and he was *so* happy, like this pure, innocent joy. It was beautiful.

Olivia

Junior was so worried about me and the babies. At home, he'd done everything for us, and he knew being on my own was hard.

"Are you doing okay?" he kept asking.

"I'm fine, but I'm more worried about you," I'd say.

"Please don't be. Your happiness is what keeps me going. I just want to see you smile, Liv."

My poor husband, I thought. *He's having to live through us now, and I spend all day depressed.*

I decided to keep that to myself and, instead, listened to Peter and Junior recount how they'd spent the last month.

Mia

After Peter and Junior were flown out of Guadalajara, they went to Mexico City and were there for a day. The next morning at six, US Marshals escorted them out of their hotel, hid them in an armored truck, and drove them into a nearby hangar, where they were placed on a US government jet. They were sent to Dallas, and as soon as they reached US soil, officials shackled them and read them their rights.

Olivia

All around them, cameras began flashing; so many, in fact, that they were temporarily blinded. As they walked onto the tarmac, Junior squinted, turned to Peter, and without words communicated what they were both thinking: *I can't believe all that we've done.* Suddenly, he felt like a terrorist. In his worst nightmare, he'd never imagined how notorious he and Peter really were.

Mia

From Dallas, they went to Milwaukee, where the federal investigation against them had begun almost a decade before. Agents shackled them, then led them into a federal building in the dead of night. The structure had been locked down as a security precaution, and Peter and Junior could hardly turn their heads without seeing an armed guard or an official from one of several different agencies. Some placed their fingers on their weapons, and many just stared. There had never been a trafficking case as huge as theirs in the United States, much less the state of Wisconsin. And the fact that they were major figures in the cartel world who'd willingly turned themselves in? It was the most remarkable case any agent there had seen.

Olivia

Peter and Junior spent one day in Milwaukee in separate prison cells, within earshot of each other. During the night, Peter called out to Junior, "Please don't sleep. Talk to me, I'm lonely." They'd been building a criminal enterprise for almost half their lives, and Peter was no stranger to captivity, but this was their first night in jail, a place they'd spent their whole lives avoiding.

The next morning, they were transported to the Metropolitan Correctional Center in Chicago. It only took an hour for them to get there;

they were in a caravan of black Suburbans, surrounded by US Marshals, that raced at top speed and blew through every red light. Barack Obama had just taken office, and we later heard that a few bystanders who saw them pass just assumed that Secret Service was moving the president.

Almost immediately after they got situated in the MCC, they orchestrated a massive reverse sting. Federal agents facilitated a few controlled deliveries, and then seized the drugs. Because of that, a lot of their workers had been arrested, but many of their wholesalers were still working the streets. When raids and seizures weren't happening, they were proffering—offering evidence and testimony to the US Attorneys—for twelve hours a day, every day. They did this for six straight months.

"We're telling the feds everything," Junior said. "Names, locations, all the ins and outs of our business, the whole bit."

Mia

Peter told us that all the proffering and recording happened in the federal building right where we were sitting, but that they were being housed in the Metropolitan Correctional Center, right across the street.

The MCC is a massive, brown, windowless building, and it's essentially a holding pen for federal criminals awaiting trial, sentencing, or placement in another prison.

"When they move us out of the MCC every day," he said, "we have twelve Marshals lead us out. They cover up the windows on everyone else's cells so they won't know who's passing by."

"As long as you're safe, baby," I said. "That's the most important thing."

God, I was naïve. That wasn't all that mattered. They didn't just need to be safe; they deserved to be treated with some basic human dignity, too.

Olivia

The MCC was hell on earth. Sure, no one was going to kill them there, but spending ten minutes within those walls was kind of like dying. Junior was always the type of person who was so selfless he never complained, but looking into his eyes every time I visited, it was hard to miss his pain and suffering. I wanted to tell him how bad I was feeling, but knowing how awful he had it and how traumatized he looked, I didn't have it in my heart to. He was already too broken.

Mia

Junior and Peter were such a big deal at the MCC that the guards there grew to hate them. They made their jobs harder because they had to jump through all these hoops just to get them out the door. So they cut their privileges, letting them have fewer showers, restricting their phone calls, and locking them down 24/7.

Olivia

While other inmates were pacing around their cells shirtless because it was so warm, Peter and Junior had been deliberately put into a cell that was so cold, the walls were covered in a thin sheet of ice. Yet the guards wouldn't give them any blankets. Peter and Junior lay together in the bed just to create body heat between the two of them. They were shaking the entire time.

The guard who checked on them at night once caught them and said, "Get the fuck out of that bed before I give you both a shot!" That was a disciplinary action that would force them each into solitary confinement, which didn't make a difference because they were already there.

Junior responded, "We're brothers, are you fucking kidding me?"

But the guard kept on. "Get out of that bed before I write you up!"

Mia

The guards finally moved them into a different cell, and when Peter walked into it, he half believed a mass murder had just gone down. There was blood on the walls, on the mattress, and on the floor. It smelled terrible. But the guards wouldn't clean it up till the next day.

The guy in the cell across from them would scream all day and night that he was going to commit suicide, then he'd rub his own shit all over the walls and the doors. The hall dividing them was so small Peter could smell it all day, so he'd just sit in the cell, put his arms over his head and think, *I'm living in hell. This is not a place for a human being to be.*

Olivia

It broke my heart to watch my husband and brother-in-law suffer. Every time I left my weekly visit, I'd get so angry that as soon as I got into my car I'd call up our lawyer, Joe, and let him have it.

"How the hell can they do their jobs if they're hurting like that?" I'd scream. "If you don't help make things better for them as soon as possible, you're going to hear from me every day of your life."

But all my calls didn't do any good. In the government's eyes, Junior and Peter were criminals, and all that mattered was that they kept feeding the feds intel.

Mia

Getting back to Olivia's house didn't provide much of a relief for us. We were still living together, but we never felt "at home." We were so consumed by what our husbands were going through that we became imprisoned in our own minds. Day by day, we were making ourselves miserable thinking about Junior and Peter, and we felt stagnant, like this could all go on forever and nothing would ever actually *happen*.

Then, in the middle of that winter, something did happen. We started feeling the heat from the people Peter and Junior were helping haul in.

Olivia

Junior had always made every day feel like Valentine's to me, but around the actual day he treated me extra special. No matter what we did, where we went, or what we gave each other, Valentine's Day wasn't just a Hallmark holiday; it really said something about our love.

That's why, just before Valentine's Day 2009, I fell into a major depression.

All I wanted to do was sit around, sulk, and think about all the good times I'd had with Junior, but Adrian and Daniela refused to let me and dragged me out of the house to get me over my funk. Brandon and I love sushi, so we all drove to a Benihana-type Japanese restaurant near my house.

After we sat down, got situated, and ordered, I got up to go to the bathroom. Just as I walked out of the ladies' room, holding Brandon in my arms, I ran right into one of the wholesalers Junior had informed on a few months before. Apparently, he was out on bond, and when he laid eyes on me, he was pissed. He got right up in my face, put his fingers to my head, and started yelling at me.

"I know Junior is telling! He and Pete fucking ratted me out!"

"What the hell are you talking about?" I was trying to sound innocent. "That's not true." I was scared out of my mind, thinking he was going to hurt me and my son, and I hugged Brandon closer to me.

"I got paperwork," he said, "and it says 'informant one and informant two' on it. Who else could that be?"

Just then Adrian walked out of the men's bathroom, saw what was happening, and put himself between the wholesaler and me.

"You need to calm down and relax," he said. "This is bullshit. How can my brothers be telling if I'm still here working? Wouldn't I be in jail, too?"

The wholesaler looked at Adrian and realized he had a good point. He backed off and shrugged. Then he turned to Adrian and said, "Can I get your number for some work then?"

This guy was *out of jail on bond*, and he was still looking to grab a few jobs. That just tells you how connected Junior, Pete, and our family were known to be.

Mia

People had expressed their suspicions to Junior and Peter directly, too. There was one occasion when Peter was on the phone setting up a drug bust, and a customer paused and said, "I need to ask you something. Are you a rat? Just be honest." Peter would deny it backward and forward, but a big part of him just wanted to fess up and answer, "Yes, I am."

He and Junior were feeling guilty. They were putting people they loved behind bars and knew their families' lives were going to be changed forever by it. These were workers who had children. Each time they helped the feds set up a controlled delivery, they were letting go of a long friendship, and it broke their hearts to turn their backs on the same people that they'd taken care of for years.

When I saw Peter every Friday, the pain showed on his face. The light he'd always had in his eyes had started to dim. He was so cold and pale all the time, and when I'd hug him, he couldn't let me go. He'd ask me to comfort him, saying, "Just remind me that I'm doing the right thing."

I lived for those Fridays, but staying home with Olivia was getting easier. Maybe we were just getting used to our new lives. We started cleaning the house every day so we wouldn't be surrounded by mountains of dirty diapers. We weren't getting new vehicles every month like we had in Mexico, so we took our cars to the shop for oil changes and new tires; even after everything they'd gone through, our husbands kept saying how worried they were about us driving in the snow. No one was running our errands anymore, so we did them ourselves. On the weekends we watched happy family movies, and it may sound silly, but they helped us see life in a positive light. We shoveled snow together and took the garbage out twice a week. Once, Olivia fell on her butt when she was hauling trash, and we both burst out laughing. As she lay there in the snow, I looked at her, smiled, and said, "I can't believe this is what our lives have become."

It was hard—our lives were like night and day compared to what they'd been six months before—but we were making it. Little did I know, though, that I'd need that strength because my life was about to become even more complicated.

CHAPTER 25

Alabama

Mia

Valentine's Day 2009, was on a Thursday, but because Olivia and I only got to visit Peter and Junior on Fridays, we decided to celebrate the day after the holiday. I used to write Peter ten-page love letters at night after Bella was asleep, so I packed one up, along with some new family photos I'd recently taken, and got in my car. When we arrived and settled into the visiting area, I turned to Olivia and Junior with a plan.

"Can you distract the guards for a little bit?" I asked.

They agreed, then cornered them and immediately began talking.

"Pete, let's go to the bathroom," I whispered.

"We can't," he answered. "Someone will catch us."

I put my foot down. "I don't care," I said.

It had been months since we'd made love, and we missed each other desperately. I knew a prison bathroom isn't the most romantic place to be with your husband, but we *needed* that closeness and would have done anything to get it. Plus, Peter needed to feel like a human being again, and, honestly, so did I.

A few weeks later, I found out I was pregnant. Bella was barely three months old.

I was shocked. But with a husband in prison and the rest of my life so uncertain, was I even just the tiniest bit worried or disappointed? Not for a second. My baby was a beautiful new beginning. In fact, having something so innocent growing inside me shielded me from what was happening to me and Olivia: the word was out about our husbands, and we'd been receiving threats.

Olivia

The DEA was receiving intel and had been tapping phones for months, but sometime that winter they'd intercepted a suspicious call. A group of armed men were standing outside a hair salon, waiting for someone they thought was me to come out so they could kidnap me.

Junior and Peter's attorney, Joe, called me in a panic with the feds on the line, and when I picked up the phone, I heard the fear in their voices.

"Liv, you're in danger," they said. "People are after you."

I hadn't been anywhere near the salon. The person inside looked a lot like me, but it was the wrong girl. The kidnappers were about to kick in the door, but the feds showed up and prevented anything from going down.

Still, the whole incident scared the shit out of me. I knew the feds couldn't intercept every call, and they wouldn't always be there to save the day.

Mia

The feds investigated one death threat after another against me and Olivia in the months after Peter and Junior were moved into the MCC. In fact, there were so many that I started to lose count.

There was one incident that stood out the most. An informant gave information that Saul Rodriguez had been staking out Olivia's house, armed and ready to kidnap her. The feds called us immediately, and they practically banned us from the state.

"You girls cannot be here anymore," they said. "The threats are coming in every direction, and we aren't going to be able to intercept every single one before it ends in tragedy. We think you should move to throw off anyone who's looking for you."

It had become a job in and of itself to protect us, and they needed to focus their efforts on the cases they had to build.

It didn't take much convincing; Olivia and I decided to leave town right away.

Olivia

We'd missed Junior and Peter's family since we'd been back in the States. While we'd gone straight to Chicago, they'd settled far away in Alabama because they wanted to be somewhere quiet and warm, far from Chicago. Besides the time Adrian had come to visit, it had been months since we'd seen them. We'd only been able to talk about Junior and Peter on the phone. They were going through the same emotions we were, and I didn't just think they could help us cope; I realized they might also be able to help me with Brandon. He'd been going through so much being away from his dad, and when we'd lived in Mexico he'd always enjoyed being with Junior's family. He missed them—we all did—and I hoped being around family would help us feel closer to Junior.

So we packed up our things, and my boys and I moved in with Daniela and Adrian, while Mia and Bella looked for their own place.

Mia

After six months in the MCC, Peter and Junior had been transferred to a county prison in Wisconsin, then to a federal facility Kansas, and we planned on visiting them every week. Life for them in Kansas was *so* much better, and Peter couldn't have been happier. The MCC had been so bad that anyplace else was going to feel like the Ritz-Carlton.

Olivia

In the middle-of-nowhere Kansas, there were fifty or more prisoners housed at a federal prison. They were all informants protected under the Witness Protection Program, and everyone, except for Junior and Pete, had been convicted and sentenced. Some were mobsters and others were drug dealers, but none were on the level of Peter and Junior. There are only a handful of these prisons in the country, and the government doesn't place just anyone who's worked with the feds there. You have to be a really big deal and be in an extremely dangerous situation.

Mia

When Olivia and I visited Junior and Peter, there was no glass separating us from them, and there was no dirty black phone you'd have to speak through. Instead, we sat on chairs in a super tiny visiting room, and Brandon, Benjamin, and Bella could actually play because they had a small area for kids. The guards were so nice to us because they saw us every weekend, and realizing how family-oriented Peter and Junior were, they treated them better. They let them hold the babies, which they hadn't been able to do in Wisconsin. It certainly wasn't like being at home, but Junior and Peter said that if they could have served their whole time there, they would have.

Olivia

They weren't locked down 24/7, so they spent their days working out, writing love letters to us, signing extradition papers, and meeting with prosecutors and DEA agents when they were needed. Even though they worried so much about our safety, they were happy because they felt closer to us, with three hundred phone minutes a month and visiting privileges every weekend.

Plus, it may sound funny, but the company was better.

"It feels good to be around people and just talk about normal things that have nothing to do with business," Junior said.

Junior's such a people person, and I knew he needed that socialization. And he *loved* our visits, which were finally regular.

I rented an apartment in Kansas and would fly up there every Friday from Alabama, staying till Sunday. I didn't care if there was a blizzard or fifteen inches of snow on the ground.

"We might as well buy our own snowplow to hook up to the front of our trucks," I joked with Mia, "because nothing's going to stop us from getting to our visits."

As much as I loved seeing Junior, it was so difficult to travel with my kids being so small. Benjamin always cried a lot on the flights, and people would give us dirty looks when he did. Prisons are never close to cities, so the drive from the airport there was two hours in the best of conditions, which they rarely were in winter. On Christmas, one of my flights was delayed because of snow, so I only got to spend thirty minutes with Junior. I didn't care; I would have driven across the country just to see him for three minutes.

When I got back home on Sunday, I pretty much had to start repacking right away for the next weekend. I constantly felt like a truck had run over me, but I knew I depended on my visits as much as Junior did. They got me through my week. Sometimes, the travel made me despise my life, but Junior always kept me grounded; he'd remind me how blessed we were that we were alive and healthy and had each other.

Most importantly, visits were the only time our boys had with their dad, and it was amazing to see the kind of bond that came out of a visit every weekend. Brandon absolutely lives for Junior. Every year, when he blows out the candles on his birthday cake, his only wish is for his daddy to come home. Benjamin doesn't know what it's like to have Junior home, but like his brother, he loves him unconditionally, and when his birthday comes around we count the years Junior's been gone.

Still, seeing their dad in prison wasn't always easy for them. In fact, for Brandon, it was actually painful.

Mia

Brandon would break down every weekend, and Peter and I felt terrible watching it. We'd hear a cry that's hard to describe; it was like he was hurting inside, and that feeling was screaming to come out.

Olivia

Brandon was the only baby who remembered his dad outside of a prison wall, so he took it the hardest. He understood what it was like to miss someone so much that it physically hurts.

Mia

Life with their dads in prison was all the babies had ever known. And for my new baby, it was going to be the same. I knew it wasn't going to be easy to keep our family close given the circumstances, but I kept telling myself, *This is your life now, and this is just what you have to do.*

Sometimes, it wasn't so bad. Compared to so many women who get pregnant with no steady partner and no support system, I had it good. In fact, Peter was already bending over backward to be involved with my pregnancy, and he had been since the beginning.

Because I couldn't call Peter in prison, I had to wait for him to call me. To feel more involved in family life, Peter always noted *all* my appointments in his calendar, plus our family events and little occasions like the day Bella got her first tooth. The first few months after I found out I was pregnant, he stored up all his phone minutes, knowing he couldn't waste them since I had big doctor's visits coming up. The day I found out whether we were having a boy or a girl, I sat on my hands for what felt like forever till he called. I knew he'd marked it in his calendar; he just hadn't been given the opportunity to use the phone.

Then my cell rang, and before he even had a chance to say "hello," I started talking. "Are you ready to teach your son how to play basketball?" I said almost breathlessly.

"I'm having a son?" he screamed.

He was so loud the whole prison probably shook, and hearing him so happy made my heart sing. Right then, I needed that pure joy, that crazy excitement, because what I refused to tell my husband was that I was having a really, really hard time living with his family in Alabama.

Olivia

Everyone's lives had completely changed when we left Mexico, but Mia and I rolled with it. Sure, it was hard, but not because we didn't have the material things we were used to, and certainly not because we regretted what Peter and Junior had done. We were proud of them! We just missed our husbands terribly and worried constantly that we were going to be killed by the cartels, who had the money and the means to track us down.

Peter and Junior's family, on the other hand, couldn't stand the fact that they started working for the government. While it brought out the best in us, it was just the opposite for them.

Mia

Peter and Junior had been their family's meal tickets. With them gone—and in such a shameful way—their parents and siblings complained all the time. There was constant fighting. When Peter and Junior told their family they had to get jobs, like normal people do, I heard my in-laws complain.

"What kind of job do they expect us to do?" they asked, genuinely confused and angry. They were just paralyzed, sitting around the house doing next to nothing.

Olivia

Junior and Peter had enabled their family members. They were so used to living in Mexico, where you pay cash for everything. In the United States, you have to have credit, and you need references to rent a house. Peter's dad was a convicted felon who'd been a fugitive for years. He wasn't a landlord's dream tenant, and he sure as hell wasn't going to get a credit card to make him look better on paper. Credit was for poor people, not him.

Mia

I don't blame them for being so self-involved, but I hated that they couldn't see how depressed I was. They complained constantly to me, assuming that I could do something, when all the while I was thinking, *How can I fix anything when I'm as lost as you are?*

My parents were so overprotective when it came to me and Bella, and I knew they would have come and packed me up in a day if I'd asked them to. But I was too ashamed to tell them that I was at my very worst. I even shied away from talking to Peter about it since I knew all he wanted was for me to be happy.

Adrian and Daniela would check on me from time to time, but they had their own lives. I felt so alone, living in my apartment with Bella, and I struggled every day. Bella was a huge baby. I'm tiny, and she was half as big as I was. People would see us out and say, "Is that *your* baby, or are you babysitting for someone?" With my belly, I could hardly pick her up. In that awful heat, I'd be pouring sweat. The best I could do was just let Bella float in a little raft in the pool all day to cool us down and tire her out. At night, I'd cook a healthy dinner for myself, we'd take a long bath, and I'd read to her. Then I'd turn on the television, let Bella fall asleep in my arms, then cry silently to myself.

In the morning, I could hardly get up, but I'd force myself to pick up Bella and go out and run errands. As soon as I put her in her car seat, she'd already be red and sweaty.

Yet no one in Peter's family offered to help me. No one.

Olivia

They just didn't understand why Junior and Peter were doing what they were doing, and it consumed them. It was like they didn't have time and energy to consider anyone but themselves, and they couldn't see the big picture. They didn't think about Peter and Junior, that if they hadn't made the decision they had, they'd be dead or in prison for life.

My father-in-law took it the worst. To him, Junior and Peter becoming snitches was the most horrible thing they'd ever done. When he'd found out his sons were cooperating, he'd screamed, "You're both cowards!" and stormed out of the house. They were the last words he'd spoken in the months before they'd turned themselves in, and since their dad never visited them in prison, it was one of the last memories they had of him. It hurt them—deeply. Peter and Junior knew that what they were doing was right, but the little boys inside of them still wanted their dad's approval.

I didn't know what to feel because I loved my father-in-law, but I felt terrible for what he'd said to Junior and Peter. Being called cowards broke their hearts. But I didn't hold it against my father-in-law; it was just the way he'd been raised.

Mia

In my family, we always greet each other with a hug and a kiss. That's just what we do. We say goodbye with a hug and a kiss, too. My dad's never been anything but affectionate and loving with me, always smiling and pleasant to be around. Sure, he gets upset about things and speaks his mind, but he's not an angry guy. He's manly, but not macho.

That's the opposite of Peter's dad. Señor had this way about him that I feared right from the first time I met him. He never smiled, and at dinner he'd get really stern and pound his fist on the table when he'd talk. I'd think, *Oh, my goodness, is he mad?* He wasn't—or usually wasn't. He was just passionate.

For the first year or so I knew my father-in-law, our conversations consisted of "Good morning!" and "Good night!" That was it. There was no small talk. There was no "Hi, are you having a good day?" And there was certainly no hugging or kissing when we saw each other. We were all business. At the time I thought, *Maybe he's so unfriendly because he already has so many sons-in-law and daughters-in-law, and having another is no biggie?* But now I realize that's just the way he was. He was set in his ways.

Peter understood this, and he went with it and spoke to him like a friend. They'd sometimes argue, usually about money, and I'd keep my mouth shut the whole time. When it was over and his dad had stormed off into another room, I'd say, "Look what just happened! You can't get out of line with your dad."

Peter would laugh. "That's just how he is, Mia. He's not really mad. It's just how he is."

Olivia

My father-in-law was a typical old-school Mexican man. He was completely different than my dad, who was encouraging and supportive and wanted me to be smart and independent, like my mom. Still, I got along with my father-in-law, and I actually really understood him. I never judged him, and I grew to love him.

When I first came on the scene, I wasn't afraid to be as strong as him. I spoke my mind, and over the years, I'd call him out if I thought he did something wrong. Sometimes it wasn't pretty, but I think he appreciated that someone was having a conversation with him, actually paying attention to him, even if it was more of a debate. He wouldn't really argue with me; he'd just smirk and smile to himself. He thought I was funny.

Once, he woke up my mother-in-law after one of our late night debates.

"Olivia is *muy cabrona*," he said, meaning I was a real bad-ass bitch who didn't take no shit.

My mother-in-law just smiled, rolled over, and went back to sleep.

Mia

I grew to love my father-in-law. Not just because he was family, but because I started to understand him. He began to seem like a normal person, not the stereotypical macho Mexican guy he tried to make himself out to be.

When I first moved to San Juan, Peter started buying horses. His hobby soon became my hobby, and our bonding time began to involve us driving to different ranches to look at horses. Nine times out of ten, his parents would come with us. Once we all traveled together to a ranch about two hours away. As we drove up to the front gate, Señor was greeted by a worker who opened his arms up to him.

"Oh, Margarito! *Buenos días!* How are you?" the man said.

"Very good and very excited to be here!" My father-in-law looked genuinely thrilled.

We got in the back of the worker's pickup truck and drove into an overgrown field. The ground was so tangled up with grass that you couldn't really see where you were going, but we got out of the truck and started walking anyway.

About ten steps in, the rancher opened his palm, which he'd filled with oats. All of a sudden these wild, beautiful horses came out from behind the trees, like magic, and began making their way through the grass toward us. I looked over at my father-in-law, and I saw his eyes light up. He began to smile, completely in awe. I don't think I'd ever seen him melt like that. Right then and there I saw his softer side, and for the first time, I felt close to him. Even though I was so scared of him most of the time, at that moment, we were close.

I try to remember those moments now when I think about him.

Olivia

My father-in-law loved his grandchildren, especially Benjamin and Bella. In Mexico, when you're light-skinned or have blond hair or blue eyes, people are like, *wow*. Benjamin and Bella are fair-skinned, and my father-in-law would always stare at them and say, "They're beautiful. Like porcelain dolls." He loved to hold Benjamin and hug him, and he'd sing to Bella until she fell asleep. He was the perfect grandfather to them at a time when they didn't really have their fathers, or at least, that constant male presence.

That's why I didn't understand why he wanted to leave. He had *everything*: a family, grandchildren he loved, and most of all, safety. No one knew where he was in Alabama, and chances were good that no one was going to come after him. But he was angry with his sons for being snitches, for taking him away from his other family, and most of all for making him flee from his home.

Mia

When you live in Mexico, you realize pretty quickly that there are people who never want to leave. They love their town, and they love their country. That's how my father-in-law was.

Olivia

That longing for home started before he'd gone back to America. In fact, after my father-in-law returned from his kidnapping, Peter and Junior bought him and my mother-in-law a mansion near our home in Guadalajara. They convinced them to leave San Juan, saying it wasn't safe. I completely furnished and decorated the mansion beautifully, and we threw a massive housewarming party for them around Christmas 2006, with a huge Christmas tree, a red, sparkly bow on the door, and a twelve-man mariachi band serenading them as they drove up to their new house. That night, my father-in-law was in tears, remembering how different his last Christmas had been.

But days later, he soured. He started talking about how much he missed San Juan, and he began complaining about being away from home to anyone who would listen.

Mia

That was the way he was in Alabama, too. Never mind that he had a wife he'd been married to for almost fifty years, and grandkids who adored him and were there almost daily. From the moment he crossed the border into the United States, he began talking about going back.

Something was calling him home, and no one was going to tell him otherwise.

Olivia

A few weeks after I moved to Alabama, I went over to my in-laws' house. No one answered the door, so I walked to the back. There, I saw my father-in-law, sitting by himself in a chair in the garden. He was staring at some flowers, deep in thought. I considered going through the gate to talk to him, but I was afraid he was going to tell me how disappointed he was in his sons. I was always defensive when it came to Junior and Peter, and the last thing I wanted to do was say something I'd regret to my father-in-law.

Suddenly, Adrian approached me. He'd come from the other side of the house, and he'd just seen me observing his dad.

I looked at Adrian and lowered my voice. "He's going to leave. He doesn't want to be here."

"You're crazy," Adrian said.

But I wasn't. I knew what I knew, and I couldn't explain why.

A few days later, in late March 2009, Adrian called me.

"My dad is gone," he said. "He just picked up and left."

Margarito Flores, Sr. had packed a small bag and driven away in his car that morning. Adrian and I didn't discuss it, but we knew where he'd gone and why he hadn't taken much with him. Apparently, everything he needed was back home in Mexico.

How could he do this to my mother-in-law? I thought. *How could he do this to his sons? If something happens to him, they won't be able to live with themselves.*

"He can't go back!" I said to Adrian. "The cartels are going to find him and kill him! What the fuck is wrong with him?"

"There's nothing we can do, Liv," Adrian said. "He's a grown man, and he knows what can happen to him. You know how he is; no one could have changed his mind."

Even though I knew he was right, I still felt guilty for not trying. No one could tell my father-in-law shit. Not Adrian, and especially not me. When he had his mind made up about something, that was just going to be the way it was, damn the consequences.

Mia

He didn't seem to mind that Mexico was a war zone. The cartel wars were raging, and in fact, they'd been escalating the entire time Peter and Junior had been cooperating.

On May 9, 2008, Arturo Beltrán Leyva's BLO army had sprayed El Chapo's son, Edgar's, car with two hundred bullets, killing him. In retaliation, El Chapo began an all-out battle on the streets of Culiacán, complete with firefights and shootouts, and there was a curfew so innocent people could avoid getting killed.

But the danger now wasn't just from random gunfire. Cartel members wanted to get revenge on Peter and Junior, and if that meant targeting their family, that was just fine.

Olivia

Margarito Sr. didn't care, though. In Mexico, there was a little church he liked to walk around in. In Mexico, he could speak Spanish. In Alabama, he lived in the suburbs, and there was no corner store you could walk to. In Alabama, there were no people hanging out in the plaza. There were no stories. There was no past.

He'd gone back to Mexico to have all of that again.

Mia

We didn't hear anything for over a month. Then one of the US Attorneys called Peter and Junior.

"We found your dad's car in the desert in Sinaloa," the lawyer said. "It had a note on the windshield warning both of you to keep your mouths shut."

There was no blood in the car, no bullet holes, and no other evidence of foul play. But I know kidnappings; I've lived through one of my own and two of my husband's. Kidnappers don't kill you in your car. They pull you out, put you in another car, and take you somewhere else. Sometimes the police will find your body, but most of the time they don't. My father-in-law fell into the latter category; he just vanished into thin air.

Olivia and I visited our husbands in prison that weekend.

"It's all our fault," Peter said. "We did this."

Junior was crying. "My poor mother. She's all alone now, and it's because of us."

"It's not. Please, stop blaming yourselves," I pleaded. I was lying, though. Their dad would have lived if they hadn't become informants. He'd still be in Mexico, betting hundreds of thousands of dollars on the horses, enjoying his wife's cooking, stealing hours here and there with his second family, sitting on the bench in front of his house on a beautiful day, and pounding his fists on the dinner table.

I missed him that day, and I've missed him every day since. We'll never know what happened—Margarito Flores's death was just one of thousands that year during the cartel wars—but we just pray that he didn't suffer. We hope that he went in peace.

CHAPTER 26

Wives at War

Olivia

On August 20, 2009, the US Attorney General, Eric Holder, unsealed the indictments against Junior and Peter. But they weren't alone; he also announced the charges against El Chapo, El Mayo, Arturo Beltrán Leyva, sixteen members of Junior and Peter's Chicago-based crew, and assorted hitmen, lieutenants, and other cartel members. In a total of fifteen indictments, forty-six men—with nicknames like Skinny, Ron Ron, and Grandpa—were charged, all because of Peter and Junior.

Mia

While hauling in the US operatives was relatively easy, extraditing the Mexican cartel players was going to be harder. Extraditions require reams of paperwork, months and months of time, and the full cooperation of the Mexican government. The feds were hoping they could do it within a few years. After all, they didn't just want to strangle the flow of narcotics into the United States; they also wanted to help Mexico end its cartel wars.

Olivia

So much was happening in our husbands' cases and all over Mexico, but unfortunately, Mia and I weren't talking to each other about any of it. By fall of 2009, we were waging our own war. Both of us were unhappy, and neither of us knew how to deal with our husbands not being with us. So we took it out on each other, and for the stupidest of reasons.

I'd stayed friends with Peter's ex, Angela, who was the mother of his older daughter, Sophia. Whenever I was in Chicago, I'd drop by her house, visit, and check on Sophia. Brandon was close to his cousin, and so was I. I'd been around her since she was born, and I looked at her like a daughter. Mia knew I still talked to Angela, and it was uncomfortable for her. She probably didn't want Angela to know certain things, or she didn't want me letting anyone else muddy the waters. Or maybe she imagined I was confiding in her, breaking our circle of trust.

Mia

In a lot of Latin families, you leave your exes in the past. That goes for your husband's ex-girlfriend, too. We're not accustomed to seeing blended families with exes, and bad feelings and harsh words are common, even expected. And when you break up with someone, your family is supposed to cut them off.

That's the way I was raised, and it's the reason I was upset with Olivia. As a woman and a wife, I felt betrayed that she was still talking with Peter's ex. When we made the decision to change our lives, we made it as a family, and I felt as if she abandoned me at my most vulnerable time. When I love someone, I love them hard, and I never turn my back on them. I worried that our sisterhood wasn't good enough, and that we were going to have to live this crazy life without each other.

Olivia

At such a sensitive point in our lives, we should have been there for each other, like sisters. So I couldn't understand why Mia was letting something like this come between us. I thought she was being so controlling.

Junior and I would talk all the time about what was going on.

"She's younger than me, and she's just being immature," I'd say to him.

"I just hope you work it out soon," he'd answer.

Junior had never had a hard time letting me know when I was wrong, and vice versa. That's part of why we made such a good team. But since he'd been locked up, the last thing he wanted to do was fight with me. He stayed quiet and sided with me.

It started coming between him and Peter and put a strain on their relationship. They'd always seen eye to eye, were always on the same page. But when it came to us, they'd do anything to make us happy.

It got so bad that when Mia and I would visit our husbands in Kansas, we'd sit on opposite sides of the visiting area. The room was tiny, too, like ten feet by twelve feet, and we wouldn't even say hi to each other. Benjamin would toddle over to Bella to try to play with her, but it still didn't break the ice.

Mia

When I hold a grudge against someone, I hang on to it forever. People think I'm sweet and delicate because I'm so soft-spoken and reserved, but inside, I'm tough as nails. I usually have my guard up. The weekend before I was scheduled to deliver my baby, I don't think I've ever been so defensive.

I went to visit Peter on Sunday, like I always did. I'd decided to move to Kansas to be close to his prison. I wasn't going back to Alabama if my life depended on it; I would have rather been on my own than be someplace where people were supposed to be helping me but weren't. I was already feeling happier, but talking to Peter two days before having my baby, knowing he wouldn't be there, set me back.

"I'm just so sorry I can't be there for you. That I can't be there for my boy being born," he said.

I'd always wanted a boy and a girl, so the fact that I was having a son was pretty much everything I'd ever wished for. I prayed every night that he'd be healthy, and I told myself that even though Peter wasn't going to be in the hospital with me, nothing was going take my happiness away. Still, with Peter sitting there apologizing, I felt completely alone. I needed him more than ever, but there was nothing he could do.

"It's all okay, Peter," I lied. "I'm not thinking of myself. I've got a baby at home and a baby on the way that need me. I'll be fine."

We both started crying, and he kissed me goodbye.

Then Olivia walked into the room with Brandon and Benjamin.

Olivia

When I saw Mia sitting in that little visiting room, I thought, *What kind of person am I that I'm not going to be there for her? She's having a baby alone, for God's sake.* I started to walk toward her, but she refused to look at me, and I backed off. We sat on opposite sides of the room all afternoon, the tension between us growing minute by minute.

When I left and got in my car, I didn't feel relieved to be away from such an uncomfortable situation. In fact, I felt guiltier than ever. So I picked up the phone and called her, and much to my surprise, she answered.

"Mia," I said. "I love you and I want to be there for you when you have the baby."

She didn't say a thing.

"I'm so sorry for everything I've done or said, and if you want me there, I'd like to go to the hospital to be with you."

There was more silence. But I wasn't giving up.

"I'm sorry I wasn't there for you during your pregnancy. I can't imagine how hard this has been for you, and I'm truly sorry for everything you're going through. I know Peter can't be there for you, and I know that I'm the closest thing that you have to him, so I genuinely want to be there for you." I kept on going. "I'd like to go to the hospital and be there for the birth of my nephew. Please let me be there. *Please...*"

Mia must have been sick of the sound of my voice because she finally broke the silence. True to form, she was polite. I don't think a day's gone by when she hasn't been sweet and courteous.

"Thank you for calling," she said. "It means a lot to me." She paused. "But I'm going to have this baby alone."

Then she hung up the phone.

Mia

My mom, dad, and a few of my aunts flew in from Chicago to be with me for the birth of my baby boy, and the morning we walked into the hospital, I'd decided I wasn't going to let the hardest time in my life consume my moment. Even with all the chaos in my life, being a mother kept me grounded, and watching my babies grow masked my sadness. So when I first saw Blake, with his curly blonde hair and light eyes, it was the most beautiful experience of my life other than having Bella. He was perfect, such a good baby, with a smile that was absolutely beautiful. I was in love and finally felt complete, and I thought to myself, *I was put on this earth to be their mom, so I'm going to give it my all. I'm going to do all the normal things that normal parents do, and I'm going to protect them, at all costs.*

I'd set up a nursery for Blake, and everything in it was perfectly in order for his arrival home. But in the middle of our first night out of the hospital, I dragged his crib into my room because I couldn't bear to have him away from me. I realized right then I never wanted to leave Bella or Blake, not for one moment.

When I took Blake to meet his dad the week after he was born, I walked in the visiting room with Blake in the car seat and Bella strapped to me in the Baby Bjorn. Peter was waiting by the door, and he had a look of disbelief on his face. He took Blake out of his baby seat and pressed his face against his.

"I love you, baby boy," he said.

From that moment on, they had a connection no one could break.

Olivia

I was feeling so guilty about Mia. I kept wishing I'd seen things her way and had honored her wishes. Not respecting Mia's feelings had tarnished our sisterhood. Even though I hadn't been trying to be malicious, I'd caused her heartache, and I regretted that.

Worse, since Blake had been born, I hadn't even spent time with him. I'd just seen him across the visiting room, bundled up in his little car seat like a tiny angel, melting all our hearts. I hated not picking him up, and I hated that I hadn't even congratulated Mia. Just by her look alone, I knew she didn't want me near her or my baby nephew. But I couldn't stop thinking, *She and I are going through something no one else in the world understands, yet we can't work out our problems together?* I was determined to make it right. Unfortunately, with her refusing to talk to me, I just didn't know how.

Then, in March 2010, something terrible happened that forced her to make the first move.

Mia

In the federal unit where Junior and Pete were housed, officials turned on the phones at six a.m. One morning in March, the sun wasn't even up when my cell started ringing. It was Peter, and he was frantic.

"They've taken Junior away," he said.

I'd been half asleep when I answered, but hearing Peter's words made me jump out of bed. "Where?" I asked.

"I have no idea. But they just took him and not both of us."

I wanted to calm him down, but I was scared shitless.

Peter kept talking, his voice shaking. "We both woke up in the middle of the night to the sound of trucks. We could see them out our cell window, ten Suburbans with their brights on. This crowd of US Marshals came into our cell and just took him. I kept shouting at them, 'Where are you taking him?' But they wouldn't say."

"Is he coming back?"

"They acted like he would be, but I know he's not."

Peter and Junior had rarely been apart since the day they were born. Especially in prison, they were each other's support system, the only thing that made the days bearable. I was devastated, probably as much as he was, and I knew Olivia would be as well.

When I hung up with Peter, I called her immediately.

Olivia

It was good to hear Mia's voice, and while it wasn't too warm or friendly, it was clear she was about to tell me something important.

"Peter told me they took Junior out of prison last night," she said.

I practically jumped out of my skin. "What the hell? Where is he?" I yelled.

"Peter doesn't know where he's gone. No one would tell him anything."

We talked for a few more minutes, then I hung up and tried to figure out what to do. I was totally torn into pieces not knowing what was going on with my husband, desperate for answers, and I lay down on the floor in a ball and cried my eyes out. I was so worried about Junior being alone. He and Peter had never really been apart, and they needed each other now more than ever.

I found out a few days later the US Marshals had transferred Junior to the New York City MCC. They'd locked down the airport, placed him on a private plane, like in the movie *Con Air*, and when it landed, the feds shut down a tunnel into Manhattan so they could drive him solo to the MCC. I knew that given the money and manpower it took to move him, he'd be at the MCC for a long time.

Mia

The reason for the move was because of a mix-up.

In Kansas, Peter had decided to show the whole world how much he loved me by putting up two enormous billboards near the highway exit we took on visiting days. In big, bold type, the first said, "Marrying you was a dream come true!" and the second read, "I love you today, tomorrow, and forever...your grateful husband." They didn't have any photos or my name on them, but Peter told me they were for me, and I thought it was just the cutest thing. It topped almost anything romantic he'd ever done.

The feds didn't feel the same. We're not sure why they were so angry, but apparently that kind of gesture was against their rules. Unfortunately, they didn't ask Peter or Junior; they just assumed that Junior was behind the billboards. They were furious and decided to transfer him. By the time they realized they'd punished the wrong brother, it was too late.

The Bureau of Prisons was so upset by the mistake that they decided never again to house them together, and now, they even have a rule that identical twins can't be in the same facility.

Olivia

The New York MCC wasn't much better than the one in Chicago. Junior had no phone privileges, so for the few months I had to wait for an authorized visit, Junior and I had zero communication, and I fell into a depression.

On our first visit, we were only allowed three hours together. That was the rule; no weekend all-day family sessions like we'd had in Kansas. When I laid eyes on Junior, I couldn't believe what I was seeing. He'd dropped twenty pounds and looked sick and pale, like he was about to break into pieces. He told me he wasn't eating the food because the kitchen staff were inmates who knew their floor housed snitches, so they urinated or put feces in it. Junior never complained, but he was at his lowest, his breaking point, and we both cried the entire visit.

An hour into our visit, a guard came into the room.

"Time's up," he said.

"But we have three hours. It's been an hour," I said as calmly as I could.

"We only have to give you an hour. Time to go." The guard walked up to Junior and led him away before I'd even had a chance to kiss him goodbye.

For the next six months, my boys and I flew to see Junior once a week, and half the time they cut our visits short. Once Junior looked out his cell window and saw me and the kids standing in the pouring rain, waiting for a cab after we'd left the building, and he broke down. He felt so guilty we were flying halfway across the country once a week and going through so much that he begged me to stop coming. I refused. After that, the first thing he'd always say when I came to visit was, "I'm sorry. I'm sorry I'm putting you through this." He constantly apologized that he'd missed seeing Benjamin for months, when he was still so small, and he hated that Brandon cried when he was led out of the room. But most of all, he missed his brother. Being separated from Peter was the hardest thing he'd ever experienced.

Since Junior had no phone privileges, I wrote him every single day. I wanted him to feel close to us, but in reality, my letters helped *me* feel close to him. They were deep and intimate, and they made me remember things that made me miss him even more.

When I wasn't writing letters, I called Junior's lawyers and the US Attorneys and begged them to do something for him. I even went to the extreme of hiring another attorney because I just needed to do something, anything, to help Junior. I had to fix his situation, so I became a total nuisance, but I didn't care. All I wanted was for Junior to get out of that fucking place.

I had no one to talk to, either. No one in the world understood what I was going through except for Mia, and she and I were still distant.

Mia

Holding a grudge against Olivia just wasn't worth it to me anymore. I was too tired. I missed the family we had and the special bond we shared, and I hated that our fight had pulled Peter and Junior apart. Olivia and I had been through the very worst and the very best times together, and the fact that we'd let anything come between us was just stupid. I wanted my sister back. And when she called one day several months into Junior's time at the New York MCC, I almost jumped for joy.

Olivia

She answered my call on the first ring, and I started talking a mile a minute.

"I was never trying to hurt you, but I know I did, and I'm sorry. Mia, I want to make things right. Please find it in your heart to forgive me. I realize that if I don't give in to your feelings, things are never going to be okay. Okay? So please know I value our friendship more than anything.

Not to mention that Junior and P need each other, and we're the only ones that can keep them close. We *all* need each other..."

"Stop. Stop," Mia said. "I forgive you. Let's put this behind us and move on. I've missed you. I've missed you *so* much."

When we hung up the phone a few minutes later, we were both sobbing.

Mia

I just had to let it go. I did what I had to do, and for one of the first times in my life, I didn't do it for Peter. I did it for myself and for Olivia.

Olivia

It took time, but we mended our friendship. Finally, I had my sister back, and thank God I did because things were about to get crazy for both of us again.

CHAPTER 27

Forfeiture

Mia

In the fall of 2010, almost two years after we'd left Mexico, Olivia and I definitely weren't living the same way we had in Mexico, with maids and new jewelry every month and garages full of fancy cars. But we had money, and we didn't realize there was anything wrong with that.

Olivia

When we'd crossed the border, we had nothing but the clothes on our backs and enough cash to buy food and gas. Knowing that we had to live on something, we picked up some money. I'll be honest; it was millions of dollars. But when you lived the way we lived in Mexico, that kind of money doesn't seem abnormal. We'd actually be downsizing in the United States. Plus, we thought, *How else are we supposed to support ourselves while we were in hiding?* In our minds, we weren't doing anything wrong.

Mia

We'd known for a long time that the court was going to order our husbands to forfeit money, goods, and property at their sentencing, but that was most likely years away. And while we knew it was possible that we'd have to give up some stuff sooner rather than later as part of the administrative process, we never dreamed the government wouldn't give us notice.

Unfortunately, the process and what happened because of it couldn't have been rockier.

Olivia

One morning in September 2010, I'd just dropped off Brandon at preschool. Benjamin was in the backseat in his car seat, and I kept looking in the rearview mirror, like I always did. Suddenly, I noticed something didn't seem right. I'd just switched lanes, and the pickup truck behind me had put on his turn signal and edged in right behind me.

My normal route home was taking the main street in town, but I instead got on the expressway. As I took the entrance ramp, so did that damn truck. I put my foot on the gas and accelerated, and he sped up just as fast as I did. I was starting to sweat and my heart was racing, so I gunned it, moved two lanes to the right, and took an exit off the highway.

The pickup was a few cars back, but it exited, too. Then suddenly, I noticed something: there wasn't just one pickup. There were three, and all of them had blacked-out windows.

I continued onto an access road, then got back on the expressway. *Oh my God,* I thought. *This is it. They've found me, and they're going to kill me.* I accelerated to about 120 miles an hour and started zigzagging to get through traffic, even jumping into the emergency lane with my gas pedal all the way down. I kept thinking, *If I crash, I'm going to flip this truck over, and my son and I are going to die.*

I pulled off the expressway once again. I couldn't see the trucks anymore, so I moved off onto a side street. As I stopped and looked at the beat-up houses on either side of the street, I suddenly realized, *Oh, shit. This neighborhood is bad news. I'm sticking out like a sore thumb in a Range Rover.* Shaking, I put the car in drive and pulled into a nearby 7 Eleven, then just sat with the motor still running.

I sat there for maybe three minutes, scanning left, then right, and looking in my rearview mirror. Believe it or not, Benjamin was sound asleep. Then, out of nowhere, I saw the three pickup trucks coming down the road behind me. I put the car in drive and floored the gas, and the pickups started chasing me again. All that was going through my head was, *I'm going to die. I'm going to die.*

My phone rang. I looked down at the screen and saw that it was Adrian.

"Someone's trying to kill me!" I screamed when I answered. "Three trucks are following me!"

"Olivia!" he yelled. "It's the feds. Calm down. I'm here with one of them, an agent named Todd. Meet me at your house."

The feds were chasing me? I said to myself. *What the living fuck were they thinking? I could have been killed!*

I made it to my house in a few minutes, got out of my truck, and started screaming at the handful of agents who were standing there.

"What the fuck is your problem? How could you do this to me and my son? We both could have been killed. I could have flipped my truck. We're here hiding, and you're going to come and expose my family like this? People here have no idea who I really am, but when they see a bunch of DEA agents, you can imagine what they're going to think. I'm fucked."

"Please, calm down," one agent said. "My name is Todd, and I just need to ask you some questions."

I was still livid. "My husband is the one cooperating, so I have no idea what you want with me. I'm not talking to you unless I speak with a lawyer first."

I pulled out my phone and called Junior's new attorney, David. He didn't answer, so I called Joe, and again, got no answer. Later on, I found out that both attorneys were at Peter and Junior's prisons meeting with them while the feds decided to ambush us.

When I finally heard back from David, he explained the discussions the feds, Junior, and Peter had had separately: they'd come to an agreement that Mia and I would have full immunity from prosecution if we met with the US Attorneys and told them everything we knew.

"So you mean Junior knew about the feds coming and didn't call me?" I asked.

"No," he explained. "He had no idea they'd be coming after you."

That's how great communication was. It was time for me to speak to the feds, yet I'd gotten no notice, apparently, and the only way to tell me was to chase me off the road.

Mia

The feds hadn't done a great job of tracking me down, either.

First, they'd gone to my house in Kansas and discovered I wasn't there. Then, thinking I might be visiting Chicago, they'd traveled to my parents' place. Realizing I wasn't there, either, they talked to one person, then another, and then finally asked my lawyer to find me. He'd been meeting with Peter, so he called me.

"I'm about to hop on a flight back to Chicago," he said. "Meet me at the airport immediately."

"Okay, I'll be right there," I said, and then got in my car.

"You're going to get called into a meeting with the feds," he said when I got to him. "You've got immunity from prosecution, but they want you to talk. You're going to have to surrender some of your possessions."

Right then, I handed him the keys to my brand new Bentley. "Take them," I said. "I know I'm going to have to give it up, so just take it now." He took the keys, and I left the car in the parking lot.

I looked calm, but I was so upset. I kept thinking, *I just gave up my car, and I'm going to have to meet with the feds any day now. Yet no one really prepared me for this. Why is this happening after everything our husbands have done?*

Olivia

At the end of 2010, Adrian, Mia, and I flew to Chicago. On separate days, each of us went to the US Attorney's office. When I walked in, there was a whole panel of DEA agents, Tom Shakeshaft, and assistant US Attorney Mike Ferrara. I looked at them sitting there, and fear shot through me. All I could think was, *Oh my God. I know I've got immunity, but what if I say something wrong?* Then I realized what I had to do: just tell them the truth, like my husband and Peter had, twelve hours a day, five days a week, for the almost six months they'd been at MCC Chicago.

"What happened the day your husbands turned themselves in?" one of the feds asked me after I sat down and got situated.

I looked at him with my eyes wide open. No one had ever asked me that, not even my husband. Adrian, Olivia, and I hadn't even talked about it. That whole traumatizing day had just laid there like a lump in my stomach since it happened. I sat for five seconds, thought about it, and immediately burst into tears.

I couldn't even talk. I felt so embarrassed; I just hadn't seen that question coming. When I finally pulled myself together, I went through everything: how and when we'd gotten the call from the DEA, saying that it was time for Peter and Junior to turn themselves in. How our husbands had had two hours to get to the Guadalajara airport. How I'd run around like a crazy woman taking down photos and video cameras. How we'd gotten a flat tire at the border.

We talked all day, and the feds peppered me with questions. Going through all the details of the last two years felt terrible, like I was living through every painful moment all over again. The agents listened carefully, never interrupting me, and when we finally finished up they only had one thing to say: "We want to know about the money you have."

Mia

The government wanted to know exactly where we got the money we'd been living on for two years, so Olivia and I sat with the feds and proffered. Then we had to account for every penny, showing exactly what we spent it on.

Olivia

Once the feds knew how much money we had, they ordered us to give it up.

Mia and I flew to Chicago and bought a few Tupperware bins—you know, the kind you put your winter clothes in, then stack up in the basement—and drove to my house in the suburbs. We pulled out each and every stack of bills we had stashed in my theater room and piled them into the Tupperware, probably ten or twelve bins. We carried them to my big Audi Q7 truck, put the backseats down, and loaded all the bins into it. They were stacked to the roof, so high you couldn't even see out the windows. As I started driving, I was so nervous. I thought to myself, *If we get pulled over and the cops catch us with Tupperware containers full of money, they're going to confiscate it before we even get a chance to hand it over to the feds.*

Then we called Junior's lawyer, David.

"Come meet us at my car," I said. "We'll be at your office parking garage in half an hour."

David had no idea what to expect, so he greeted us in the garage with a big smile on his face. Then he stepped back, saw the clear Tupperware in the back, and practically jumped out of his skin.

"What the hell am I supposed to do with all of those?"

"David," I said, "the government wants this money, and we can't live with it. Please take it."

David looked positively baffled. "What am I going to do, leave this in my office? I'm not going to be responsible for this."

"I'm sorry I put you in this position," I said, "but you're a smart guy, and I need you to figure it out."

He made a phone call to the feds, then said, "Let's get back in the car."

We drove to the bank on the corner, right near his office, and together, we deposited the cash into Junior's account. It would stay there till sentencing, when he and Peter would forfeit it. You should have seen the looks on the tellers' faces when we dragged those bins in. They were like, *What the fuck is going on here?*

Except for that one moment, the whole episode was frustrating, but pretty soon, I came to understand that the feds had just been doing their jobs. They had to do a thorough investigation, and they had to follow procedure. Even though my husband and brother-in-law might have been the most important cooperators in US history, that didn't mean they or we got free passes or any type of special privileges.

Mia

Almost immediately, Olivia and I actually felt great. We wanted to start a new life and have a clean slate, and that meant getting rid of everything. We needed to clear out all that dirty money and fancy stuff that had come from a criminal past. We'd been living with dirty money, and we wanted it gone. A part of us had been living in la-la land, with me driving around in a Bentley like it was just the way life was. It was time to fall off the cloud nine we'd been on in Mexico and accept reality.

CHAPTER 28

Arrests

Olivia

When Junior and Peter began cooperating, they started a chain reaction of indictments against the entire North American drug trafficking network. Early on, the dozens of players hauled in through raids on their stash houses and warehouses were low-level workers, mainly dealers and wholesalers. But by the end of 2009, the domino effect was in full force, and US Attorneys were reeling in bigger and bigger fish across the country.

Mia

The indictments weighed on Peter and Junior, and the whole time they were proffering, they tried to convince some of their associates and workers to turn themselves in. Peter told me that while the prosecutor and DEA agents were sitting right next to him listening in, he would practically beg his associates to cooperate. He'd say, "You're about to get caught, but you can save yourself. We can help you."

He didn't want them to go to jail because he genuinely cared about them and their families, and he knew they might face life sentences. But many refused. They were arrested and charged to the full extent of the law.

Unfortunately, that wasn't the worst that happened to many of them. In December 2010, Kiley Murray, a close friend and associate of Peter and Junior's, was shot to death while he was out on bond. Kiley had always lived large; he had a six-bedroom, six-bath mini-mansion about 150 miles west of Chicago, and his neighbors assumed he was a former NFL player when he moved in. In reality, he was helping Peter and Junior traffic drugs throughout Chicago, and he was eventually charged with conspiring to distribute cocaine and heroin. In this business, people will murder you out of fear you might snitch, and we assumed that was the case with Kiley.

I was the one who told Peter, and he took it so badly.

"Remember the first time you met him?" he asked me.

"Yeah, he was such a good friend to you and your brother. He lived like a celebrity. They didn't call him Hollywood for nothing."

"I was planning to ask his forgiveness next time I saw him. I wanted to say I was sorry and tell him I loved him. Now I'll never have that chance."

The whole time my husband was waiting for his plea agreement, from 2009 on, it was just like that, one arrest right after the other. Someone would be caught, and it would lie heavy in his heart. I'd be there to pick him up, but I knew he'd never fully shake off his guilt.

Olivia

But at the end of the day, their cooperation gave us protection. Just look at what happened with Saul Rodriguez.

Mia

If you can believe it, Saul was still out to get us.

Peter and Junior had a longtime courier named Sosa, who was like a brother to them. In the period of time my husband and brother-in-law were trying to convince him to turn himself in, Sosa heard through a friend that Saul was looking for Olivia because he wanted to kidnap her. Because Sosa had always been close to our family, he didn't want anything happening to her, so he decided to cooperate and told the feds about Saul's plot.

Olivia

Officials couldn't arrest Saul right away, though. In order to do so, they had to set him up. Peter and Junior came up with a plan.

Mia

The idea was for Sosa to start badmouthing Peter and Junior, then tell Saul that he knew where my husband and brother-in-law had stashed six hundred kilos. He knew that Saul wouldn't be able to resist getting his hands on it, so he tried to convince the DEA that this was the perfect way to nab Saul. It took a long time, but the feds finally went for it, and Sosa was willing to help out.

Sure enough, on April 9, 2009, Saul took the bait. The DEA filled up a blue cargo van with bricks of fake cocaine, parked it in front of a suburban Chicago warehouse, and had Sosa call Saul's associate and tell him the address.

"The key is in a Doritos bag inside a green garbage can," he said.

Five of Saul's guys showed up to rob the van, geared up in bulletproof vests, ski masks, and guns. They were busted by the feds, and all of them were sentenced to life, except for Saul.

Olivia

I can't tell you how happy I was that Saul got arrested. I don't wish prison on anyone, but I hated that guy. He was nothing but a thief who tortured and killed people for a living, and everything about him just made me sick.

In the scheme of things—and I mean the whole North American drug trade—Saul was nothing. Junior and Pete had their eyes on the prize, and they'd always imagined the government would go for people like Chapo and El Mayo and the BLO immediately. Not seeing them do that was frustrating.

Mia

After all, every other federal organization in Mexico seemed to be hard at work trying to dismantle the cartels. They'd even killed one of the big guns.

Olivia

On December 11, 2009, the Mexican Navy's elite special forces raided a Christmas party being thrown by Arturo Beltrán Leyva, and in an exchange of gunfire, four people were killed and Arturo fled. Five days later, on December 16, two hundred Mexican marines located him in a small town an hour north of Mexico City, raided his safe house, and in a ninety-minute firefight, killed him and five of his associates; one marine also died.

Mia

Then, one of the "good guys" decided to decorate Beltrán's bullet-ridden body with dollar bills, like some sick joke out of a gangster film, and photos flooded the internet. In retaliation, BLO members stormed a candlelight vigil for the dead marine and killed his mother, aunt, brother, and sister.

Olivia

Nothing so dramatic—so critical in stopping the drug trade—had happened between Mexico and America, though. Chapo, El Mayo, Vicente, and all the other suppliers were still at large, and the United States just seemed to be focusing on the little people in their conspiracy: the US-based distributors and dealers like Saul. Junior and Peter thought the DEA wasn't prepared for just how many players they'd arrest, and it drove them nuts.

"They're going backward," Junior would say. "We're giving them the biggest people in the world, the most wanted, and they're starting at the bottom of the ladder."

Then the feds got Vicente, and we all realized they actually *were* using the information our husbands were giving them.

Mia

Vicente was arrested in Mexico City on March 19, 2009, and charged with trafficking over a billion dollars' worth of cocaine and heroin.

Peter and Junior signed his extradition papers, and the most significant cartel member the United States had ever captured was transported to Chicago in February 2010.

Olivia

Vicente had never been your average drug lord. While most narco juniors drive around in Lambos, Ferraris, and Maseratis and dress themselves in designer clothes, red bottoms, and iced-out jewelry, Vicente seemed humble. He wasn't looking for everyone to cater to him. Instead, he was serious about his business, and that's why he'd become number three in the Sinaloa Cartel.

Junior got along with Vicente and talked to him pretty regularly. Vicente was charming and sophisticated almost all the time, but on occasion, Vicente displayed these really strange quirks. One of them was that he liked to blow shit up.

Once Junior went to visit Chapo in the mountains. Vicente was there, surrounded by a crowd of guys in military gear. It wasn't any big thing for cartel bosses to have militia with them, but Vicente liked to be around guys with hand grenades and AK-47s just a little bit more than most people. This time was no different.

Vicente turned to Junior and said, "Hey, look at that truck over there." He pointed toward a brand new pickup truck, with dealer plates and shiny leather seats.

"That's a nice truck," said Junior.

"It is," answered Vicente. "But watch this."

Vicente motioned for one of his guys, who then walked over with a rocket launcher in his hand.

"Ready. Aim. Fire!" Vicente yelled. Then Junior heard a huge *boom* and jumped back as the truck burst into flames.

I guess blowing shit up was just Vicente's thing.

Mia

Vicente was one of the last cartel members Junior caught on tape, so we figured that was why the feds jumped on his case faster than everyone else's. Maybe the trail of evidence was shorter, or possibly it was because Vicente was already feeding the US government information about rival cartels. Snitching like that wouldn't have been unusual, in fact; it's believed that the Sinaloa Cartel became so powerful because they would rat out other cartels' members, in an attempt to dismantle their organizations.

Olivia

Because of Vicente's position and all that our husbands had on him, Junior and Peter were going to have to testify against him.

Well before the trial date, Vicente hired a dream team of lawyers from New York City, who argued that the US government promised Vicente immunity in exchange for intel while he was in Mexico. In their minds—and his, too—he had carte blanche as long as he was feeding the government info.

Mia

As Vincente's trial approached in 2012, Junior and Peter's faces were plastered all over TV because they were the biggest witnesses against him, and his was one of the biggest drug cases ever to happen in a US court of law. Unfortunately, the proceedings kept getting delayed again and again.

Worried about the upcoming trial and the threats we'd been receiving, eight DEA agents drove up to my house in blacked-out minivans, Chevy Tahoes, and a working van so that they could sweep my home for bugs and tracking devices. They asked me to wait in the kitchen with my babies as they brought out these huge pieces of surveillance equipment that looked like something out of the movies. While they were sniffing around, I peeked out the window and saw two agents lying on plastic under my car, holding flashlights to search the undercarriage. When they were finished, they came inside and spoke to me.

"You should look under your car once a week," they said.

They hadn't found anything, but that didn't mean I never would.

Unfortunately, Olivia had suffered something worse, and her whole life was about to be turned upside down.

Olivia

Saul Rodriguez was an orderly at the Chicago MCC while Vicente was being held there, awaiting trial. Saul was allowed to move around freely, doing odd jobs around the center, and he befriended Vicente and gained his trust.

At the time, my first husband, Leo, was imprisoned there, too. Saul knew I'd been married to Leo, so he cozied up to him, trying to get information from him about where my parents lived. He knew that Vicente wanted to kill Peter and Junior, so Saul's brilliant plan was to sell this information to Vicente. He even went so far as to transfer $6,600 into Saul's lawyer's account for it.

Even though Leo snitched on me and sent me away to prison, I'm sure the last thing he wanted was to see the cartels kill me or my parents. In exchange for a sentence reduction, he talked to the feds, and prosecutors ripped up Saul's plea agreement for tampering with a federal witness. Saul's now serving forty years.

Unfortunately, Saul getting punished once again didn't ensure a happy ending. The feds took his threat so seriously that they relocated my parents from the home they'd lived in for twenty years. My innocent parents who had worked so hard to give me a decent life, and who had loved me unconditionally despite all I'd put them through, had to uproot their lives and move to another neighborhood, far from everything and everyone they knew. Junior and I felt horrible. My mom and dad didn't deserve to be affected by any of this, and Junior and I will forever live with guilt for the burden we put on them.

Mia

The dangers posed didn't end there. In fact, they only got worse.

Olivia

In August 2011, I had moved to the Midwest and was beginning to settle in. I'd just unpacked all our things and was trying to make my kids and myself feel at home.

One night I was looking out my window, which I do routinely, and I noticed a man sitting outside my house in a car, with a blue light shining up into his face. I realized right away he was staring at a computer.

What the hell? I wondered. *This can't be good.*

I immediately ran into the living room and unplugged my router, turned off all the lights, and lay down on the couch. Every hour or so for the rest of the night, I'd stand up in the pitch dark and walk to the window to peek out and see if the man was still there. Sure enough, all night long, he sat in his car on his computer, and all night long, I panicked, thinking, *This guy is going to kick in my door any minute and kill me and my children.*

The next morning, I didn't take my kids to school and refused to let them go outside to play. I crawled on my knees past my windows, standing up and crouching so I could peek out and try to get a visual of him. I started to write down his schedule, which didn't consist of much except him leaving for fifteen minutes or so every now and then. I just assumed he was driving to Walmart so he could go to the bathroom.

One of my neighbors called the cops, and they showed up while the guy was on one of his fifteen-minute pee breaks. When he returned, they questioned him, and the man drove off. Just before the police left, though, I walked out of my house, pretending to be a concerned citizen rather than the focus of the guy in the car, and cornered them.

"Did you find out who that man is?" I asked innocently.

"He's a private investigator working on a case," the officer said. "And we can't tell him to leave. He has every right to be here."

I walked back inside, defeated. I wanted more than anything to march up to his car, bang on his window, and tell him I knew exactly who he was working for. I wanted to get up in his face and scream, "You're working for the cartels, you fucking coward. How can you live with yourself knowing that your boss wants to kill me and my kids? I hope you rot in hell."

I called the feds, and they told me they were sending agents to investigate, but I needed to get my things and leave immediately.

That evening, I packed up my car in the garage, waited for the man to drive away, put my boys in their car seats, and drove to a hotel as fast as I could and never looked back. We lived there, in hell, for six months.

The three of us were crammed into a tiny room with two double beds. The hotel removed the desk and office chair, and I stacked up

Tupperware bins full of all of our possessions. One had teddy bears in it, another held toys, another had books, and the rest held clothes.

After we woke up in our little beds side by side, I'd open up the mini fridge, take out a half gallon of milk, and serve cereal. After breakfast, I'd put on Brandon's and Benjamin's backpacks, and we'd walk through the lobby, where the maids and front desk staff would wave at them and say, "Have a good day at school!" I'd drive them to school, go back to the hotel, lock my door, close the blinds, and sit in the dark all day.

But when it was time to pick the boys up, I always had a smile on my face. "This is so much fun! It's a mini vacation!" I'd say.

I don't know who I thought I was kidding. At night Brandon would cry that he just wanted to go home, and in the dark I would lie and cry silently so that he couldn't see or hear me. My breaking point was when I came back to the hotel after his kindergarten graduation, and he threw himself on the bed in a little ball and screamed, "I just want Dad!"

I wanted the exact same thing.

I started questioning whether or not cooperating was the right thing to do, wondering, *If this is hurting my kids and feels so wrong, how can it be right?*

I knew I was being selfish, but all I could think about was how much pain and suffering my family was going through. We did this for a normal life, but running for your life in the middle of the night was not normal.

After six months, the government finally relocated me to a different state. The US Attorney investigated who had hired the PI, but they weren't allowed to tell me their findings. Maybe I'll never know. All I can do is be thankful that no one killed me or my kids.

CHAPTER 29

Grand Jury and Plea Agreements

Mia

When Peter and Junior agreed to become informants and turn themselves in, they formally and legally admitted they were criminals. This acknowledgment didn't change during their years of proffering, although then, they were protected: anything they said couldn't be used against them in a court of law.

Olivia

In order to face indictments, they had to sit in front of a grand jury, which they did from December 2008 to June 2009, during their time at the Chicago MCC. Federal grand juries are typically larger than those in state courts—they can contain anywhere from sixteen to twenty-three jurors. In front of these average Chicago citizens, Junior and Peter were prepared to be 100 percent truthful, incriminate themselves, and tell on everyone they cared for. They knew they were going to be charged, but for what was still in question. That would depend on the grand jury testimony and the government's thorough investigation to make sure all that they'd said was true.

Mia

Peter and Junior had to go in front of a grand jury maybe a dozen times, and it was one of the hardest things they'd endured in the whole course of their cooperation. Standing before the grand jury, they had to

read out every criminal act they'd committed while they ran their organization. Every single terrible thing.

It made Peter feel awful. He didn't even want me to read his sworn
statements, let alone his kids one day in the future.

"I'm so ashamed," he told me on one Sunday visit. "When I turned
myself in, I wasn't proud of what I'd done, but at the time, I thought I
should be forgiven. Now, I'm not sure anyone should ever forgive me."

Olivia

Junior was so nervous before his first grand jury appearance, but he wasn't
the only person on edge. The whole thing was such a big deal that before he
and Peter walked in, officials cleared the entire court. Even the parking lot
was empty. When they walked in, Thomas Shakeshaft was sweating pro-
fusely. Apparently it was a big day for everyone, even the US Attorney.

Mia

The moment Peter stood in front of the grand jury and stated his
name, all those people staring at him in disbelief made him feel humiliated. In the drug world, he felt normal, even respected. Out there in the
open in a court of law, he felt so vulnerable, like such a criminal, that it
was hard for him to think straight.

Olivia

Tom Shakeshaft broke down their whole case, walking the jury through
everything: from the very first day they started, when they sold their first
thirty kilos, to their peak, when they had a $2 billion empire. Then, he let
the grand jury ask Junior and Peter questions. Pretty soon, the talk turned
personal; everyone was so intrigued with them.

Mia

At one point, someone on the grand jury stopped in the middle of his
inquiry, stared at them, and said, "Are you guys going to write a book or
make a movie?"

Olivia

Finally, the grand jury considered the testimony, read all the evidence, and handed over the indictments in August 2009. When Mia and I first read them, we were overwhelmed.

"This is a lot to take in," I said to Mia.

"Yeah," she answered. "Reading everything Junior and Peter did on paper is different than living it every day."

Mia

Those indictments were hard pills to swallow. Junior and Peter had always wanted to protect us, so in a lot of ways, we'd been shielded from the whole truth of what they did. They never wanted us to worry, so in Mexico, they made our lives feel almost normal.

Still, we didn't feel lied to, and we certainly weren't mad at them. Sure, we were disturbed to see everything in print, but we knew that Peter and Junior changing their lives had all been done for us and our children. They'd become the men they promised us they'd be and that we always knew they were.

Olivia

After the indictments were handed over, the US Attorneys and Peter's and Junior's lawyers set to work on a plea agreement.

Plea bargains are essentially contracts that are governed by layers upon layers of statutes, rules, guidelines, Department of Justice policies, and case law. In their plea agreements, Junior and Peter would accept all that they'd been charged with. They'd take responsibility for the distribution, the manufacturing, the trafficking, you name it. Then, they'd agree to a range of years that the judge might sentence them to—and it could be five years or five times that.

Sounds straightforward, right? It was actually a living hell. It was this complicated, painful process that began June 2012, four long years after they left Mexico, and took two months.

Mia

Over that whole summer, people were angry, and I don't just mean at each other; they were angry at *us*. The US Attorneys went back and forth with our lawyers, then our lawyers went back and forth with Peter and Junior. Both sides were eager to settle, and because of that, our lawyers pressured Junior and Peter.

"Do you know how many kilos of cocaine you sent into the United States?" one of them once asked.

"Yes, why?" Peter asked.

"Because it was so much that most people would get life in prison. You need to sign this plea agreement. Stop fucking playing games."

Peter was pissed. "Why are you scolding us? You're our lawyers. You're supposed to be on our side."

Peter and Junior loved their lawyers, and so did we. They'd slaved away for them. Joe, especially, had been on their side since way before they were on the international stage. Junior and Peter never lost sight of that. But everyone in a situation like theirs wants the best deal. Of course they were going to fight.

Olivia

I was making calls to David and Joe and his legal team day in and day out, and after weeks of endless conversations they began to get really frustrated with me. We weren't seeing eye to eye. They were advising us, pleading with Peter and Junior to sign, and we were giving them every reason why they shouldn't. It became a nonstop screaming match.

Things got so bad that our lawyers grew tired of explaining themselves to me. I stopped getting straight responses, and sometimes I'd just get a one-word answer, which is almost as bad as no answer at all.

Mia

I'd have to pass messages from our lawyers to Peter, then relay his questions back to them because in prison, you don't get special privileges to call your lawyer whenever you want. It has to be a matter of life and death. All this back and forth every day felt endless. There were so many calls I started to get dizzy every time the phone rang.

Olivia

Our lawyers wanted Peter and Junior to sign a plea agreement for ten to sixteen years, but I couldn't comprehend why they should settle for that. I thought they didn't deserve a day more than ten years after everything they'd done. They'd jeopardized their lives when they worked undercover in Mexico. They'd given the government every major player in the cartels on a silver platter. On top of that, they'd voluntarily turned themselves in to serve their time and pay for their crimes. Theirs was the biggest case that had ever touched the Chicago office. Bigger than Al Fucking Capone.

Plus, their intentions had always been good, light years more honest than anyone else in the drug trade. I tried to spell this out to our lawyers.

"In this business, many men use their money and power to hurt and kill people," I said. "Our husbands have been robbed, kidnapped, and almost left for dead, and not once have they gone out for revenge or been violent. Doesn't that count for something?"

Apparently, it didn't. I knew there were hitmen for the mob, with bodies stacked up and hidden away, who had been offered better deals for cooperating. These guys were in and out of jail in less than ten years.

I guess that shit only happens in New York City, I thought.

Mia

When things didn't go our way, we assumed the worst: that the government didn't need our husbands as much anymore since Vicente was now cooperating.

Whatever was going through their minds, the US Attorneys were playing hardball, not budging one inch. They were offering Junior and Peter ten to sixteen years, and that was just what it was going to be.

After two months, Peter finally decided to sign his plea agreement. He did so the day before Junior did, and then he appeared in front of the federal judge.

Olivia

Unlike civil and criminal cases in state and county courts, federal courts don't use juries to approve plea agreements and determine sentences. Instead, there's one appointed official who reviews them and later decides how many days, weeks, or years a defendant gets. In Junior and Peter's case, the judge who was going to decide their fate was the chief judge for the United States Court of the Northern District of Illinois, Ruben Castillo.

Mia

Like Peter and Junior, Judge Castillo had done better than his parents. He'd been born in Chicago to a Puerto Rican mom and a Mexican dad and was the first member of his family to go to college. When he was appointed by Bill Clinton to the US District Court in 1994, he was the first Latino federal judge in the state of Illinois. Castillo had grown up in a tough neighborhood, and many of his friends ended up in prison.

Olivia

In a lot of ways, he and our husbands were two sides of the same coin. But while one had gone to law school and risen to the highest ranks of his profession, the others had run the most lucrative drug operation in the United States. We all knew that growing up in a bad neighborhood is very different than being raised in a home where you're trained to sell drugs, but still, we all wondered: *Is what makes them similar and different going to make him sympathetic, or repel him?*

Mia

When Peter walked into the courtroom, Judge Castillo was sitting in his oversized chair, front and center, way up high, looking like he was playing God. The courtroom is built to make you feel intimidated, but Peter was experiencing that and more.

"I was humiliated," Peter said. "But I was ready to apologize. I couldn't believe the destruction I'd caused in my life and the lives of others."

I wasn't there, but Peter told me that while Judge Castillo read out his charges, he'd never felt sorrier about anything. He wanted to denounce his whole life right then and there.

"Still, I wished I could tell the judge one good thing about myself," he told me.

But he knew he was fooling himself. The time for defending himself was over; he had to be man enough to stand in front of a judge, feel intense remorse, and accept his fate.

Olivia

Junior couldn't imagine being alone, in jail, for sixteen years. Our babies and Samantha and Sasha were growing up without him, and the six-year difference he was fighting for determined whether he'd be home before Brandon graduated from high school. He might even miss his girls' college graduations. Junior and I love each other enough to get through anything, but it's our kids we worry the most about, and we knew that a few years makes a huge difference in a young child's life.

So when our lawyer, David, called me one evening and pleaded with me not to let Junior make the biggest mistake of his life, I didn't know what to think. *Do I fight, like I always have, or do we just accept it?* If there's anything I've learned in my marriage, it's to trust my husband 100 percent, and so I decided to agree with Junior, whatever he wanted to do.

Junior fought to the very last day, right up until the minute the US Marshals flew him to Chicago. When he landed, Tom Shakeshaft and David were there to greet him.

"Peter already signed the papers, Junior," David said.

The US Attorney added, "And if you don't sign them, too, it's possible the judge will rip up the plea agreement, and you'll be looking at life."

Junior was shocked and hurt, and he knew he was backed up against the wall. He and his twin brother had always been on the same page, but Peter had gone ahead and signed the papers without telling him.

Why the hell did my brother do that? he thought to himself. *Now I don't have two legs to stand on.*

Deep down, he realized what had really happened. Peter hadn't done anything wrong, and he'd never meant to catch Junior short. It had just been too hard trying to negotiate through their attorneys. For the first real time in their lives, at such a critical moment, they hadn't been able to communicate. They hadn't been able to read each other's minds.

As Junior signed his plea agreement, minutes before going in front of the judge, tears fell from his eyes. In a room full of men, all of whom were staring at him at his most vulnerable moment, he felt degraded. Worse, he worried that he was giving up, that he was letting me down.

Then, as he stood before Judge Castillo, who was draped in a big, black cloak, with the United States of America emblem behind him and the stars and stripes beside him, Junior felt the power of the court. When Judge Castillo read him his charges, he fully understood the severity of his crimes and the harm he'd done to society, and he realized: *I'm ashamed of the damage that I've caused, and I'm ready to pay for my crimes. It's the right thing to do.*

Judge Castillo pulled his glasses down and said, "Mr. Flores, do you understand everything that you're admitting to?"

"Yes, Your Honor," he answered. Suddenly, he knew he'd done the right thing, and later, he told me as much.

"Liv, we've been living in this bubble. I can't believe everything we did; it sounded so bad. I can't believe I fought with my attorneys and almost lost my deal. I could have spent the rest of my life in prison. I'm so grateful I got the plea agreement I did. I realize now how severe my case was."

"We're going to get through this. I'm proud of you," I said. Then I added, "How are you feeling?"

"Relieved."

He looked it. Right then and there, I knew our attorneys had been right, and I felt bad for second-guessing them and giving them such a hard time. They'd had his best interests at heart, and I'd just been so passionate, so determined to have my children grow up with their dad. We'd risked our lives, after all, and our husbands were going to have years and years in prison to think about it.

CHAPTER 30

Sentencing

Olivia

Sentencing was scheduled for Tuesday, January 27, 2015, and getting to that day had taken forever. We'd waited over two years since Junior and Peter had signed their plea agreement.

Mia

Over all that time, the government had had to make sure all testimony that Junior and Peter had given them was fact, and they had to corroborate their testimony with other witnesses. They weren't in a hurry; on a case this big, they *had* to do things right.

Olivia

But for two years, we all hung in the balance, and we were worried about so many things. One of them was the judge.

Mia

Judge Castillo had served on something called the Federal Sentencing Commission, which was a committee that outlined the levels that determine sentences for federal crimes. We were so afraid of him because, clearly, having been on that committee, he believed in the federal guidelines, and he was there to enforce them.

Olivia

Federal crimes go up to level 43, weighing what your crime is with your criminal history. Given all that they'd done, Junior and Peter were off the charts. They would have been looking at life if they hadn't cooperated.

But here's the thing. The judge could throw out the plea agreement and sentence them to whatever he thought was best; 99.9 percent of the time the judge would go with the US Attorney's recommendation, but there was still that 0.1 percent chance he might go with something else entirely.

Mia

The other issue at hand concerned something called a 5K.1.1 motion, which the US Attorney had recently filed. A 5K.1.1 asks the judge to consider a defendant's "substantial assistance to authorities" when he hands down a sentence. The US Attorney had practically gushed about Peter and Junior when he wrote his recommendations, saying they "voluntarily broke away from their positions in the highest echelons of the cartel world to transform themselves into extraordinary witnesses." Then he made clear that they were the biggest drug informants in US history, having done more to dismantle the drug trade than anyone, and he and the other prosecutors hoped Judge Castillo would reduce the sentence to something at or near the low end of the ten to sixteen years outlined in the plea agreements.

In the weeks leading up to sentencing I was really counting on the 5K.1.1 motion the US Attorney had filed. I mean, I wasn't ignoring the fact that everything was ultimately up to the judge, but Peter and I thought things might swing in their favor.

Besides, I thought, *If they don't deserve the ten years, then who does?* They were fully committed to cooperation from start to finish, and without a doubt never lost sight of the reason why they did this in the first place. They'd risked their lives and the lives of the people they loved the most. They set the bar high when it came to cooperation, and were a great example of people who truly wanted to change. Not just that, but their case was the biggest drug conspiracy case in US history.

Olivia

After Junior and Peter risked their lives in Mexico, and after everyone they'd helped bring in, I believed passionately that they shouldn't do a day more than ten years. Junior's lawyer had been reluctant to agree with me because he didn't want to piss off Judge Castillo, so before sentencing, I hired a new lawyer from New York to come in with a fresh set of eyes. I thought Jim, the new attorney, might push for ten, but instead, he did the opposite.

"I think you should accept the fact that they might get sixteen," he said. "It's as simple as that."

It wasn't what I wanted to hear, so even though it hurt, it was the reality of things. Suddenly, I saw the big picture, and by the time sentencing day rolled around, I was prepared for the worst and hoping for the best.

Mia

I couldn't believe it when sentencing day finally arrived. This was it. Everything we'd done and gone through together was going to come to an end in just a few hours. Everything depended on one man who had my future and the future of my children in his hands. His decision was going to determine my happiness.

Peter was trusting someone else, too. Just before sentencing, he said, "I'm leaving it up to God to decide our fates. It's all up to him."

Olivia

That day I had such mixed emotions. I was so eager to know Junior's future, but I was terrified about the outcome. I lay on my bed, staring up at the ceiling, feeling paralyzed. Deep down, though, I kept thinking, *Junior and I love each other so much that we can withstand anything. Our relationship is rock solid, so whatever the judge decides won't break us.* But most of all, it was our children I was stressed about.

Mia

It snowed a lot on January 27, so Bella and Blake were home from school. I hadn't said a thing to them about what was happening, but I think they knew something was up; they'd been following me around the house all day, almost obsessively. I'd been giving them tons of hugs and kisses, but it hadn't helped. I'd basically barricaded myself in my room to clear my head and pray, when I heard a knock on the door.

"Mommy, can we play Chutes and Ladders with you?" asked Bella.

"Sure, baby, sure," I answered, relieved someone was taking sentencing off my mind. "Whatever you need."

Olivia

We all felt so vulnerable because of our kids. Brandon and Benjamin had been babies when Junior turned himself in, doing the right thing so our children would have a better future. But here was the irony: they were growing up without seeing their father every day. In doing "the right thing," we'd ended up hurting them.

It got worse before sentencing, too; I was so stressed that I'd had trouble even focusing on my boys. I wasn't present *at all*. I was constantly upset, Junior was always sad, and my poor babies kept asking for their daddy to come home. I knew it was taking a toll on Brandon, especially. He cried when we left our visits, he cried before he went to bed, and he even cried in the shower, for God's sake. So I took him to a child psychologist. I didn't go into the extent of our situation, like what Junior had done, but I told her my husband was in prison.

After a few months of sessions, she and I met separately, and she reassured me.

"You and your husband are doing the best you can. You're good parents," she said.

"But my boys are a wreck," I pleaded. "All they want is for their dad to come home. I'm a protector, and I feel like I've let Brandon down through all of this."

She looked at me and got really serious. "There are fathers who are so consumed by work and don't give their children the undivided attention they need. One day your husband will come home, but for right now your kids have 100 percent of Junior every single weekend. He's a great dad, and you're both doing the right thing for them. When they're grown up, that's what they're going to remember."

Right then, I decided: *Whatever Junior's sentence is going to be, it's not going to change us as a family. We've sacrificed more than most, and that's made us closer.*

Still, my heart just ached for Junior to come home sooner rather than later.

Mia

The day of sentencing, Peter and Junior were everywhere on the news. They even started trending on Yahoo. The TV broadcasts kept flashing a photo of them when they were sixteen, and suddenly, Peter became that teenager I met a million years ago. I started to remember being in my early twenties, so crazy about him, and how he always left a rose on my front doorstep, or how he'd call me at work just to brighten up my day.

I wanted so badly to be with him, but I couldn't. Our lawyers had told us not to come, that it was far too dangerous. So on the most important day of our lives, instead of holding my husband's hand, I was home playing Chutes and Ladders.

I'd even called my lawyer that morning. "I'll go to the court in a wig. I'll disguise myself. I just need him to know he's not alone."

"No," he said. "This is open to the public. You think people aren't going to try to find out if his wife is there? If I see you there, I'll drag you out myself."

Olivia

That morning, Mia and I called each other every hour.

"I've heard nothing," I'd say. "Have you?"

"No," she'd answer. "But the lawyer promises he'll call me."

Mia

I finally unplugged the TV just to be sure I wouldn't find out that way. I needed a real, live person to talk to when their sentences were announced.

Then, just before lunch, I start getting texts from my family, one after the other after the other.

"Are you okay?"

"Did you hear?"

"I'm praying for you."

Oh God, I thought. *I hope it's not bad news.*

Then my phone rang, and it was Olivia. Her lawyer had just told her everything.

Olivia

From the minute they sat at our kitchen table in Guadalajara and decided to become informants to the day they walked into court to find out their fates, Junior and Peter had never stopped helping the government. In fact, the morning of sentencing, they'd had a meeting with the feds to discuss yet another superseding indictment out of San Diego: the extradition of El Mayo's sons, Mayito Gordo and Mayito Flaco. They signed those papers, followed by papers for La Puerca's sister.

Mia

Then, they walked into Judge Castillo's courtroom, sporting beige prison uniforms and buzz cuts, and were greeted by the US Attorneys and their assigned DEA agents, who'd flown in because they were now stationed in different parts of the country. Peter and Junior hadn't laid eyes on each other in almost five years, and they hugged and cried when they met. They hadn't expected to be reunited until they came home from prison.

Olivia

It was a media frenzy, but who stood out were a few Mexican women sitting in the first row, their eyes burning holes in the backs of the twins' heads. Peter and Junior assumed they were related to some of the people that they'd cooperated against, but they never turned around.

Mia

The US Attorneys started by giving a full account of Peter and Junior's crimes and cooperation—from the minimum of sixty tons of cocaine they'd trafficked into Chicago over the years to the fact that their cooperation was "unparalleled" in the city's history and resulted in dozens of national and international arrests and convictions. While the attorneys made a point of saying that their cooperation wasn't 100 percent perfect, calling particular attention to the 276 kilograms of cocaine they'd trafficked without telling the government and the fact that they'd arranged for the pickup of drug proceeds, they still showered them with praise.

Olivia

"They cooperated at the height of their criminal enterprise," said US Attorney Michael James Ferrara, who'd replaced Tom Shakeshaft after he stepped down. "These two defendants are the most valuable cooperators this district has ever seen in the context of a drug case, and as well, Your Honor, in the context of international money laundering related to drug-trafficking charges." Then he gave specifics, saying, "A massive criminal enterprise used to exist here in Chicago…it no longer exists, and they are directly responsible for that."

Mia

He concluded by asking the judge for a sentence at or near the low end of the plea agreement, concluding ten years would be best because their cooperation had been "unprecedented, extraordinary, historic, incomprehensible," words hardly ever used in a federal court room by a US Attorney. A man who'd spent almost seven years working tirelessly to prosecute Peter and Junior practically begged the judge to go easy on them.

Olivia

Next, Junior and Peter addressed Judge Castillo, each taking turns. Junior went first, followed by Peter. Choking up, they both took full responsibility for their crimes, for the damage they'd caused, and for putting their families in harm's way. "I know my actions deserve the greatest punishment," said Peter, "and I'm grateful that the government has asked you to consider my work as a cooperator."

Mia

Then it was Judge Castillo's turn to speak.

"I think growing up in Chicago under different circumstances, both of you gentlemen probably would have accomplished a great deal if you had been law abiding because there's a lot of things you are, but stupid is not one of them." Calling them "the most significant drug dealers that I've had to sentence in twenty years on the bench, and that's saying a lot," he didn't skirt the fact that their crimes were "devastating" and "horrific."

Then Judge Castillo paused and removed his glasses, looking them in the eyes. Sounding as stern as you'd expect of a judge who'd gotten as far as he had, he pointed out that their cooperation was imperfect and cited the 276 kilograms they'd trafficked without telling the feds. He admitted that while it was terrible they'd lost their father because of their cooperation, tens of thousands of others had lost their lives because of drugs. Because of *their* drugs.

Olivia

Then, the judge gave them fourteen years and ordered them to forfeit more than $3.5 million dollars. He said he would have given them twelve years, closer to what the US Attorney had recommended, if they hadn't trafficked the 276 kilos.

The 276 kilos that had probably saved us our lives.

My lawyer sent me a freakin' text message with the news. When I called Mia right away, she lost it. When I say she lost it, I mean all you could hear was her scream and fall to the floor.

Mia

I was devastated. I kept thinking to myself, *This is not what we planned. This is not what we did everything for. Fourteen years is not what we risked our lives for.*

Olivia

For one of the first times in my life, I shut my mouth and listened to Mia sobbing. I didn't say a thing.

In my mind, though, I was thinking, *What are you upset about? Have you not been listening to me?* I'd spent the last seven years fighting with Peter's lawyer, obsessively calling Junior's lawyer, spending money on a fancy Manhattan lawyer, and even picking lawyers up at the airport to drive them to Junior's prison. All those miles and hours and money, and they'd all told me the same thing: "Junior and Peter might get sixteen years."

Yet Mia and Peter had acted like it was a given that they were going to get ten years. At one point, Mia had even said, "I think they'll get time served."

I'd shot back, "You're out of your mind! They're going to get sixteen years because the attorney I hired from New York is sure of it. We really have to listen to what these attorneys are telling us. Mia, I want ten years just as much as you do, but I'm just trying to prepare you so you don't fall apart if the worst happens. We've been consumed by this for too long, and we've been thinking with our hearts and not with our heads. We have to be logical."

She wouldn't even discuss it. "No, that new lawyer is full of shit. They're going to get ten."

Anytime I'd talk to Mia I wanted to shake her. I felt like she was living in the Twilight Zone. All I could think was, *What planet are you living on? What are you telling my brother-in-law? What is he telling you?*

But on the phone that day, I shut my trap. I was done arguing, and I knew we just needed to be close. We were all we had in the world, on this little island together, just the two of us. No matter how differently we felt about sentencing or how we were dealing with it, all we could do was hold hands and get through this mess together.

Mia

The hardest part that day was pulling myself together so I could tell Peter's daughter, Sophia. I knew she was waiting for good news, and I wasn't sure how to break just the opposite to her.

I decided all I could do was be honest, then encouraging. "We love you, sweetie," I said. "Please be strong; this will be over soon."

When Peter's lawyer called me later that afternoon, I realized how much I needed that kind of pep talk myself.

"I'm not going to give up," he said.

"What?" I asked. I was genuinely confused; I felt so defeated I'd crawled into bed and expected I'd stay there for days.

"I mean I'm going to keep fighting. There's still hope. But you just keep supporting him. It's all you can do. Be the wife you've always been, that he needs you to be."

He was right, and it was as true then as it is now: being a good partner is the best I can do. Peter's done it for me, and I'll do it for him.

When Peter called me the next day—literally the first minute he could get to the phone—we couldn't even speak. We just sat on the phone together and cried, feeling the exact same pain. For the first time we couldn't hold each other up. We both felt so helpless that I started to wonder if my lawyer was all wrong. *Maybe there isn't any hope?* I worried. Then I managed to choke a few words out.

"I love you so much, Peter. Everything is going to be okay."

"I love you, too," he said. "And I'm sorry I let you down."

"You didn't," I said. "I will *always* be proud of you."

Even as Junior and Peter have gone off to serve their sentences, Olivia and I have never stopped feeling honored by what our husbands did. Especially now, when we've seen their cooperation rewarded in the biggest ways possible.

CHAPTER 31

Bringing Down El Chapo

Olivia

When Judge Castillo sentenced Junior and Peter, he acknowledged the risks they'd taken, recognizing that even though they were getting fourteen years, they were actually leaving with life sentences. He said, "You and your family members...will always have to look over your shoulders and wonder every time you're outside in a vehicle and you see a motorcycle come up behind you...if that is the motorcycle that is going to take your life."

Mia

At the time, those words were cold comfort to me. But now, I realize that he wasn't just stating the obvious: that what Peter and Junior had done was nothing short of putting their lives on the line. He was also recognizing our husbands—and by extension, us—as people, not criminals.

Olivia

He, as much as anyone, realized that we'd all be living the rest of our lives in grave danger. And because of that, Junior and Peter were going to be taken away to two of the most secure prisons in the country.

Mia

Under the umbrella of the Federal Bureau of Prisons there's a little-known initiative called the Witness Security Program. Created in 1970 to protect informants who testify against drug traffickers, terrorists, members of organized crime, and other major criminals, it now serves only five hundred inmates, which is less than one half of one percent of the US prison population.

Because they're typically involved in ongoing federal investigations, these inmates are safeguarded with the highest levels of security and are kept at prisons off the radar. If there's even the slightest risk to them—whether from the outside or the inside—they're relocated to another prison immediately. Their identities are secret, their families are typically in hiding—as we'd be—and when they're released, they enter the Witness Protection Program and are protected by the US Marshals.

Olivia

When Junior and Peter left sentencing, they were taken almost immediately to these separate federal prisons to serve their fourteen-year sentences. For six of those years, however, they were credited for the time they served, meaning they'd see an additional eight years behind bars.

Right now, they live with former mob bosses, drug traffickers, hitmen, and kidnappers. They're surrounded by organized criminals, so in many ways, it's not that different than the life they'd lived before, except that each of these men is now a federal witness.

Mia

Their cooperation didn't stop when they went to jail, either. They've kept working with the feds and signing extradition papers, leading to the arrest and extradition of cartel members including Mayito Flaco, Mayito Gordo, Felipe "El Ingeniero" Cabrera Sarabia, Alfredo Vásquez-Hernández (aka Alfredo Compandre), Tomas Arevalo-Renteria, La Puerca, La Puerca's sister Guadalupe "La Patrona" Fernández-Valencia, and El Mencho.

Junior even almost testified in one of the drug trade's biggest cases: Mochomo's scheduled trial in February 2016.

Olivia

Before the trial date, the US Attorney from DC visited Junior with Mike Ferrara because they wanted my husband to be one of the main witnesses. There were several other witnesses, but the difference was that Junior's a US citizen, and not only does he speak English, but he actually trafficked 1,800 kilos of cocaine he received from Mochomo into Washington, DC. With Junior on the stand, jurors were going to be astounded how close the cartel boss's drugs hit home.

I did *not* want my husband to testify, and I told him as much.

"Somebody might kill us all," I said.

He took me seriously, but he was firm. "Liv," he said, "they might reduce my sentence because of my testimony. A few more years home with our children could make a world of difference for them."

That was just like Junior; there's nothing he wouldn't risk just to be there for his children.

My worst fears came true before the trial, though: the witness list was leaked, and the family members of two cooperating witnesses were killed. One was the wife of Chino Anthrax, one of Chapo's main hitmen, and the other was Rey Zambada, El Mayo's brother's son. Granted, these murders both happened in Mexico, but I knew the cartels could easily cross the border, so I didn't feel safe.

Still, nothing could change Junior's mind about testifying. He was determined, and the US Attorneys from DC and Chicago even debriefed him to get him ready for the stand.

It never happened, though. The morning of the trial, Mochomo's attorneys learned that Junior was on the new witness list. We suspect he looked at his name and realized his case was sunk, that it was a slam dunk for the prosecution, so Mochomo pleaded out at the end of February 2016.

Mia

Olivia called me in April 2016 to tell me about a murder case she'd just seen on the news. She said eight members of an Ohio family had been found shot, execution style, at their rural home. The hitmen left three young children, including a four-day-old, alive, but the rest were pretty much slaughtered. Authorities found hundreds of illegal marijuana plants around the property, and a link to a Mexican cartel was suspected.

"That poor family." she said. "This is a nightmare."

"Yes," I said, "And we can't let it happen to us."

Still, this is our life, and it's a real possibility, especially with the extradition of Joaquín Guzmán Loera, aka El Chapo, the most wanted man in the world.

Olivia

During the first couple of years Junior was in prison, he'd sometimes get really serious, look at me, and say, "They're going to find Chapo."

"There's no way," I'd tell him. "He's too well hidden, too powerful."

Year after year, though, Junior insisted that would change. He'd say it to me, the feds, and his lawyers. Nobody believed him, and they'd laugh and say it would never happen. After a while, everyone was so sick of hearing him, they'd all tell him at the same time, "Shut the fuck up!"

Mia

Chapo had always been a ghost to me. When we were in Mexico I'd overhear conversations between him and my husband and Junior, but I'd never met him. All I knew was that he played a huge part in their business, and every conversation with him was full of personality and ended really pleasantly. If he was just some voice way off in the distance to me, I imagined he was phantom-like to the world as well. There was no way anyone would ever haul him in.

Olivia

But, sure enough, on February 22, 2014, it happened: El Chapo was captured by Mexican police at a beachfront hotel in Mazatlán.

When Mia and I found out, you could have picked our jaws up off the floor. We knew it was almost unbelievable, but in this crazy life of ours, anything was possible.

When the news settled in, though, the whole thing became nerve-wracking. I went to visit Junior that weekend, and we were sitting in the visiting room watching TV. Chapo was on every channel, with Junior and Peter's faces plastered next to his. Every time the guard changed the channel, whether it was the Spanish channel or CNN or whatever, you'd see the same thing.

It was terrifying, and as I held hands with Junior, trembling, I started to think once again, *My life has been hell since the night we sat at the kitchen table and decided to cooperate. And it's never-ending. Was this really worth all this stress and heartache?*

Mia

Then on July 11, 2015, El Chapo escaped, like Houdini himself, from his prison cell through a mile-long tunnel that had been burrowed underneath his shower stall and led to a nearby house. I was visiting Peter in prison the next day, which was a Sunday, when a prison security guard walked up to the table where we were playing a game with our kids.

"I'm sorry," he said, "I'm going to have to cancel your visit."

"Why?" Peter asked, shocked. This hadn't happened in years.

"Chapo was captured. We have to lock you up for security. And we're worried prisoners are going to start rioting."

My heart dropped. I kissed Peter goodbye and was escorted out of the prison, and as soon as I felt the cold air against my skin, I felt lost. Sure enough, that fear of the unknown that had haunted me for years crept up once again.

I didn't talk to Peter for almost a week, but I saw his face everywhere on the news, and it was heartbreaking. All I could think was, *I want more than anything to talk to him about this,* but I just couldn't. Then I'd call his lawyer, who was encouraging and said lots of helpful things, but he still didn't know what would come out of this situation.

Olivia

I called my lawyer, too, and he mentioned that Junior and Peter were going to have to testify against El Chapo.

"Because of that, it may be time for you to go into the Witness Protection Program," he said.

That was the last thing Mia and I wanted to do with Junior and Peter still locked up, so I wasn't convinced.

"If we do that, there's no guarantee we'll be close to them," I said.

"It might be smart," he answered.

For the first time ever, I was starting to get a bad feeling that he might be right.

Mia

Safety is always a concern for us. Olivia and I each have dozens of email addresses—one for our kids' teachers, one for our families, one for corresponding with each other about this book. When we call the cable company to report a problem, we have to remember which phone number we've given them. We even hire private investigators every few months to make sure there's no trace of us out there.

In the weeks after Chapo escaped, Junior and Peter were all over the news, witnesses started coming out of the woodwork, and word about the case spread. People started playing songs called "Narco Corridos," describing what the cartels would do to Junior and Peter if they found them. On blogs people began threatening our families. Average Joes who hadn't known who Chapo was for most of their lives wore shirts and hats with his face on it, and people dressed up like him for Halloween. I was disgusted. I couldn't believe people were looking at the most dangerous man in the world—one who'd killed an obscene amount of people, many of them innocent—as a celebrity.

Needless to say, all of this put Olivia and me at huge risk. In 2014, we felt more exposed than we'd ever been.

Olivia

El Chapo was in a Mexican prison for most of 2014. I've been to jail in Mexico, and believe me, it's different than in the United States. Someone like El Chapo could have anything he wanted. Money, his business, even women. In Guadalajara, we used to live near a drug kingpin named

Caro Quintero, and our neighbors said he'd come home from prison to his mansion on the weekends.

Mia and I knew people were going to help El Chapo while he was locked up, and that's why we weren't at all surprised when he escaped.

Mia

El Chapo got out through a hole in the shower floor of his prison on a Friday morning in the middle of July 2015. That weekend, Olivia and her kids were in town to visit me and Peter, and at first we all thought it was a hoax.

Then, once again, we started seeing Junior and Peter's faces all over the news channels, and our lives became a big three-ring circus.

Olivia

Everyone started calling us. My family called, hysterical, and said, "What are you going to do? He's out there!"

"We'll be fine," I said. "We've been living this life for so long. We've been keeping ourselves safe for years and years."

I always like to sugarcoat everything for my family, so I didn't want anyone to worry about us, but the truth was, we were terrified. El Chapo had all the discovery of what exactly our husbands had said throughout their cooperation. In the drug world, betrayal is the ultimate death sentence, and we were literally driving ourselves crazy just thinking about it. It's like we became prisoners in our own minds.

Mia

We didn't stop feeling that way until the Mexican Navy's special forces captured him in northwest Sinaloa on January 8, 2016, just over six months later.

Soon after that, Peter and Junior signed his extradition papers, which was so nerve-wracking. I kept thinking *When Chapo's lawyers receive them and see Junior's and Peter's signatures, he's going to lose it.* The damage was done, and we all waited nervously.

Olivia

Just over a year later, on January 19, 2017, El Chapo was extradited to the United States. The next day, he pleaded not guilty to seventeen indictments, and he's now in solitary at the Manhattan Metropolitan Correctional Center.

If El Chapo stands trial, Junior and Peter will serve as the star witnesses against him, and their conversations on tape will serve as the damning evidence needed to convict him to the full extent of the law.

Mia

Because of that, Liv and I thought long and hard about going into the Witness Protection Program. Now we have no choice but to enter that next chapter in our lives. We thought we could wait until our husbands are released from prison, but as mothers, we have to protect ourselves and our young children from the harsh realities we face.

Chapo living on US soil is very different than him hiding out in Mexico. Some of his kids live in the United States, and our husbands are going to be the star witnesses against him. How are we to know something won't happen to us before then?

Olivia

With Peter and Junior being the only people who've gotten Chapo on tape, the case officials were pulling together in Chicago was the strongest one. But I guess the US Attorneys in New York City fought a little harder to get him there. Mike Ferrara worked like crazy on this case since 2008, and more than anyone, we thought he deserved it. His time and attention were incredible; he and his team put their blood, sweat, and tears into getting El Chapo, and if anyone knows the ins and outs of the case, it's the Chicago office.

The reality of the situation is that we're terrified about El Chapo being *anywhere* in the United States. When they extradited Vicente, we were scared out of our minds. The thought of Chapo here produces a much, much deeper feeling of fear.

Mia

Our husbands are the ones who put Chapo away, and his people want revenge because of it. Mexican cartels contain the most ruthlessly violent individuals in the world. All the people at the top believe in is making money and having power, and they'll do whatever it takes to hold it.

Olivia

Our husbands felt differently. They didn't think that world was worth losing their lives for. They wanted to walk their daughters down the aisle and watch their sons grow into extraordinary men. They just didn't believe in the cartel life any longer, and neither did we. But El Chapo did, and that's why he—and not our husbands—will die behind bars.

Afterword

Olivia

For the last eight years, I've been hanging in the balance between my past and the future. In 2008, my life in Mexico was lavish. Now, I live a simple life. In the Witness Protection Program, Junior and I aren't sure what the future will hold, but we'll have each other and our kids, and that's all we really need.

Mia

In the past, life was about living and loving every moment. Now, I spend a lot of time looking ahead and waiting. The last eight years have been me waiting for my husband to call, to sign his plea agreement, or to be sentenced. Now, we're waiting for Peter and Junior to be released, which will happen no later than 2021.

Olivia

In 2021, Benjamin and Bella will be finishing up middle school, and Blake will be about to start. Brandon will be thinking about getting his driver's license and starting to consider colleges. Even though he's just a little boy right now, he says he wants to go to Harvard. This doesn't surprise me or Junior; we tell him every day that we believe in him, and that he can be whatever he wants to be.

What's come out of the last decade, though, is that he'll never know the drug trade, because we've shielded him from that life.

Mia

Through sports, great schools that teach morals and ethics, and normal activities like playing Minecraft or going to the jump park on their birthdays, Olivia and I try to give our kids as much stability as possible. More than that, we want to show them they have options and choices their dads never had; when Peter and Junior were in elementary school, they were fishing marijuana out of gas tanks, and when they were in high school, they were setting up an illegal, multimillion-dollar business. Drugs were all they'd ever known. We want our children to be normal kids and understand there's a whole other world out there.

Olivia

While we try to make their lives feel as stable and routine as the next kid's, we don't want them to think that prison is a "normal" place. Sure, it's where Daddy lives now, but it won't be forever.

But because Brandon is almost ten and remembers a time when Junior lived with him, that's been hard. He understands that there was a "before" and "after," and sometimes he struggles to reconcile the two.

For example, two years ago, we visited Junior, like we do every week. We walked in and headed to the prison playroom, and while Brandon started playing with Legos, Junior, Benjamin, and I caught up. Out of the corner of my eye, I saw Brandon building something that looked like an enclosed pen, and as he put a few plastic animals inside, he spoke up, looking a little embarrassed.

"Daddy, look at what I made."

"Is that a zoo?"

"No," he whispered. "I can't tell you what it is. It's a swear word."

Junior was so reassuring. "It's okay, baby. You can tell me."

Brandon approached his dad and whispered in his ear. "It's jail."

When I pulled myself together and digested what he'd just said, I asked, "Where did you learn that word?"

"From *SpongeBob*."

"I don't ever want you watching *SpongeBob* again!" I said, half in shock. But I should have known better. As much as I try to protect him and keep him in a bubble, he's not a naïve little boy anymore. He's learning to accept reality and understand what makes his life different.

This year, Junior talked to him about what prison is. "I'm here because

I made bad choices," Junior said. "And I have to pay for my mistakes. But you, son, are going to learn from them and make better choices. You're a good boy with a big heart. You're super smart, and I know you'll make me proud and be someone great."

Loving his dad unconditionally, Brandon won't disappoint him. I'm sure of it.

Mia

We can't lie to our children about the reality of their lives. When Bella and Blake are ready to ask why their dad is in prison, and I think they're old enough to understand it, I'll explain it to them as gently as possible. In fact, I've already had to.

Last year, Bella told her friend that her dad lives "in a cage." When her friend expressed concern, Bella came home and told me what she'd said. I thought about the situation and tried to explain what secrets were.

"Bella," I said. "In our family we don't keep secrets from each other. We try to tell each other everything. But family is family, and what goes on in our house and what goes on in our family has to be kept between us."

Explaining this to my little girl was heartbreaking, but it was for her own safety. Now, when her friends ask what her dad does, she says, "Oh, he lives in another town." She doesn't feel like she's lying because, outside of our family, you don't have to tell everyone everything.

Olivia

We can't dance around some issues with them, though. Mia and I have each moved more than five times in eight years, and we have to be honest with our kids that we're getting a new house because Daddy is, too. It hurts me that we have to keep putting our children through this, but luckily, they're used to change, so when we find them new schools, doctors, and sports teams, they view it as an adventure. They're good at making friends, and seeing their dads every weekend makes them happy. In fact, they often think their dads are the nice ones, since we're home every day, forcing them to clean their rooms and go to bed on time.

Samantha and Sasha have been wonderful influences on my boys, and they're now in high school making straight As. We have open communication with them, so they know everything, and they're learning every day from our experiences and the sacrifices we all made.

Xavier is all grown up, and he's so close to the girls that they consider each other real brothers and sisters. Now that Junior's away, he's stepped in and become a second father to Brandon and Benjamin. I'm so blessed.

Mia

Bella and Blake are great kids. It's amazing how polite, happy, and well mannered they are. The only complaint I have about them is that they fight with me because I don't let them use their iPads Monday through Thursday. Other than that, I can't say they've been really affected by all of this, except that they miss their dad.

Olivia

Living in fear is a curse. You can't sleep, and you jump out of bed at even the smallest noise. You constantly look out the window. You won't answer your doorbell if it rings, and you're so paranoid you're often sick to your stomach. You don't trust anyone, and you keep your conversations with your neighbors to a minimum. You avoid small talk because the last thing you want is for anyone to figure out who you are. Sometimes, you even keep your children from playing outside because you're afraid something could happen to them. Because I live in fear so much, I've suffered panic attacks that have made me feel like I'm about to die.

Mia

Luckily, though, writing this book has helped with that terror. Since we first started it, I've had many ups and downs and sometimes felt like I was reliving my nightmares. This book brought me to places I thought I'd left in the past, and that I'd never have to think about again. Even though I've cried, and felt anger, my choice to write this book was probably one of the best decisions I've ever made. It brought back sweet memories with my husband that overshadowed the bad ones, and it allowed me to let go of negative emotions that I'd buried.

With the help of this book, I've learned to live for today. I was guilty of wishing and hoping the years would fly by, until one day I saw both my children growing up right before my eyes. Now, I've learned to savor moments despite my circumstances. I now realize I have more than I ever thought I'd have: a husband that I adore and love, and amazing children that give meaning to my life. I have everything a woman could ask for; I just had to get through a few dark times to make it to the light.

Olivia

Through writing this book, I've learned that at times you have to look backward to move forward. I, like most people, don't want to live in the past. I want to put it far behind me, learn from it, and progress.

Writing this book was the hardest thing I've ever done because it forced me to confront the fears and the shame I had about my past decisions. Reliving embarrassing moments was very hard on me, and at times, I felt like I didn't recognize who I once was. But I had to stay true to myself. In order to do so, I had to be completely transparent and brutally honest. I now believe that facing and dealing with my fears has prepared me to better face my future.

Through my journey, I've learned about myself. I don't regret my life, and my past does not define me. Through my painful struggle, I've gained wisdom from many life lessons, and they've molded me into the person I am today. I'm now more resilient, a stronger woman, a better mother, and a more loving wife. In this journey of self, I realized what's important in life: my family.

I grew up in a family who gave me unconditional love and showed me that family is everything. Despite coming from a good home, I made bad decisions and lost myself along the way. When Junior came into my life, he softened my heart and showed me how to love the right way. I showed him the true meaning of love and family. Not wanting to lose his family, he chose to change his life. He made the ultimate sacrifice for us, and because of it, our children will have a better future. When Junior comes home my life will come full circle, and we'll give our children the simplicity of love and family.

In the end, I'm optimistic that one day, when our children read this book, it will help them understand and appreciate Junior and me. I hope that the decisions and sacrifices that we made will one day be reflected in our children, and that we'll be able to give them a life far different than the one we initially chose to live. Hopefully they'll understand that, through bad choices and good, we had the courage and the love to change our lives and make things right. Junior and I want more than anything for them to grow up to be better people than we've been. We want to see them go to college, get their degrees, and make the world a better place. And if all goes right, one day, they'll understand that everything we went through was for them.

—January 2017

Acknowledgments

From Mia:

I owe so much to my beautiful children, Bella and Blake, who are the center of my universe, and who represent the very best of me and then some. As your mother, I brought you into this world, but you both gave me life. You are my true happiness, and I am so proud to be your mommy. I love you both.

Sophia, I love you so much, and it has been a privilege to be in your life and to watch you flourish into a beautiful young lady.

My wonderful mom and dad have loved me through everything, and they gave me the template of what it is to go above and beyond for your children. I love you both tremendously.

To my sweet sister and brother: I will always be here for you. Thank you for all of your understanding. You both are amazing, and I am so proud to be your sister.

To the rest of my family, thank you for your love, companionship, and words of wisdom and support. You are ALL truly the best.

Endless thanks to my in-laws, who accepted me into the family, got past the hard times, and remained close through it all. I will never forget the great times we had. Thank you to my mother- and father-in-law for bringing the love of my life into this world. Only because of you, my children and I are blessed with the greatest man. I promise to take care of him and love him for the rest of my life.

The deepest of thanks to my brother-in-law for all his many sacrifices. Junior, I love and admire you, and I will never forget everything you have done for us.

Olivia, thank you for this incredible journey. You always made the unbearable bearable, the regular days special, and the best days a little sweeter. Thank you for your friendship and dedication to me. I love you.

From Olivia:

Brandon and Benjamin, you are the sons I always dreamed of having. Because of you, I strive to be a better mother every day. When your dad and I decided to change our lives, we never realized how much you would have to sacrifice. We're sorry for all your pain. We hope you understand we did this for you, so our family could have a normal life and because you deserve a better future. You are truly amazing boys who will grow into extraordinary men one day, and knowing that makes this all worthwhile. I will forever be by your side to guide you and keep you safe. I hope you will forgive us and understand that your dad and I love you and are willing to do anything for you.

Xavier, there are no words to describe the love I have for you. I'm sorry for all that you've been through. Because of my choices, you lived a hard life. It amazes me to see the man you've grown to be. You're everything a parent hopes their child will become. You're smart, compassionate, and have a beautiful soul. I can walk with my head up high because of you. You've made me proud and blessed me in so many ways. To your brothers and sisters you are the true definition of a role model.

Samantha and Sasha, I love you. Thank you for sharing your dad with me. You are the daughters I've always wished for, and you've brought so much happiness into my life. I'll always be here to love and support you. You've been amazing daughters and sisters, and without you our family wouldn't be complete.

To my loving parents: I don't know if you'll ever read this. If you do, I know it's going to be hard. I am sorry that I let you down. This is my story, my life, and I apologize for all the heartache I've caused. Through it all, you have given me unconditional love and support. I am a better daughter, mother, and wife because of the imprint you've left on me and the morals and values you've instilled in me.

To my beautiful sister: You've been protective of me, taken care of me, and have always been by my side. You have never judged me, have always given me the best guidance, and have blessed me with your wisdom. I have always looked up to you, and I am forever grateful for your love and friendship.

Peter, thank you for putting our family first. I admire your strength and courage, and all that you have to endure will never be forgotten. Thank you for being a great friend; you mean so much to me, and I love you dearly.

Mia, you are my best friend. Thank you for always being there for me when I need strength, encouragement, or just a shoulder to cry on. Who else understands me but you? There aren't many people who can comprehend what we go through, and I'm so glad we have each other. I couldn't have gotten through this without you.

Finally, to my in-laws: You've traveled down this road with us, and your life has been affected in so many ways. I know it's been hard. We've been through so much together, and still, you have opened your hearts and been there for us. No matter what, we'll always be family. Suerga (my mother-in-law): Thank you for being so sweet, kind, and loving. I love you and will always be here for you.

From Mia and Olivia:

A special thanks to our readers: After reading our book, you may have different opinions and may even judge us, but all our mistakes were just the ingredients that have made us into the wives and mothers we are today. People like us aren't given the chance to show the world we are human just like everyone else. We cry when we are hurt, we laugh when we are happy, and we love our family just like you. We hope you understand our message: that the life we once had doesn't define who we are today, and by reading this book you've witnessed a family that would go through the toughest obstacles for a chance at a simple, beautiful life together.

To our attorney and his wife: Thank you for not judging us, but instead believing in us. You opened the doors for us, and this book wouldn't be possible without you. You have always gone the extra mile and have our best interests at heart. Thank you for being our friends.

Thank you to our husbands' criminal attorneys for all your hard work over the years, which continues today. For receiving our phone calls at all hours and answering our never-ending questions, we're so grateful. Yes, we're a handful, but I hope you now understand. We are sure there are many attorneys who wouldn't have taken the case. We are grateful to you both, especially to Joe, who put himself in harm's way to be there for his clients. You have dedicated time that took you away from your family and spent so much energy fighting for us. We will be forever in debt to you.

Thank you to everyone involved in the making of this book. Coming from where we came from, we never thought we'd be given the chance to publish our life story. We feel honored and privileged to be surrounded by such wise and intelligent people. You all saw past the stereotypes and took us for who we are. We never thought we would receive such touching and profound comments and praise. We will forever hold your words in high esteem.

To our TV/film agents: Thank you for believing that our story should be out there for the world to see, and for giving us the opportunity to take our project to the next level. We have an awesome team!

We're ashamed of our past lives, but we couldn't be prouder of the decision we made. Writing this book was one of the most difficult things we've ever done, and we thought about not going through with it many times. But we realized that if this could help change someone's life, it would all be worth it. We wanted to do something positive and hopefully inspire someone who's living this lifestyle. Too many families and children have suffered, and if everyone thought of the people they love the most, they, too, could change their lives and put an end to the many dangers drugs pose to the world today.

We're extremely disheartened and saddened by the drug problem today. So many people are addicted and dying, and we hope our and our husbands' difficult decisions have made an impact in helping to end this epidemic.

Olivia's life is a living testament to the fact that a person can overcome the torment and misery that is an abusive relationship. She has lived through and survived these relationships, and we're hopeful that our story will empower women and give them the strength to love and value themselves and find true love like we have.

Thank you, reader, for letting us tell you our story.

Sources

Chapter 1: Olivia
   Tanvi Misra, "Why Chicago Is Still the No. 2 U.S. City for Mexican Immigrants," *The Atlantic*, Citylab, October 9, 2014, accessed November 8, 2016, http://www.citylab.com/housing/2014/10/why-chicago-is-still-the-2-us-city-for-mexican-immigrants/381304/.

Chapter 3: Junior
   Annie Sweeney and Jason Meisner, "A Dad's Influence: How the Flores Twins Learned the Drug Trade at Home," *Chicago Tribune*, May 7, 2015, accessed November 8, 2016, http://www.chicagotribune.com/news/ct-father-flores-brothers-met-20150507-story.html.

Chapter 5: The Heat Is On
   Annie Sweeney and Jason Meisner, "How Twins from Little Village Rose to Win the Trust of Drug Kingpin El Chapo," *Chicago Tribune*, March 28, 2015, accessed November 8, 2016, http://www.chicagotribune.com/news/ct-flores-brothers-drug-cartel-met-20150327-story.html.
   Annie Sweeney and Jason Meisner, "A Dad's Influence: How the Flores Twins Learned the Drug Trade at Home," *Chicago Tribune*, May 7, 2015, accessed November 8, 2016, http://www.chicagotribune.com/news/ct-father-flores-brothers-met-20150507-story.html.
   Sun-Times Staff, "Final Round: Cartel Twins vs. Cop-Backed Kidnapper," *Chicago Sun-Times,* April 15, 2016, accessed November 8, 2016, http://chicago.suntimes.com/news/final-round-cartel-twins-vs-cop-backed-kidnapper/

Chapter 7: Guadalajara
   Duncan Tucker, "The City of Guadalajara Is the Money Laundering Capital of Mexico," *Vice News*, June 14, 2015, accessed November 8, 2016, https://news.vice.com/article/the-city-of-guadalajara-is-the-money-laundering-capital-of-mexico.

Juan Montes, "Deadly Mexican Cartel Rises as New Threat," *Wall Street Journal*, May 15, 2015, accessed November 8, 2016, http://www.wsj.com/articles/deadly-mexican-cartel-rises-as-new-threat-1431509401.

Chapter 9: El Chapo
Michelle Garcia, "Court Docs Raise Questions about Mexico Sinaloa Cartel Narrative," *InSight Crime*, November 12, 2013, accessed November 8, 2016, http://www.insightcrime.org/news-analysis/zambada-trial.

Chapter 15: "This Is Going a Little Too Far"
Charles Bowden, "Mexico's Red Days," *GQ*, June 30, 2008, accessed November 8, 2016, http://www.gq.com/story/juarez-mexico-border-murder-drug-war.

Jason Meisner, "Chicago Brothers Detail How Mexican Cartel Moved Cocaine by Jets," *Chicago Tribune*, November 11, 2014, accessed November 8, 2016, http://www.chicagotribune.com/news/ct-mexican-cartel-cocaine-transportation-met-20141110-story.html.

Chapter 26: Wives at War
US Attorney's Office, "Three Alleged Mexican Drug Cartel Leaders and Twin Brothers Who Ran Chicago-Based Distribution Crew among Dozens Indicted in Chicago as Part of Coordinated Strike against Drug Traffickers," FBI.com, August 20, 2009, accessed November 8, 2016, https://www.fbi.gov/chicago/press-releases/2009/cg082009.htm.

Chapter 28: Arrests
Steve Schmadeke, "Six Charged in Elaborate DEA Operation," *Chicago Tribune*, April 23, 2009, accessed November 8, 2016, http://articles.chicagotribune.com/2009-04-23/news/0904221240_1_cocaine-drug-dealers-drug-enforcement-administration-sting.

Chapter 30: Sentencing
Jason Meisner, "14 Years for Chicago Brothers Turned Informants in Takedown of Cocaine Cartel," *Chicago Tribune,* January 27, 2015, accessed November 8, 2016, http://www.chicagotribune.com/news/local/breaking/ct-flores-brothers-cartel-sentencing-met-0128-20150127-story.html.

Chapter 31: Bringing Down El Chapo
BBC News, "El Chapo: Mexico to Extradite Drug Lord to US 'by February,'" *BBC News*, October 16, 2016, accessed November 8, 2016, http://www.bbc.com/news/world-latin-america-37663107.